Civil Society Impact on the EU Climate Change Policy

TRANSNATIONAL PRESS LONDON

Books by TPL

Civil Society Impact on the European Union Climate Change Policy
Turkey's Syrians: Today and Tomorrow
A Defining Moment - Transnational Nursing Education
Revisiting Gender and Migration
Economic Survival Strategies of Turkish Migrants in London
International Operations, Innovation and Sustainability
Overeducated and Over Here
Image of Istanbul: Impact of ECOC 2010 on the city image
Women from North Move to South: Turkey's Female Movers from the Former Soviet Union Countries
Turkish Migration Policy
Conflict, Insecurity, and Mobility
Family and Human Capital in Turkish Migration
Little Turkey in Great Britain
Politics and Law in Turkish Migration
Turkish Migration, Identity and Integration
Göç ve Uyum

Journals by TPL

Migration Letters
Remittances Review
Göç Dergisi
Border Crossing
Journal of Gypsy Studies
Kurdish Studies
Transnational Marketing Journal

Civil Society Impact on the EU Climate Change Policy

Selma Şekercioğlu

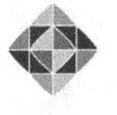

TRANSNATIONAL PRESS LONDON

2018

Civil Society Impact on the EU Climate Change Policy

by Selma Şekercioğlu

Copyright © 2018 by Transnational Press London

All rights reserved. This book or any portion thereof may not be reproduced or used in any manner whatsoever without the express written permission of the publisher except for the use of brief quotations in a book review or scholarly journal.

First Published in 2018 by TRANSNATIONAL PRESS LONDON in the United Kingdom, 12 Ridgeway Gardens, London, N6 5XR, UK.

www.tplondon.com

 Transnational Press London® and the logo and its affiliated brands are registered trademarks.

This book or any portion thereof may not be reproduced or used in any manner whatsoever without the express written permission of the publisher except for the use of brief quotations in a book review or scholarly journal.

Requests for permission to reproduce material from this work should be sent to: sales@tplondon.com

Paperback

ISBN: 978-1-910781-58-6

Cover Design: Gizem Çakır

www.tplondon.com

Contents

Contents i
About the author ii
List of abbreviations iii
Preface 1
Introduction 3
Chapter One: Conceptual framework 9
Chapter Two: The evolution of EU environmental policy and the role of the institutions 35
Chapter Three: The evolution of the European Union climate change policy and organizations 61
Chapter Four: The influence capacity of the EU wide civil society organizations within the Union 131
Conclusion 183
Index 205

About the author

Dr Selma Şekercioğlu is a lecturer at Nişantaşı University in Istanbul, Turkey. Şekercioğlu received her PhD in Political Science and International Relations from Istanbul University. She completed an MA in EU Politics and International Relations at Marmara University and BA in International Relations at Istanbul University. Her research focuses on the EU acquis on renewable energy and climate change politics, non-governmental organizations's relations with the EU and decision-making processes.

List of abbreviations

ACRE:	Alliance of Conservatives and Reformists
ALDE:	Alliance of Liberals and Democrats for Europe
CAN:	Climate Action Network
CAN Europe:	Climate Action Network Europe
CCS:	Carbon Capture and Storage
CDM:	Clean Development Mechanism
CERs:	Certified Emission Reductions
COP:	Conference of the Parties
COREPER:	Perminent Representatives Committee
CPI:	Climate Policy Integration
CSO:	Civil Society Organization
DG:	Directorate General
ECJ:	European Court of Justice
ECCP:	European Climate Change Programme
ECSO:	Environmental Civil Society Organization
EEB:	European Environmental Bureau
EP:	The European Parliament
EPE:	Energy Policy of Europe
EPI:	Environmental Policy Integration
EPP:	European People's Party
EPPO:	The European Public Prosecutor's Office
ERU:	Emission Reduction Unit
ETS:	Emissions Trading System
EU:	European Union
FoE:	Friends of the Earth
FoEE:	Friends of the Earth Europe
G4:	Green 4
G10:	Green 10
Greens/EFA:	European Greens/European Free Alliance
GNP:	Gross National Product
GUE:	European United Left
IPCC:	International Panel on Climate Change
JI:	Joint Implementation
LULUCF:	Land Use, Land Use Change and Forestry
NAMA:	Nationally Appropriate Mitigation Actions
OPEC:	Organization of Petroleum Exporting Countries
R&D:	Research and Development
SEA:	The Single European Act
S&D:	Progressive Alliance of Socialists and Democrats
TFEU:	Treaty on the Functioning of the European Union
UN:	United Nations

UNFCCC: United Nations Framework Convention on Climate Change
USA: United States of America
WWF: World Wide Fund for Nature

Preface

For some time, climate change has been one of the issues that has most attracted the interest of the academic world as climate change related challenges are increasingly important. Thus, the number of studies about climate change policies have grown.

While formulating the research, the lack of EU climate policies in the literature – the backbone of this book – was spotted and thus the aim is to offer a basis for future studies.

It is the author's personal preference that the book does not include a chapter related to Turkey. Most academics in Turkey who focus on EU-Turkey relations avoid studying the EU's microstructure. Hence, with this book, I aim to make a difference in order to expand the field of EU studies into Turkey too.

I would like to thank my supervisor Professor Faruk Sönmezoğlu who supported me during this study. I would also like to thank Dr Özlem Terzi and Dr Semra Cerit Mazlum for their valuable comments and contributions to the study through committee meetings. I would also like to express my gratitude to Professor Gencer Özkan, Dr Hakan Güneş and Dr Sevgi Uçan Çubukçu, who encouraged me and offered different perspectives for future research.

Last, but not least, I thank my dear family for always being on my side during this research and for their encouragement. I thank Gizem Sucaklı for her helps during the translation period of the book. I also thank all my friends for their understanding and support over the years.

Şekercioğlu

Introduction

Environmental disasters in the 1990s revealed the inadequacy of the measures that were in place since the 1970s. Industrialization imposed various pressures on the environment such as air pollution and water pollution. In 1972, after the Stockholm Conference, the first action plan was drawn and implemented in 1973 in the EU. This was the first step for legislation on environmental issues.

With the Single European Act, it became possible to speak of environmental policy as de jure. With the foundation of the Directorate General of Environment in 1981, it can be stated that legislation on environmental issues had been institutionalised. However, considering specific legislation to climate change, it can be seen that the EU policies started to take shape after 1990. The Commission laid the foundations for a climate change policy by publishing two reports in 1988 and in 1990 on greenhouse gases. During the preparations for the Rio Conference, the number of civil society organizations concerned with environmental issues in the EU rapidly increased. Hence, EU climate change policies and the emergence of civil society organizations active in this field dates back to the early 1990s. In the 2000s, climate policy was transformed in parallel with international developments and evolved into what it is now.

The influence of civil society also increased during this time and became more visible. The emphasis on the necessity of democratic participation in Article 10, and the necessity to make a dialogue with civil society in Article 11 of the Treaty of Lisbon are the results of this process. Thus, the activities in this field enabled the emergence of a concrete outcome.

Climate change policy of the EU is an interesting field. International developments and the increasing number of climate change-related global disasters have paved the way for new legislation on this issue in the EU. Along with this increase in legislation, new academic studies on the climate policy of the Union have emerged.

The democratic structures in the EU allowed civil society organizations to influence the decision-making process. In fact, the Commission, which is considered to be the most bureaucratic of all EU institutions, began to include civil society in its own decision-making mechanisms. Within this framework, in addition to meetings such as partner meetings to exchange opinions and to inform, online consultation processes have been initiated.

In this respect, it can be said that the relationships of EU institutions and civil society seen a transformation. This transformation in the EU has been the subject of many studies. The studies in this field can be grouped into three. The first is the descriptive studies analysing the transformation in the EU's policy of environment and climate change; the second is lobbying studies analysing the relationship between EU institutions and interest groups; and the last one covers the studies of influence analysis.

The first group is considerably important for showing the progress of the field of policy. The second group is important in the first place for seeing the progress of present lobbying studies specific to the climate. As climate change has an influence on every single EU citizen, the lobbying studies differ from traditional lobbying. Moreover, especially in addition to professional lobbyists involved in the activities defending the interests of the business world, it can be observed that civil society organizations, besides specializing, are also professionalized in the field of lobbying.

The lobbying activities are conducted by the CSOs fundamentally divided into two groups. Accordingly inside lobbying and outside lobbying activities can be analysed. While inside lobbying includes interviews through professional lobbyists, outside lobbying is used to define activities such as actions and protests participated by large masses. To analyse the influence caused by such outside lobbying activities, because of the difficulty to follow the actions directly, it was decided for this book to focus on the analysis of the inside lobbying activities. Thus, within the book, the focus was not on the actions of CSOs but on the persuasion relation with the institutions.

Here, the difference of inside-outside lobbying is actually not very clear. Because during the examination of CSOs, the disintegration of the activities of CSOs using both methods may not be possible. Considering this pre-acceptance, although the differentiation between inside-outside lobbying may seem to have a facilitative role, it should be indicated that the analysis may generally include both components. Because making a differentiation here may cause an uncertainty and to reflect this uncertainty in the minimum level, mostly reports and lobbying of institutions rather than actions were focused on.

Thereby, the next dimension of lobbying studies is the studies of influence, measuring the success levels. These studies of influence can be done from many different viewpoints. There are coding studies that undertake formal text analysis as well as studies trying to perform influence analysis by using the methods of survey or interview. However, as the frame of influence has not yet been completely drawn, it can be observed that different approaches in the literature on this subject has been developed.

Here "influence" can be used extremely ambiguously. In this sense, it is highly difficult to draw the border of influence. To overcome this, special emphasis was made on the conceptualisation of "influence". The concept through the emphasis on the formation of political decision as it had been used in the works of Heike Klüver. Here, at what rate do the people who want to have an influence in the political decision have a share in the output of the political decision, is being looked at.

During the initial planning of the study on which this book draws upon, in addition to descriptive studies, work on lobbying and political influence has been researched and integrated into the discussion. The book focuses on the emergence of climate change policy and examines the roles of the EU institutions in the process of developing policies in this area. Furthermore, the civil society organizations' role in this process and their influence on the final outcomes are examined.

The main focus of this book is the growing influence of civil society on sustainability over time. However, this argument needs to be tested. Thus, it is meaningful to study the period after the Kyoto Protocol when the participation of civil society reached at high levels. For this reason, two periods are important: first, the period after 2000 when the arrangements following the Kyoto Protocol recommendations increased and second, the period between 2009 and 2014 when the Treaty of Lisbon was set.

The historical process will be handled under three sub-chapters. These chapters are the periods between 1990–2000, 2000–2009 and 2009–2014. The first period is when the developments on environmental and energy policies gained speed. The second period starts with the First European Climate Change Programme and examines the period until the Treaty of Lisbon. There were two European Climate Change Programmes effective in this period; the first was in 2000 and the second in 2005. In the third period, the developments after the Treaty of Lisbon and Kyoto Protocol, especially the foundation of Directorate General for Climate Action in 2010 are also discussed in this book.

Thus, also the organ(s) of the EU through which civil society organizations can exert influence are analysed.

- What is the role of civil society in the formation of EU climate change and energy policies?

- Through which umbrellas did civil society have an influence on policies, especially such as the Climate Change package that connects the fields of climate change and energy?

- At what rate did the opinions of civil society find a field of application in EU acquis and at what rate does it reflect the requests of civil society?

According to these questions, to analyse the aforementioned influence, a frame of analysis was formed to explain the two theories most relevant to the subject, which are "liberal intergovernmentalism" and "multi-level governance". The goal is to show the change in the decision-making mechanism.

Hence a review of literature and , a formal text analysis were carried out, and interviews both with EU institutions and civil society representatives were conducted. The method that is determined here is the analysis of texts, such as proposals and declarations submitted by the Commission by manual coding, and the analysis of instructions that are the corrections and final decisions of the Parliament and their detection of differences by comparative reading. In this process, if an online consultation is organized, in the cases when there can be no consultation with the answers loaded into the system by their CSOs or when these documents cannot be reached, then the reports prepared by civil society is analysed.

Therefore, the differences or similarities between official texts and civil society reports could be revealed. The civil society institutions that are analysed within the book are environmental civil society organizations. As seen in several studies, organizations with actively growing operations during the period of 1990–2014, organizations focused on the environment (such as Greenpeace, European Environmental Bureau) and studying specific to climate change (such as CAN Europe) were chosen. The selection of these civil society organizations was drawing on a list of such organizations published in a pioneer study titled "Environmental NGOs" by Rudiger K. W. Wurzel and James Connelly. The organizations identified as most influential on the EU climate policy were WWF, FoE, Greenpeace, CAN Europe and EEB were chosen to be included in the research.

The selected organizations were needed to comply with the criteria below:

    - To be actively engaged in the subject of climate change and energy

    - To do activities that would have an influence on EU policies

    - To be active during the period of the research

- To be organized EU wide/to be able to reach member countries through national institutions

- To be included in G10.

A qualitative study was considered to be appropriate for collecting information. Accordingly it was tried to reach out to those authorities who could answer the questions about the relationship of CSO-EU institutions. The collected data were then compared with literature data and the affirmation/falsification of the present literature was made.

This book aims to explain the evolution of the EU, governments and civil society organizations through a new concept of "intertwined asymmetrical relation" and it is suggested to use this concept in further studies on the EU, especially for the explanations in the field of climate change.

The concept not only includes the complicated structure of the EU decision-making mechanism, but also the symbiosis created by different components; because of the actors' different positions, this concept also reflects the qualification of this relation as asymmetrical. Together with being rather inclusionary from these aspects, it can also be used in studies analysing long-term changes, as it also reflects the transformation during the process.

The first chapter of this book presents the conceptual framework and the background to the EU decision-making mechanisms and the foundation of lobbying. This is followed by the data and methods used in the research on which this book draws upon. The EU decision-making mechanisms and lobbying are discussed in reference to the literature.

The second chapter discusses the evolution of enviromental policy within the EU. First, the general process of environmental policy and then the institutional structure, decision-making mechanisms and inner organization of the European Union institutions of Commission, Council, Parliament and Court of Justice are explained. The chapter ends with an evaluation of lobbying.

The third chapter offers a background to the climate change and energy-related climate change policies. Legal texts analysed form an essential part of this chapter. Strategic Documents and the Connecting Texts are analysed separately in a comprehensive fashion, from the proposal to enactment stage.

In the second part of the third chapter, EU-wide CSOs are separately analysed, including their evolution and reports about legal documents.

In the fourth chapter, I present and discuss the findings. In reference to the background given in the previous chapter, CSOs' reports are discussed. The analysis shows the relations between the CSO reports and official reports. Then the ways of the CSOs' participation in the decision-making process are examined. This chapter also discusses the ways in which civil society influences the decision making mechanisms.

After discussing the findings, this book ends with a concluding discussion over the findings and suggestions for future research and policy making.

Chapter One
Conceptual framework

It has been attempted to explain the EU process through different theories for the last 60 years. These theories are generally used according to the characteristic of the study, from more extensive and general theories to more micro theories.

In studies concerning the EU, classic realist, neorealist and institutionalist approaches that are frequently used in the literature of general international relations theory are avoided; studies grounded in intergovernmentalist integration are preferred. As Pollack states, most theories on the EU explain the characteristic of its integration rather than decision making.[1]

Studies on the environment, energy and civil society are generally handled under the frames of "multi-level governance" and "democratic representation theory".

In EU grounded explanation perspectives, there is the functionalism movement defending that integration will gradually increase on one side, and theories concentrating on state-centered and intergovernmentalist bargains on the other.[2] Generally, while for the grounding the view suggested by the new functionalism movement multi-level governance is used, to explain intergovernmental bargains, liberal intergovernmentalist theory is used. Where institutions are analysed, both edges of the present theoretic polarization are mentioned. In order to analyse the link between the states and institutions and thus civil society and to see the rate of consistency of the theoretical ground with practical ground,

---

[1] Mark A. Pollack, "Theorizing EU Policy-Making," *Policy Making in the European Union,* edited by. Helen Wallace, William Wallace and Mark A. Pollack, (Great Britain: Oxford University Press, 2005), 15.

[2] Ben Rosamond, *Theories of European Integration*, (Great Britain: Palgrave, 2000), 131.

the theories of multi-level governance and liberal intergovernmentalism are used. Furthermore the fundamental development of this process is examined to analyse the influence of the enlargement of the union authority to policy production process.

Bargains between the states on the subjects and thus the correlation between the attitudes of the states, and the way that the management is taking in related different layers about these topics are examined. However, in Moravcsik's works, it is already stated that power in the EU is divided vertically between The Commission, Council, Parliament and Court and divided horizontally between local, national and transnational levels.[3] Based on this, both theoretical approaches are handled as complements of each other.

The concentration on governance rather than EU integration is focused on; however, considering the current EU literature, no narration can be made without mentioning the integration. For this, Moravcsik's liberal intergovernmentalism theory is analysed to emphasize the integration and to enable the governance to be better understood.

The principle of democratical representation creates a more suitable ground for the studies focusing on the measurement of civil society's influence. Democratic representation means much more than representative democracy and enables the notion of democracy to be handled in detail.[4] Especially in reports prepared by the Commission, consultations to obtain the the views of civil society and accepting this as a standard procedure, is distinguishing in this way. The Commission does not use the principle of representation officially sonot to ruin the existing balance between the EU institutions. While the Parliament becomes integrated with representative democracy, the Council seems to be integrated with participatory democracy. Here it can be said that the principle of representation aims to legitimize its system through the interests of the EU.[5]

Decision-making theories in general

In order to look at the process of policy making, one single conceptual framework is not adequate. With different factors (such as sub-national, national

---

[3] Andrew Moravcsik, "In Defence of the 'Democratic Deficit': Reassessing Legitimacy in the European Union," *Journal of Common Market Studies* 40, no. 4 (2002): 610.

[4] Elizabeth Monaghan, "Making the Environment Present: Political Representation, Democracy and Civil Society Organisations in EU Climate Change Politics," *Journal of European Integration* 35, no. 5 (2013): 602.

[5] Monaghan, "Making the Environment Present", 607.

and supra-national) that are impossible to examine from a single perspective, it is necessary to have a different focus than classical studies. Moreover, with the various studies on decision making, different perspectives to evaluate have been developed. Today decision making processes can be analysed by notions taken from different viewpoints. Unlike an idealist perspective – although standardization is not possible with new studies – it is possible to create a road map.

The approach of decision making not only has an important role to play in foreign policy decision making and in foreign policy analysis, but also helps to explain the state complexity in international systems.[6] Because the decisions that are the outcomes of the states being analysed, its emergence as a public decision gives way to many different behaviour patterns to make sense.

Generally it will bring out more effective results if in the literature, the outcomes of the rationalist and behaviourist approaches are not handled separately but on the contrary in today's conditions to be handled together with their similarities. Rational choice theory while basically trying to place the foresight that in foreign policy decision makings it is acted rationally, psychological factors come forward together with behaviourist approach. Depending on the subject to be analysed, any of these approaches can offer a more effective research perspective. In literature mostly subjects on security and economy are handled from a rationalist perspective and these researches where numeric values become prominent are associated more with rationality. Also in cases where numeric asessment is not very determinant, it can be stated that the behaviourist researches come into prominence.

Studies including decision making approach are generally handled in the frame of foreign policy analysis. Thus also here it will be reflected similarly.

The decision-making system, with the effect of the EU making its decisions according not only to one single state but to the demands of the member states, can be seen as a kind of foreign policy decisions system until a different understanding is developed.

In Snyder and his team's classical definition, decision making is "a process which results in the selection from a socially defined, limited number of problematical, alternative projects of one project intended to bring about the

---

[6] Chris Alden and Amnon Aran, *Foreign Policy Analysis* (New York: Routledge, 2012), 14.

particular future state of affairs envisaged by the decision makers"[7] When seen from this view, decision is a state of making a choice among the choices.

There are five types of decisions according to Mintz and DeRouen. These are; one-shot (single) decisions, interactive decisions, sequential decisions, sequential-interactive decisions and group decisions.[8] Within this decision-making process it is possible to analyse many different variables. Even if the subjects analysed on foreign policy are generally singular, most of the time they are related with a series of foreign policy decisions and are a follow-up of a behavior pattern. The meaning of interactivity is that two or more states are included in the process of foreign policy decisions.

Snyder, at this point, claims that the most fundamental part of decision making analysis is the questioning of who becomes involved in a decision, how, and why? Here automatic assignment or negotiation can come into question.[9] In other words the choosing of the ones to be assigned in the decision-making unit get determined either automatically or by various negotiations. The stage of foreign policy decision-making is one of the subjects that the literature is most engaged in.

However, foreign policy decisions are made by the individuals working in the related field and that the changes occuring in present structures can cause different decisions to come out.[10] Because of this, it would be meaningful to look in what way do the decision makers involve in the process of decision making.

According to Snyder, decision makers should be examined in the frame of four different concepts. Firstly the discriminatory behaviour of the decision makers in their relations with the conditions and other actors should be analysed. Then, the existence of a purpose, the importance that is advised for the condition and at last the standards of acceptance need to be evaluated. These concepts can generally be classified as "perception", "choice" and "expectations".[11]

---

[7] Richard C. Snyder, H. W. Bruck and Burton Sapin, "Decision making as an Approach to the Study of International Politics," *Foreign Policy Decision Making (Revisited)*. Edited by. Richard C. Synder, H. W. Bruck, Burton Sapin et al. (New York: Palgrave Macmillan, 2002), 78.

[8] Alex Mintz and Karl DeRouen, *Understanding Foreign Policy Decision Making* (New York: Cambridge University Press, 2010), 16.

[9] Synder, Bruck and Sapin, "Decision making as an Approach", 84-85.

[10] Faruk Sönmezoğlu, *Uluslararası Politika ve Dış Politika Analizi* (İstanbul: Der Publishing, 2014), 302.

[11] Richard C. Snyder, H.W. Bruck and Burton Sapin, "The Decision-Making Approach to the Study of International Politics," *Foreign Policy Decision-Making: An Approach to the Study of International Politics*.

Decision makers tend to shape their behaviours as a part of social structure according to this structure. The purposes that decision making is required divide into various categories. Different decision makers in their own social structure, can have a voice in long or short-term planning. For example the first unit to influence the decisions on the subject of environment can be named as the Ministry of Environment. Here it needs to be pointed out that the same subject can be considered by many different units but generally only one of them has full authority.

Foreign policy decisions are under the influence of many different factors as outcomes of decision making process. According to Mintz and DeRouen, the factors determining foreign policy decisions are decision environment, psychological factors, international and domestic factors.[12] Thereby the idea of the states to behave rationally, has changed in passing time. Especially thinking that the foreign policy studies change depending on time, country or countries to be analysed, using different variables together become important in this respect. When appropriate the behaviours of state presidents can be analysed in the frame of psychological factors and when appropriate the country's foreign policy behaviours spreading over time can be analysed in the frame of rationality hypothesis. Comparative analysis used by the behaviourists are one of the most important studies to influence the change in the surrounding of foreign policy analysis.

As a necessity of globalizing world, as foreign policy behaviours and domestic policy behaviours cannot be separated in theory, foreign policy decision makers and its environment cannot be analysed as in classical theory with sharp environment and the same categorization. From time to time in the fields that the attention of the public is drawn to and in the fields influencing the domestic policy directly, citizens can participate directly in the forming of state's foreign policy behaviour and can invalidate classic methodology.

In a state the existence of a civil society that can influence the foreign policy decisions shows the chance for that state's citizens to participate in the state practice in broader fields.[13] Thus civil society networks emerging in these states by building supra-national structures, can become components of pressure in making international decisions. EU wide active civil society institutions are also

---

edited by. Richard Snyder, H.W. Bruck and Burton Sapin (New York: The Free Press of Glencoe, 1962), 202 - 203.

[12] Mintz and DeRouen, Understanding Foreign Policy, 4.

[13] Christopher Hill, *The Changing Politics of Foreign Policy* (China: Palgrave Macmillan, 2003), 187.

considered to cause such an influence. Especially after the analysis of findings from the field, this will also be discussed.

As it can be seen, the change in classical decision-making mechanism caused the divergence from the approach that was developed for the military competence to be used power focused and that found itself in realist perspective. In the proceeding period it can be said that the pluralistic approach, able to include many components to itself, was of influence. In the last period however, with the increase of the roles of global actors, the studies examining foreign policy decision making should be taking more variables into consideration.

The theory of liberal intergovernmentalism

The theory of liberal interngovernmentalism is one of the popular theories of 90s found by Moravcsik. This theory, in which the states are positioned as fundamental actors and thus on the subject of integration, intergovernmental bargains in related fields and the role of the present institutional structure are examined, claims to make an extensive analysis. Accordingly, the theory indicates that it is a large hypothesis positioned in a wide social sciences theory and that it is prudential.[14,15] According to Moravcsik: "EC can be analysed as a successful intergovernmental regime designed to manage economic interdependence through negotiated policy co-ordination".[16]

Within this framework it can be stated that a theoretical platform is made in the frame of economy causing intergovernmental mutual dependence and being the main component of the theory. Moravcsik, seeing the criticism of the new realist movement thinking of the EU as a formation created by two polar world of the post-war era, as one of the basic elements of his theory, was especially influenced by the neoliberal institutionalist works that he associated with Keohane.[17]

The theorist, suggesting realist, institutionalist and constructivist criticisms in his proceeding works, claims that these theories fall short to create opposite arguments against liberalism and that it is not possible to explain the concept of "socially constructed" without using the substructure of liberal theory.

---

[14] Andrew Moravcsik, "Preferences and Power in the European Community: A Liberal Intergovernmentalist Approach," *Journal of Common Market Studies* 31, no. 4 (December 1993): 474.

[15] Andrew Moravcsik, Frank Schimmenfelling, "Preferences and Power in the European Community: A Liberal Intergovernmentalist Approach," *Journal of Common Market Studies* 31, no. 4 (December 1993): 68.

[16] Moravcsik, "Preferences and Power", 474.

[17] Rosamond, *Theories of European Integration* (Great Britain: Palgrave, 2000), 142.

In this sense the distinguishing feature of liberal theory comes not only from its getting involved in the system and interstate relations but also of its getting involved in the changes of inner state.[18]

As Rosamond states, Moravcsik using both liberal theory including national choice formations and interstate strategic bargaining process in his theory, conflicts with Putnam's two level game theory. Putnam measures the legitimacy sources of the groups that by creating a metaphor trying to hold the power in national policies and that have a voice in international relations.[19] In fact on the one hand it represents the effective group trying to increase its influence on domestic policy decisions and on the other hand it represents the state with intergovernmentalist bargaining chain. Therefore basically the behaviours of foreign and domestic policy, by effecting each other, necessitates an integral analysis. Especially in recent years when interstate interactions has gained speed with the influences such as globalization, examining domestic and foreign policy apart from each other with sharp lines, has become harder. Thus in a supranational organisation like EU where states take a stand in certain fields and increase their mutual dependencies, two level analysis offers a rather enlightening framework of analysis.

Moravcsik claims the theory of liberal intergovernmentalism to be composed of three basic components. These three components can be lined up as such: "the assumption of rational state behaviour, a liberal theory of national preference formation, and intergovernmentalist analysis of interstate negotiation". Rational state approach is examined in two different dimensions. First the governments define the interests of the states and these interests form the demands of the states. Later these governments by pressing on the political system of European Union, try the decisions to be made in this way and create a bagaining field for themselves. And this can be evaluated as an offer.[20] (See Table 1)

Because of the distinctive supra-national structure of EU, it should be stated that decision making mechanism is also distinctive. Moravcsik mentions the influence of three different components on this subject. First of all the intergovernmentalist negotiations here are made totally voluntarily and without enforcement. In bargaining process, much information can be reached and the cost of operation of the bargain is low.[21] Thereby as it is easier to create a

---

[18] Andrew Moravcsik, "Taking Preferences Seriously: A Liberal Theory of International Politics," *International Organization* 51, no. 4 (Autumn 1997): 513-515.

[19] Rosamond, Theories of European, 136.

[20] Moravcsik, "Preferences and Power", 480-481.

[21] Moravcsik, "Preferences and Power", 498.

cooperative atmosphere and the uncertainties are few, the decisions find more sound application area.

Table 1: The liberal intergovernmentalist framework of analysis

Liberal Theories (International demand for outcomes)	Intergovernmentalist Theories (International supply of outcomes)
Underlining societal factors: Pressure from domestic societal actors as represented in political institutions	Underlying political factors: Intensity of national preferences; alternative coalitions; available issue linkages
↓	↓
NATIONAL PREFERENCE FORMATION ■▶ Configuration of state preferences ■▶ INTERSTATE NEGOTIATION ■▶ OUTCOMES	

Source: Andrew Moravcsik, "Preferences and Power in the European Community: A Liberal Intergovernmentalist Approach," Journal of Common Market Studies 31, no. 4 (December 1993): 482.

In any case, mutual decisions rather than unilateral policies, prevent some countries to be excluded as a result of a possible coalition. However the relativity of the alternatives to be too many, may increase the bargaining power of the state. Finding a common ground can cause interstate differentiations to decrease and can give the opportunity to countries with low standards to increase them. In cooperations like the protection of the environment and the consumer, it is aimed to unite around a shared value. Thus shared policies can be produced.[22]

---

[22] Moravcsik, "Taking Preferences Seriously", 528.

Here, in decision making, the negativity and positivity of policy externalities are also effective. At the same time considering the states having different interests in different fields, the stage of bargaining can come to conclusion by package offers created by the mutual devotion of the states and by every state having the highest profit for itself.[23] Thereby an "asymmetrical interdependence" gets created.[24] Here it is necessary to indicate that the choices and decisions of the states are changeable depending on the subject and the time.

This theory, besides focusing on intergovernmantalist bargaining and negotiation processes, also attributes a distinct significance to EU institutions because of EU's distinctive status. Institutions, while increasing the effectiveness of the bargaining process, also strengthen the autonomy of the national political leaders.[25] Other than the temporarily formed institutions of other international organizations, these institutions possess a continuous structure and while providing ultimate communication in interstate negotiations, also empowers the state leaders to be more effective in the possible problems that may occur in national policy. EU, firstly, with the application of qualified majority separating from other international regimes, caused the definition of political risk to change. Besides, with the creation of a technical institution positioned in equal distance to all the states like the Commission, it leads to the development of an understanding of integral interest.

Integration, in this sense, despite the fact that it starts with the formations such as free circulation or common tariff walls, later on turns its face to legislations in fields such as environment.

However the agreement to be reached and the common position to be developed may not be as concrete as in economical fields. Integration, with its basic form, represents the concrete economical interests. In Moravcsik's works no concrete sample can be seen on other fields but it was only tried to be shown by a general narration. Accordingly:

> *The core of EU activity and its strongest constitutional prerogatives still lie almost exclusively in the area of trade in goods and services, the movement of factors of production, the production of and trade in agricultural commodities, exchange rates and monetary policy,*

---

[23] Moravcsik and Schimmenfelling, "Liberal Intergovernmentalism", 69.
[24] Moravcsik, "Taking Preferences Seriously", 523.
[25] Moravcsik, "Preferences and Power", 507.

> *foreign aid and trade-related environmental, consumer and competition policy.*[26]

Therefore the theory is limited with economy related fields. In the formation of the theory, it was being highly selective and a limited amount of parameters were used and the fundamental institutional outcomes were tried to be examined.[27] In other fields it is emphasized that more extensive authorization belongs to nation states and these fields are relatively excluded. The reason for this is that these fields mostly require technical information and cannot only be examined politically. The biggest criticism to the theory concentrates on this point.

According to Pollack, these criticisms can be gathered in two groups. In the first group there are the theories of rational choice and historical institutionalism. While rational visions in Moravcsik's theory is accepted, the role of the institutions during policy making processes not being sufficiently examined and the theory being unable to enlighten the daily problems are being criticized. The second group is Sociological Institutionalism and Constructivism. Here, methodological individualism and the acceptance of rational choice are being opposed to.[28]

When the criticisms are seen generally, first of all the claim of creating a large hypothesis is being criticized and it is emphasized that in large hypothesis more questions need to be answered. In a sense, the scope of the theory is narrower than its claim. Besides, although social activities are emphasized in general, no analysis on these activities on the subject of their influence on foreign policy is made. On the contrary the privileged appearance that the state directors will attain is only emphasized.

Considering the fact that the influences of EU institutions cannot be much analysed and the difficulty to make a differentiation between the demands of the states and EU institutions, the capability of the theory to be applied in practical field decreases. Again, the activities of the institutions bearing supranational qualities such as EU institutions and European companies cannot sufficiently be examined. The reason for this is because of the analysis of history

---

[26] Moravcsik, "In Defence of the 'Democratic Deficit'", 607.

[27] Moravcsik and Schimmenfelling, "Liberal Intergovernmentalism", 85.

[28] Pollack, Theorizing EU Policy-Making", 19.

making events and of the theory being developed in such a way that it cannot answer the analysis of daily developments.[29]

However it forms an important ground in terms of seeing the role of the states in the formation of policy fields. In order to overcome the present ambiguity, in the proceeding part, the theory of multi level governance, which will enable the analysis of the role of supra-national institutions more elaborately and more effectively and which will present the biggest criticism against the theories adopting intergovernmentalist approach, will be handled.

The theory of multi-level governance

Before proceeding to the theory of multi-level governance, it would be meaningful to mention the analysis of level in international relations. Although there have been debates in the studies of international policy, on the subject of the analysis of level, to Sönmezoğlu, there are five levels of analysis that are generally used. They are, "individual/ group, state, international organizations, sub-system and global system". Furthermore these levels of analysis can be handled under two titles that are the actor and the system.[30] While handling a subject, the analysis of level or analysis of units are being looked at. According to this, the studies are usually done by looking at the analysis of level or the analysis of units in the studies analysing the actors.[31] In this context, in the studies of foreign policy, if the examination is made from the analysis of level, the subject is handled through different levels like the individual, the state or the system and in the studies where analysis of unit is used, it is handled through the actors.

In the studies on EU, this analysis of level takes another form. Accordingly, in literature, generally there are studies making analysis in the local, national and EU level as in the theory of multi level governance. According to Tatiana Romanova, in institutional studies on EU, three different levels are taken into consideration: intergovernmental, transgovernmental and transnational.[32] The transnational level generally includes non-state actors. In this context CSOs and transnational companies are the main subjects for the researches to be made in

---

[29] Michelle Cini, "Intergovernmentalism," in *European Union Politics*, edited by. Michelle Cini and Nieves Pérez Solórzano Borragán, 3rd ed. (United States: Oxford University Press, 2010), 101-102.

[30] Sönmezoğlu, *Uluslararası Politika*, 82-83.

[31] Nuri Yurdusev, "Analiz Seviyesi" ve "Analiz Birimi": Bir Ayrım Argümanı," *Uluslararası İlişkiler Journal* 4, no. 16 (Winter 2007-2008): 4.

[32] Tatiana Romanova, "The Partnership for Modernisation Through the Three Level of Analysis Perspectives," *European Politics and Society* 16, no. 1 (2015): 46.

this level. Because of the intertwined structure of the EU, transgovernmental and transnational levels create the most suitable ground for the studies on EU.[33]

According to Risse-Kappen, the existence of these analysis of level in EU studies are explained with the intertwinement of domestic and international fields in the system of EU.[34] Thus, unlike the classical international relations literature, in EU studies, the levels of analysis determined for foreign policy cannot be used or an explanatory frame in the same level cannot be created.

The theory of multi level governance, unlike the theory of liberal intergovernmentalism, is not emerged to explain the integration but emerged from the structural policy studies done in the aim of explanation of the EU structure created by the process.[35] In a sense, the new regime is being looked at. Especially the new regime in which the influence of the borders are decreased, the authorizations of national governments are limited and from domestic to supra-national, the inclusion of different components is conceptualized this way. From this aspect, it distinguishes itself from the theories focusing on classical interstate relations or the ones proposing more integration.

In this sense, it is emphasized that the EU policy making process is "characterized as mutual dependency, subsidiary functions and overlapping authorizations." It is important to point out that the post-sovereign identity of the Union cannot be linked up with traditional borders and that the political authority cannot be constituted by governing from only one place.[36]

In the theory of multi level governance, although the state holds the directorial power, the EU cannot only be seen as state centered. Also, the EU cannot be handled as a federal state consisting of supra-national institutions. The main purpose is to measure the interaction of the political actors in different levels. Generally, this interaction system of the EU is called "a horizontally as well as vertically asymmetrical negotiating system."[37]

---

[33] Romanova, "The Partnership for Modernisation", 48.

[34] Thomas Risse-Kappen, "Exploring the Nature of the Beast: International Relations Theory and Comparative Policy Analysis Meet the European Union," *Journal of Common Market Studies* 34, no. 1. (March 1996): 54.

[35] Ian Bache and Stephen George, *Politics in the European Union* (Great Britain: Oxford University Press, 2006), 33.

[36] Dimitris N. Chryssochoou et al, *Theory and Reform in the European Union*, 2nd ed. (Great Britain: Manchester University Press, 2003), 50-51.

[37] Rosamond, *Theories of European,* 110 (in Marks, Nielsen et al., 1996, p.41).

Marks et al summarized the three basic arguments of the theory in opposed to the theory of intergovernmentalism: These are;

>*1) Collective decision making involves loss of control for the governments of individual states.*
>
>*2) Decision-making competencies in the EU are shared by actors at different levels, not monopolized by the governments of states.*
>
>*3) The political system of member states are not separate from each other, as Moravcsik assumed, but are connected in various ways.*[38]

In contradiction to Moravcsik's rational model, here, the idea of seeing the states as rational decision makers became impossible. Because states are unable to decide on their own but with the influence of different mechanisms such as the components of civil society and state mechanism. These mechanisms can time to time cooperate with the similar groups of other states beyond their national borders in the EU. Thus, the decision making process transforms into a complicated structure.

According to Rosenau, governance, in this sense, is a more comprehensive expression compared to governing. Accordingly it expresses the inclusion of the individuals and institutions through civil society and informal establishments to the system. In this system whereas European Council and Council of Ministers present a more intergovernmental appearance, the Commission and the Parliament present a more supra-national characteristic.[39] As it is, the EU's governing and decision making system is open to the influence of different variables. This is also the driving power of the transition from governing to governance.

The biggest objection here is to two level analysis. The approach of two level game frequently used in state centered analysis, gets criticized because of the ignorance of the participation by the actors' in different levels and because of not using the argument produced by the theory of intergovernmentalism. In this sense, as Rosamond states, multi level governance is a more pluralist concept than liberal intergovernmentalism in the way of its handling the state.[40] In this way it handles the pluralism, similar to new functionalism.

---

[38] Bache and George, Politics in the European, 34.

[39] Andrew Jordan, "The European Union: an evolving system of multi level governance or government?," *Policy and Politics* 29, no. 2 (2001): 199.

[40] Ben Rosamond, New Theories of European Integration," *European Union Politics*, edited by. Michelle Cini and Nieves Pérez Solórzano Borragán (United States: Oxford University Press, 2010), 116.

In two level game, national states provide the connection between domestic and international levels.[41] New functionalism on the other hand, similar to liberal intergovernmentalism, distinguishes between "low" and "high" politics. Accordingly the ones in low politics can be depoliticized by europeanisation.[42] In this case, in the studies on EU and policy fields, it is possible to make a different analysis depending on the political field that the subject is included.

Gary Marks remarks the three basic arguments opposed and ignored by state centered view. First of all, "history making" decisions themselves are not a result but a start (post decisional process). Thus, not only one incident, but the process created by this incident should also be analysed. And this requires the analysis of daily decisions and technical committees. Second of all, there is a distribution of power from subnational actors to supranational actors. Third of all, with the representation of EU by national interest groups, EU has become some sort of a Regional Europe, the influence of national states has decreased and even in some cases they were left out of the bargaining process. Fourth of all, states lose their autonomy from place to place. Most of the time even, they cannot estimate how their decision will be applied with what sort of a legislation and its results. At last, multi level governance is a new movement starting from 80s and probably it will develop further.[43]

The criticisms to multi-level governance are stated as such by Jordan: First it is an amalgam rather than a new theory. Second, it is insufficient in creating a testable hypothesis and in explaining the basic components of integration. Third, states are still important actors and the autonomy of subnational actors are being exaggerated. Fourth, the role of subnational actors seems more likely to be determined from upwards to downwards and the upward role is not very much emphasized. Fifth, rather than subnational actors, international authorities are emphasized. Sixth, the independent actions of subnational actors do not mean they can give shape to the results. At last, it is thought that the EU's interaction in international field is ignored by multi level governance.[44]

As it can be seen, the theories of liberal intergovernmentalism and multi level governance are both in the level to be used in the analysis of policy making processes. These theories are used in this book within the examinations showing different attitudes between both EU level and the countries.

---

[41] Risse-Kappen, "Exploring the Nature", 55.
[42] Risse-Kappen, "Exploring the Nature", 56-57.
[43] Andrew Jordan, "The European Union: an evolving", 200-201 (in Marks and the others, 1996, p. 41).
[44] Jordan, "The European Union: an evolving", 201.

As it was stated in the beginning of the chapter, the concept of levels of analysis frequently used in similar researches in the literature of international relations, is not used here. Because of this, in this book it is prefered to use the explanation frames produced especially for the EU.

As Lenschow stated, the making process of European environmental policy, transformed into a regime, from being a political production process. It is claimed that this transformation is within the frame of three different variables. Accordingly, firstly the policy making process not only reflects the governance structure in the EU but also gives shape to it. Secondly as the EU policy making process has influence on the states, it can be said that the states has also influence on the process of policy development. Lastly, the EU, as one of the new actors of international environment policy, is also influencial on the system of international governance.[45]

The transformation of the environmental policy to a regime, obligates the examination of its components. The three variables mentioned by Lenschow, which are the EU level, state level and international level, are coherent with the theoretical ground that will be used by this book. Within this framework, especially in parts two and three, both the development process of environment policy and the theories indicated in the examination of the EU institutions, offer an influential area of usage.

With the emphasis that will be made to the intergovernmental negotiations during environmental policy development, the ground offered by the theory of liberal intergovernmentalism could be used. On the other hand, together with the development of political fields, the theory of multi-level governance is used in the examination of multi-level governing system. In institution examinations, especially while examining the structure of the Council, the roles of the countries are emphasized. In a sense, the distinguishment of leader/laggards in literature is tried to be shown and the process of intergovernmental bargaining is considered. Here, the only and main reason to dwell on the bargaining process is to show the formation process of the decisions. Therefore an extensive country influence analysis is not planned. In other institutions, the role followed by taken decisions and their activities to domestic level are to be shown. However no detailed analysis is done here.

---

[45] Andrea Lenschow, "Environmental Policy in the European Union: Bridging Policy, Politics and Polity Dimensions," *Handbook of European Union Politics*, edited by. Knud Erik Jørgensen, Mark A. Pollack and Ben Rosamond (Great Britain: Sage Publications, 2006), 422.

The expansion of the Union jurisdiction

The expansion of the Union jurisdiction is a fact that can be evaluated within historical continuity. The Treaty of Rome, which formed the EU, determined a jurisdiction on the policy areas such as common commercial policy to be organized within the Union. With the proceeding treaties, the subjects within the jurisdiction of the Union expanded. With the deepening strategy of the EU, new legislations were formed in the fields under the authority of the EU. The start of increase in authorization, especially with the European Single Act, reached its peak with the Treaty of Lisbon. In the EC's decision-making mechanism, the method of "co-decision" to be transformed into ordinary mechanism during this deepening process is also an important factor.

During the process of transformation of an economy-based union to a political union, the jurisdiction fields of the member countries expanded by including fields such as agriculture, trade, competition, energy, and money, together with property, service, capital and freedom of movement of persons – which are the basic necessities of a common market.[46] The roles of the national legislative organs decrease and these institutions, according to Karakaş, use "dependent authorization with regards to legislative prerogative." In this sense, national parliaments share their legislator authorizations.[47]

In the foundation of the EU's jurisdiction lie the Treaties of Maastricht, Amsterdam and Nice. Within this process, institutional structuring was transformed. Every new treaty has the aim of strengthening the legal position.

With the Treaty of Nice, four basic changes were brought about: "The greatness of the Commission and its compound, the weightage of the vote in Council of Ministers, the adoption of qualified majority instead of the consensus in decision making procedures, and amplified cooperation."[48]

With the Treaty of Lisbon, the EU's institutional structure changed even further. The three pillar structure was removed and the necessary legal background was prepared in order for the decision-making mechanism to function better, within the frame of democratic principles. In this sense, the participation of different stakeholders in the decision-making mechanism within the frame of participatory democracy, which is important in terms of our subject, is

---

[46] Işıl Karakaş, "Avrupa Birliği'nde Egemenlik Yetkilerinin Devredilmesi Sorunsalı," *Avrupa Birliği Hukuku*, edited by. İdil Işıl Gül and Lami Bertan Tokuzlu (İstanbul: Şefik Matbaası, 2003), 43.

[47] Karakaş, "Avrupa Birliği'nde Egemenlik", 44-45.

[48] Erhan Akdemir, "Avrupa Bütünleşmesinin Tarihçesi," in *Avrupa Birliği – Tarihçe, Kurumlar ve Politikalar*, edited by Belgin Akçay and İlke Göçmen (Ankara: Seçkin Publishing, 2012), 50.

guaranteed at the highest level. By increasing the integration of national parliaments with the system, especially in the frame of subsidiarity, a communication network was established from domestic to supra-national level.

The expansion of the EU's jurisdiction increased prominently after the Treaty of Maastricht and with the following treaties. With the Treaty of Lisbon, the jurisdiction transferred to the EU expanded even further. Seen in this context, it may not be possible to talk about a specific subject coming under only one kind of jurisdiction. Different aspects of the same subject can come under different jurisdictions with different legislations. Within this scope, according to Tezcan: "the jurisdiction transfered to EU by the member countries are not homogeneous."[49]

As Tezcan points out, the EU has four different competencies. These are: exclusive competencies; shared competencies; employment area competencies with economic and monetary issues; and supporting/coordinating competencies.[50] Decision-making processes start with these competencies. During this process, especially from the Treaty of Lisbon onwards, the principles of subsidiarity and commensurateness were focused on more clearly.

The addition of methods such as the open coordination method to the decision-making mechanism was also important to prevent problems occuring during the decision-making process, especially during the period up until the Treaty of Amsterdam. Although there is a legal arrangement dimension in intergovernmental negotiations, after the Treaty of Amsterdam, both additional methods to the decision-making mechanism and studies on the addition of different levels from domestic to supra-national to the decision-making mechanism, indicate a new process of evolution.

European Union decision-making mechanisms

The main purpose of creating this part is to provide a solid background for the detailed analysis, especially in chapters two and three. While looking at the main components of climate change policy and the role of the institutions, the functioning of the decision-making mechanism will gain importance. In this section, the basic components of the subject rather than an extensive narration, will be explained.

---

[49] Ercüment Tezcan, "Avrupa Birliği'nde Politika Yapımı / Karar Alma," *Avrupa Birliği – Tarihçe, Kurumlar ve Politikalar*, edited by. Belgin Akçay and İlke Göçmen (Ankara: Seçkin Publishing, 2012), 284.

[50] Tezcan, "Avrupa Birliği'nde Politika Yapımı", 284.

The decision-making mechanism of the EU is multi-leveled. The authorizations on decision-making change according to the legislations concerning the subject. In areas delegated to the authority of the EU, we can talk about the decisions, made at EU level. However, in subjects included in the national government jurisdiction, such as tax, decisions are made on a national level. On the other hand, changes depending on time may be seen in a political field. As will be seen in the second chapter, it is possible to say that environmental policy has undergone a tremendous change over time. Environmental policy is both given partly under the EU's jurisdiction, and with the formation of principles such as the subsidiarity principle, environmental management is tried to be started from local government. Thereby, by attributing a different importance to local governance, it is possible to suggest multi-level solutions.

In the process of EU decision-making, which is also called the legislative process, the European Council, EC and EP are included. For legislation to be created in the related field, the proposal comes from the European Commission, and with the decisions of the Council and the EP, it becomes law. A request can also be made by the Council and the EP to the EC to create a proposal. The outcomes of this legal EU decision-making process are regulations, directives, decisions and non-binding recommendations.[51] New actors in the technical and consultative level are added to the decision-making process, for example the Committee of the Regions founded with the treaty of Maastricht and EU agencies whose numbers are nearly 350.[52]

According to the Treaty of Lisbon, decisions to be made within the frame of ordinary legislative procedure together with the codecision procedure. Within the frame of extraordinary legislative procedures on the other hand, the procedures of consultation and assent are used.

The co-decision procedure became a part of the EU decision-making mechanism with the Treaty of Maastricht and became ordinary EU legislative procedure with the Treaty of Lisbon. This procedure, which may be valid for the related fields in the first pillar of the three pillar structure foreseen by the Treaty of Maastricht, after the Treaty of Amsterdam started to be used more by the shifting of fields from the third pillar to the first pillar and finally with the

---

[51] Alex Warleigh –Lack and Ralf Drachenberg, "Policy Making in the European Union," *European Union Politics*, edited by. Michelle Cini and Nieves Pérez Solórzano Borragán (United States: Oxford University Press, 2010), 212-213.

[52] For detailed information see Ercüment Tezcan, Avrupa Birliği'nde Politika Yapımı / Karar Alma," *Avrupa Birliği – Tarihçe, Kurumlar ve Politikalar*, edited by. Belgin Akçay and İlke Göçmen (Ankara: Seçkin Publishing, 2012), 281-318.

Treaty of Lisbon after the removal of the pillar structure, became valid for all the fields under the jurisdiction of the Union. (See Table 2).

With the Treaty of Lisbon, the differences between the procedures disappeared and the necessity for all ordinary legislative processes to be created by a single procedure was emphasized. With the emergence of this procedure, the jurisdiction of the EP expanded. According to this, hereafter, the EP is to be involved in a major part in the decisions to be made for the Union. While EC proposals are being prepared, the potential economical, social and environmental results are considered and the positive and negative results of the decision are reported in an impact assessment.[53] In these reports, public participation is also very important. CSOs, local authorities and representatives of industrial enterprises related to the subject can help to shape the report by presenting their own opinions.[54] In the EC's proposal, all the related directorate generals' approval needs to be taken and this enables the EC to act as one.[55]

The proposal prepared by the EC is presented to the European Council and the EP simultaneously. The EP presents its opinion. If any changes are asked by the EP, the Council either accepts the amendment together with this change or the Council itself proposes a change. Next comes the process called the second reading. The EP may accept this change as it is, may reject it or may ask for a change. If it rejects it, the amendment is not accepted. If the EP asks for a change, the EC and the Council analyse these changes.

According to the report of the EC, voting takes place in the Council. In the case of still not coming to an agreement, a Conciliation Committee is formed to try to reach a conclusion. The Committee sends the outcome to the Council and EP again. During this third reading, both the Council and EP may block the process.[56]

The consultation procedure has been valid since the Treaty of Rome in 1957. Accordingly, amendments prepared are presented to the Council and the EP. The decision of the EP is non-binding for the Council and its decisions may not be the same.

---

[53] "Impact Assessments," *European Commission,* Accessed December 1, 2013, http://ec.europa.eu/governance/impact/index_en.htm.
[54] "Consultations," *European Commission*, Accessed December 1, 2013, http://ec.europa.eu/yourvoice/consultations/index_en.htm.
[55] Warleigh –Lack and Drachenberg, "Policy Making in the European", 216.
[56] "How EU Decisions are made," *European Union,* Accessed December 1, 2013, http://europa.eu/eu-law/decisionmaking/procedures/index_en.htm.

Table 2: The distribution of EU research fields according to the decision-making method

Fields to make decisions with common decision procedure	Fields to make decisions with consultation procedure	Fields to make decisions with confirmation procedure
-Principle of non-discrimination based on nationality -Freedom of movement and residence -Free movement of employees -Social security for migrant employees -Rights of foundation -Transportation -Internal market -Employment -Cooperation in customs -Struggle with social exclusion -Equality of opportunity and treatment -Application of decisions related to European Social Fund -Education -Vocational education -Culture -Health -Protection of consumers -Trans-Europe Networks -Application of decisions related to European Regional Development Fund -Research -Environment -Transparency -Struggle with fraud statistic	-Police and judicial cooperation in criminal matters -Revision of treaties -Discrimination based on gender, race, ethnic, religion, political view, disability, age or sexual preference -EU citizenship -Agriculture -Policies related to freedom of movement of people like Visa, asylum, migration -Transportation (in situations effecting seriously on certain regions) -Rules of competition -Tax regulations -Economical policies -"Developed cooperation" – for example, legislations allowing countries to work together even in contradictive situations	-Certain tasks of European Central Bank -European Central Banks System/in the status of European Central Bank -Transformation -Structural funds and reconciliation funds -European Parliament election procedures -Determined international treaties -Acceptance of new member countries

Source: "Decision Making Mechanisms," European Union Turkey Delegation, Accessed December 1, 2013, http://www.avrupa.info.tr/tr/avrupa-birligi/ab-nasilcalisir/karar-alma-mekanizmalari.html.

The approval prodecure is valid for actions such as signing new international treaties and accepting new member states, and was added to the decision-making mechanism with the European Single Act (ESA) in 1987. According to this, without the approval of the EP, the decision cannot be legalized by the Council.

Before the ESA was introduced, in Council intergovernmental negotiations, decisions were reached by unanimity, whereas with the ESA, decisions are made by the qualified majority. While fields such as tax and new member acceptancy need to be decided by unanimity, in other issues the decisions can be made with the qualified majority.

In the practice of qualified majority, the member countries have 352 votes in total in proportion to their population. These predetermined voting rates are valid in all negotiations. For example while Germany has 29 votes, Malta has 3 votes. In order for a decision to be reached, there are the rules that firstly 260 out of 352 votes need to be in this direction, the majority of the countries need to be decided in this direction, and 62% of the population need to be represented. In 2014, double majority voting became valid. However until April 1, 2017, in case of requesting from the countries, voting on conservancy was possible. Accordingly, in order for the related decision to come out, at least 15 countries (55%) and 65% of their population need to vote in the same direction.[57]

In the first reading, decisions to be made in the EP are made with a simple majority. In the second reading, if the EP's changes are approved by the Council, the decisions are made with simple majority. If there is a change in the Council, then they are made with absolute majority.[58] In the Conciliation Committee where members of the EP vote with absolute majority, the members of the Council vote with qualified majority or with unanimity. In the third reading, the amendment is accepted with simple majority by the EP, and with qualified majority by the Council.[59]

The influence of lobbying in the European Union

Over the last 30 years of its evolution, the EU decision-making mechanism has been influenced by lobbying operations. The expansion of the EU jurisdiction and the first authorization of legislation being in the hands of the EC brought

---

[57] "Council of the European Union," *European Union*, Accessed December 2, 2013, http://europa.eu/about-eu/institutions-bodies/councileu/index_en.htm.
[58] According to absolute majority voting, in the case of voting in the same direction by more than half of the voters, then the final decision is made accordingly.
[59] "Legislative Powers," *European Parliament*, Accessed December 2, 2013, http://www.europarl.europa.eu/aboutparliament/en/0081f4b3c7/Law-making-procedures-in-detail.html.

out the need to examine the content of the operations and their ways to perform these operations of the interest groups carrying out lobbying operations.[60]

Lobbying is of academic interest because it is very common not only in the EU but in Western politics in general

According to the socialist parliamentarian Marc Galle, a lobbyist is: "anybody who acts on the instructions of a third party and sets out to defend the interests of that third party to the European Parliament and other Community institutions".[61] Lobbyists try to influence studies on EU institutions through the institution they work for or they work together.

Lobbying operations can generally be gathered under two main titles: inside lobbying, and outside lobbying. While inside lobbying makes direct contact with decision makers with the aim of influencing political outcome, outside lobbying operates with the aim of molding public opinion and increasing public support to influence the political outcome.[62] When the lobby preferences of the institutions are examined generally, employers' organizations are good at using inside lobbying operations and CSOs on the other hand mostly try to influence the decision making mechanism through outside lobbying operations.

In the 1990s, the operations of the interest group increased with the transition to the Common Market. Apart from the institutions carrying out traditional lobbying, groups that are to be directly influenced by the related decisions, along with the expansion of the Union jurisdiction, have an influence in Union decision making. Thus, lobbying operations conducted through institutional channels of the EU rather than through national lobbying operations will be discussed.

After 1993, ever-increasing lobbying operations and competitive environment started to evolve, especially with the EC's and the EP's encouragement of interest groups and their funding. While lobbying operations in the '90s concentrated mostly within industry and trade, in the 2000's, institutions conducting lobbying operations diversified with the development of social right claims.

---

[60] This study includes groups such as interest groups, CSOs, laborer and employer unions, companies, professional unions that are organized and have the purpose to influence political decisions.

[61] Justin Greenwood, "Regulating Lobbying in the European Union," *Parliamentary Affairs* 51, no: 4, (1998): 590.

[62] Andreas Dür, Gemma Mateo Who lobbies the European Union," *Journal of European Public Policy* 19, no. 7 (September 2012): 973.

In the early 1990s – before the Treaty of Maastricht – the EP was under the influence of intense lobbying operations and therefore the need to organize these operations was felt. For this, Marc Galle was asked to prepare a report. In his report, published on October 1992, he suggested that lobbying operations had to be accredited and their inclusion into the EP had to be followed more carefully. With the aim of providing information and supporting an increase of democratic participation, the Commission – in return for Parliament's making legislation – published the Sutherland Report to prevent any decrease in participation. In return, after the elections of 1994, another socialist parliamentary member, Glyn Ford, expressed his opinion that stricter rules needed to be established for lobbying operations coming from outside, in his report for the EP. On the other hand, the focus of the Nordmann Report was mostly on parliament members; it emphasized the need to make a list of the lobbying operations that entered the EP, their presents to the parliamentarians, the support they provide, and the necessity to create a more transparent environment. Generally, the legislation of the increasing lobbying operations has been a subject open to debate among the parliamentarians.[63]

In such an environment, both public and special interest groups started to develop new and direct lobbying strategies. This process cannot only be examined with the influence capacity of interest groups, but also with the EU's transparency in decision-making mechanism, its guarding the democratic participation principles, and its pressing in this direction. According to Coen's research, nearly 40% (24% companies, 4% think tanks, 11% governmental and regional authorities) of the interest representation in the EC and the EP is made up of individual actors, rather than interest groups. Besides, most of the lobbying operations at EU level are directly conducted through the EC; here the decisions to be made by the qualified majority is an important issue[64] because the influence made during the preperation of an amendment by the EC and the influence made by the decision making of the Council are considered to be the same.

According to Klüver's[65] study, interest groups aiming to influence EU institutions can be analysed through information supply, citizen support and economical power. Within this supply, offering is of key importance. The more technical the subject to be regulated, the more the institutions need information

---

[63] For the detailed process analysis see Justin Greenwood, "Regulating Lobbying"
[64] David Coen, "Lobbying in the European Union," *DG Internal Policies Briefing Paper*. 2007. http://www.eurosfaire.prd.fr/7pc/doc/1211469722_lobbying_eu.pdf, 4-6.
[65] Heike Klüver, *Lobbying in the European Union* (Great Britain: Oxford University Press, 2013a). Also see Heike Klüver, "Lobbying as a Collective Enterprise: Winners and losers of Policy Formulation in the European Union," *Journal of European Public Policy* 20, no. 1 (2013b): 59-76.

and are open to the influence of lobbies. Information supply can be provided first to the EC which makes a political formulation, then within the decision-making mechanism of the Council and the Parliament. In this respect, the decision-making mechanism can be examined under two titles: formulation and decision making.

The subject to be regulated is one of the determinant factors in terms of the quality of lobbying operations. In this sense, both the quality of the subject and the amount of stakeholders influence the decision-making process about the subject to be regulated. Moreover, in the second stage of decision making, there may be an increased need for information compared to the first stage. During the evaluation of the proposal prepared by the EC, the need for information can be greater because of the considerable work load and possible lack of suitable specialists. However this situation is out of question for the Council. The states operate in the Council at the information provided by their own ministries and national interest groups. By playing a key role in providing the EU's democratic legitimacy, it results in the EC trying to include many interest groups together with CSOs into the policy-making process during decision making.

The "consultation" relationship with CSOs in the 1960s and '70s, changed into "partnership" in the 1980s to early '90s and into "participation" from the late 1990s.[66]

The EC's strategy to include interest groups in the decision-making mechanism takes its shape in the frame of transparency policies. In order for democratic participation to take place, which is seen as the solution for problems originating from the directorial mechanism, some mechanisms were developed to allow CSOs' input and exchange of ideas. There are several ways for interest groups to present their opinions to the EU.

The first is organizing various meetings to provide opinions from interest groups. This method, generally used in the first part of the consultation regime, is still used. Second, a civil society website is brought into service, through the EC's website. Through this website, reports prepared by CSOs are loaded on exposure drafts. It is certain that these reports have an influence on the final legislation. The aim of the system is to take different opinions on the subject and to make legislations accordingly. The online consultation procedure, in terms of bringing the present influence and the success of the system into the open, is important in this sense.

---

[66] Christine Quittkat and Barbara Finke, "The EU Commission Consultation Regime," *Openining EU Governance to Civil Society Gains and Challenges*, ed. By. Beate Kohler Koch, Dirk De Bièvre and William Maloney (Mannheim: CONNEX Report Series no: 5, February 2008), 184.

Because of the increasingly complicated structure of the EU level lobbying activities, policies conducted by interest groups started to be proactive, rather than reactive.[67] In this sense, the success of lobbying activities is achieved by new political attempts at the Union level, rather than traditional methods. Changes in the EU legislation forces the EC to be the center of lobbying activities.

In order for lobbying activities to influence institutions, they need to make strategical preferences. These strategical preferences shape the sources that the institution owns. Sources such as financial instruments, legitimacy, representability, experience, specialty and knowledge, influence the success of the activity.[68] While deciding the use of these sources, at which point of decision making will the lobby take place, is needed to be made clear. Lobby activities need to focus either on agenda setters or on veto players.[69]

Likewise, the process of deciding which sources, in what way they will be used, and what kind of activities will take place, are examined under the strategical preferences of national unions. Institutions that are rich in terms of sources are more successful in lobby activities.[70] In this sense, it can be observed that Labor Unions are luckier in terms of sources, compared to other organizations. When the activities influencing decision-making mechanisms are examined in general, more importance is given to lobby activities of the groups that study only on one topic and that may have an interest in the area that is to be regulated.

Lobbying can be seen as a kind of relationship that creates a mutual dependence. Institutional reliability and long-term relationships are fundamental in active lobbying. In terms of climate policy, the powerful interest groups providing these conditions are industrialists and CSOs. While industrialists focus on subjects such as competition, economical development, production costs, for CSOs, achieving a global solution is top priority. The general lobbying activities conducted by these groups are founded not only to influence one political field, but also to influence further political steps. Generally, this also obtains more successful results. When the activities of interest groups within this context are

---

[67] Coen, "Lobbying in the European Union", 6.
[68] Dür, and Mateo, "Who lobbies the European", 971.
[69] Tora Skodvin, Anne Therese Gullberg and Stine Aakre, "Target group influence and political feasibility: the case of climate policy design in Europe," *Journal of European Public Policy* 17, no. 6 (2010): 855.
[70] Coen, "Lobbying in the European Union", 6.

examined, the lobbying studies of industrialists are more intense compared to CSOs.[71]

While the costs caused by lobbying activities are handled by the institutions undertaking those activities, the benefit that occurs at the end of the lobby activity gets distributed among different groups.[72] Therefore, the influence of lobby activities affects a wide range of groups in society.

---

[71] Anne Therese Gullberg, Rational Lobbying and EU Climate Policy," *International Environmental Agreements: Politics, Law and Economics*, 8 (2008a): 161-178.

[72] Skodvin, Gullberg and Aakre, "Target group influence", 854.

Chapter Two
The evolution of EU environmental policy and the role of the institutions

Beginning of the EU environmental policies can be dated back to 1970s. According to the literature, legislations on environment started to take place globally after the Stockholm Summit in 1972. Environmental disasters were main trigger for environmental legislations. With producing norms on the environment and with common legislation, steps to prevent environmental disasters and to change wrong governing dynamics that create these disasters, were being taken.

According to Bomberg, the most important reason that environmental disasters occur is the expansion of urban areas together with the increase of energy consumption, and the use of motor vehicles with the effect of economical welfare in the post-war period.[1] The change in consumption patterns and economical development resulted in environmental disasters such as Seveso, Chernobyl and Sandoz.

According to Budak, the developments that led the EU to make legislations on environment can be categorized under three titles: ecological, economical and political. Ecological reasons include the problems caused by air pollution and waste management. The economical reason is the necessity of the legislation of competition conditions created by the internal market which will try to preclude conflicts emerging from the transnational governing and legislation differences.

---

[1] Elizabeth Bomberg, *Green Parties and Politics in the European Union* (London: Routledge, 1998), 34.

The political reason is the necessity of environmental legislations to provide the life standards for the citizens.[2]

The transformation of the EU jurisdiction and governing practices with the treaties in the 1990's also caused changes and improvements in the environmental policy. The environmental issues to be transnational and the need for a common planning process brought out the necessity to establish legislation and a follow-up system at the EU level.

For example the will that emerged in respect of "Integrated Pollution Control" led by the UK, is important for giving the community the authority to control. With the Council Directive on Integrated Enviromental Pollution prevention and control in 1996, the EC was authorized with the integrated pollutions' prevention and control.[3]

The EU felt the need to make a legislation for its directorate generals. Although the Directorate Generals of Environment and Energy were established separately, they can be evaluated together because of the negative externality and environmental pressure created by the energy production processes. The necessity to create a coordinated political production to support energy production systems that cause less negative effects on the environment, such as renewable energy, and to solve problems that have global areas of influence, i.e. climate change, emerged from the negative relation of environment and energy production, was brought out.

The need for coordinated political production necessitated the foundation of Directorate General of Climate Action in the 2000s Regulation within the EU emerged as a result of policies from Northern countries that are named as "Green" states and constituent states such as Germany that are leaders in technological development. Legislation is not at the desired level because of the influence of Union members such as Poland owning coal intense energy production and members such as Italy that could not interiorise the environmental legislations.

Member states that are leaders in technological developments, such as Germany, think coming to an agreement at EU level is not only important for the environment but also for providing the continuity of economical conditions. For example, principles that focus on the solutions of technical problems such as the Polluter Pays Principle tried to incease interest in new technologies at EU level in the same supportive level as Germany. To overcome huge financial

---

[2] Sevim Budak, *Avrupa Birliği ve Türk Çevre Politikası* (İstanbul: Büke Yayınları, 2000), 111.
[3] Budak, Avrupa Birliği ve Türk Çevre Politikası, 66-67.

Civil Society Impact on the EU Climate Change Policy

burden, structural funding was given and studies in this field were supported. However, considering the distribution of these funds, the share spared for studies on the environment is a small percent.[4]

One of the most important breakthroughs of the EU and the environment is the wish to be the world leader on this matter, and with the influence of CSOs the principle to produce a policy open to the influence of different social layers. The activities of the Green Parties within the EU still provides a political contribution that not many states can reach. Both in national parliaments and in the EP, the existence of Greens causes an influence in the political production processes, even if at a minimum level.

General process of the EU environmental policy

Within the evolution of the EU environmental policy, it can be said that the EU had a coherent period with the "deepening" strategy. The evolution of the EU environmental policy can be handled in three different periods, which are: 1972–1987, 1987–1992, and from 1993 to the present.[5]

These periods generally present a coherent view with the EU treaties; the ESA and the Treaty of Maastricht are the turning points. Here, the intention of development is not only measures to be taken solely for the aim of protection, but also the preparation of a legal basis that will help the political field to act in a planned way. In other words, this expresses the transition to proactive political production process from reactive political production. In addition to this, waste management – constituting the basis of the policy in the beginning – became a more extensive political field than the studies in the field of air and water pollution[6], in which basic measures needed to be taken. (To see the changes that came with the treaties, see Table 3.)

---

[4] For detailed information see Budak, *Avrupa Birliği ve Türk Çevre Politikası*, 77-78.

[5] Andrea Lenschow, "Environmental Policy," *Policy Making in the European Union*, edited by. Helen Wallace and William Wallace (Great Britain: Oxford University Press, 2010), 309.

[6] The studies on waste management go far back to 1970s. The Directive 2008/98/EC issued on this subject in 2008 is the last waste framework directive and it is the most extensive legislation. See http://ec.europa.eu/environment/waste/framework/framework_directive.htm.

The most important reason for EU's activies on environment in the 70s is the aim to increase the air quality. Starting from 1980s, many directives, decisions and strategy reports have been issued about air quality. See http://ec.europa.eu/environment/air/legis.htm.

Another subject given importance by the Union is the protection and management of water. The scope of the water include Water Framework Directive, drought, flood, struggle with climate change and drinking water planning and the strategies are created in this direction. See http://ec.europa.eu/environment/water/index_en.htm.

Şekercioğlu

The EU's production of a policy on the environment can also be expressed with the transformation of its internal policy. A considerable part of environmental problems hold a transnational and international quality and this necessitates a new transformation in international policy. The legislations in certain fields in the first period are an expression of this foresight: water quality, sea pollution, waste contol, air quality, nuclear radiation, hazardous chemicals, energy preservation, pesticides, noise pollution, genetic modification, forestry, and animal health.[7,8]

The Paris Summit of European Economic Community in October 1972 is acknowledged to be the start of the EU environmental policy. In this summit, a declaration about environment and consumer policy was issued and the Commission was assigned to produce an action plan on the subject of environment protection.[9] The measures taken on the subject of environment started with the First Action Plan, which was prepared by the Commission and approved in 1973. The environmental policy of this period primarily included subjects about trade and legislations were made based on the provisions of common market in the treaties.[10]

Although there were economical concerns at first, legislation on issues such as air pollution, and acid rain – which hold a transnational quality – started to gain importance together with the forcing power of the pioneer states. These measures aimed to improve the living condition of the EU population. The emphasis on living conditions originated from the Treaty of Rome, where no

---

The protection of nature and bio-diversity became a more visible political field with the diversification of fauna and flora within the area of the Union. See http://ec.europa.eu/environment/nature/index_en.htm.

Apart from these subjects, the fields of protection of soil and noise pollution are also included in environmental policy planning. See

http://europa.eu/legislation_summaries/environment/soil_protection/index_en.htm,

http://ec.europa.eu/environment/noise/home.htm.

At last, with the foundation of EU Civil Protection Mechanism in 2007, it can be stated that a cooperative atmosphere is being tried to be created. See

http://europa.eu/legislation_summaries/environment/civil_protection/index_en.htm

[7] John Vogler, "The External Environmental Policy of the European Union," *Yearbook of International Cooperation on Environment and Development 2003/04*, edited by. Olav Schram Stokke and Øystein B. Thommessen (London: Earthscan, 2003), 65.

[8] Within the current content of EU environmental policy, climate change, sustainable development, waste management, air pollution, protection and direction of water, protection of nature and bio-diversity, protection of soil, civil protection and noise pollution are to be seen. Within this framework, many variables from the chemicals to the air and soil quality, from the condition of seas to development of industry, are being evaluated.

[9] Christoph Knill and Duncan Liefferink, "The Establishment of EU Environmental Policy," *Environmental Policy in the EU*, edited by. Andrew Jordan and Camilla Adelle, 3rd ed. (London: Routledge, 2013), 13.

[10] Lenschow, "Environmental Policy", 309

reference was made to the environment, and arise from the evaluation of the environment to give a legal framework to the subject in Paris Summit.[11] In this way, they tried to overcome the lack of norms regarding the protection of the environment in the first period.

The measures taken on the environment influence the economical activities of the EU beause of the Common Market and create commercial handicaps. Before the ESA was created, 120 directives, 27 decisions and 14 regulations were issued between 1973 and 1985.[12] Within this period, the delegations of certain subjects to the EC created an external competence and this required the states to participate in negotiations concerning the environment. The needed compliant atmosphere for the common market to function properly can be provided in this manner; environmental issues were shared between the states and the European Community.[13] In order for the Commission to continue its study more at ease, the Directorate General of Environment was founded in 1981. Since then, the EC's environmental studies have been conducted by Directorate General of Environment.[14]

The second period of European environmental policy started with the ESA in 1987. With the ESA, the purposes, principles and decision-making mechanism of the European Community were determined and its area of jurisdiction was drawn. Its importance on the environment is that its legislation was arranged under a new title, some environmental decisions could be made by the qualified majority in the Council and the increased authorization of Parliament. With the application of a qualified majority, it attempted to overcome the issue of policy production being stopped by the vetos of member states.[15]

---

[11] Christoph Knill, Duncan Liefferink, **Ibid**, p. 15.

[12] Bülent Duru, "Avrupa Birliği Çevre Politikası", **Avrupa Birliği Politikaları**, Der. Çağrı Erhan, Deniz Senemoğlu, Ankara, İmaj Publishing House, 2007, (online), http://kentcevre.politics.ankara.edu.tr/duruabcevre.pdf, (27/03/2013), p.2.

[13] John Vogler, "The European Union as a Global Environmental Policy Actor", **The European Union As a Union in International Climate Change Politics**, Ed. Rüdiger K. W. Wurzel, James Connelly, London, Routledge, 2011, p. 23.

[14] The environmental studies are not only conducted by the Commission's Directorate General of Environment but also by EP Environment, Public Health, Committee of Food Security, EU Council, Economic and Social Committee, Regional Committee, European Investment Bank and European Environmental Agency. The first duty of the Commission here is to constitute a coordination among related institutions and comprehensive EU policies. In the first period between the years 1973 and 1981, 5 experts on environment worked under Directorate General of Industry. This situation is the most important indicator on why the objective of Environment and Common Market was conducted together in the proceeding period.

[15] Vogler, "The External Environmental", 66.

Table 3: Significant treaty changes affecting EU environmental policy

Year signed	Year in force	Treaty	Changes affecting environmental policy
1957	1958	Rome	-No mention of environment
1986	1987	Single European Act	-Environmental Title added -Article on environmental policy integration added -Qualified Majority Voting (QMV) for the internal market
1992	1993	Maastricht	-'Sustainable growth respecting the Environment' becomes one of the tasks of the Community (Article 2) -Environment title strengthened to include mention of 'precautionary principle' -Integration Article (Article 130r) was reinforced -The number of policy areas where the Council could adopt environmental legislation using QMV was extended -Co-decision strengthened the role of the European Parliament in developing environment policy
1997	1999	Amsterdam	-Article 2 strengthened so that 'Sustainable development of economic activities' made an explicit objective of the EU -Integration Article given more prominence (Article 6) -Co-decision becomes the normal process for agreeing environmental policy
2001	2003	Nice	QMV changed to establish a double majority of member states and votes cast
2007	2009	Lisbon	-Environment Title (174-176, TEC) substantively unchanged but numbering changed (now Articles 191-193, TFEU) -Integration Article now Article 11 -Article 2 strengthened so that the EU shall work for the 'sustainable development of Europe' and the 'sustainable development of the Earth' (now Article 3, TEU)

Source: Andrew Jordan and Camilla Adelle, "EU Environmental Policy: Context, Actors andPolicy Dynamics," *Environmental Policy in the EU*, edited by. Andrew Jordan and Camilla Adelle (London: Routledge, 2013), 4 (Based on A. Farmer's "Manuel of EU Environmental Policy" study).

During the preparation period of the ESA, many people, especially the Greens, criticized the possibility of the increase of economical activies within the internal market causing environmental disasters and public health problems. Beyond environmental concerns, the criticisms on the threat of the rights of the employees intensified in this period. Nevertheless, the ESA is also seen as a representative of important developments on the subject of environmental legislation. Thereby, it became possible to talk about an enviromental policy as de jure.[16]

Together with the Third Environmental Action Plan formed in this period, the principle of high levels of protection was put forward and protective measures were emphasized (for the fundamental contents of the Environmental Action Plans, see Table 4). With these conditions, the integration of the enterprises on environment and the other policy areas of the EU were provided. The most significant policy produced in this period is the principle of "rectifying pollution at source," especially formed by bringing legislations on emissions.[17] The principles of "the polluter pays," "precaution", and "the principle of integration" are still internationally acknowledged principles put forward by the EU in this period. The subsidiarity principle was put forward by the First Environmental Plan and entered into agreement with the ESA.[18]

The environment, being handled under another title, began to change its status and was evaluated together with legislations on economic integration. Although the purpose of the ESA was to deepen economic integration, singular environmental legislations came out as the means of producing independent policies on the environment. Together with these legislations, ordinary practices gained a legal basis.

According to article r, clause 130 under the 7th title, environmental activities of the community have the aim of preserving, protecting and developing the quality of the environment; contributing to human health; and using natural resources vigilantly and rationally. If achieving these aims are easier at community level, it proposes the Community to go into action. Member countries finance and apply these applications.[19]

This situation, put forward by the ESA, continued until the Treaty of Maastricht – the beginning of the third period of environmental policy. After the Treaty of

---

[16] Bomberg, *Green Parties,* 36-37.
[17] Andrea Lenschow, "Environmental Policy," 309.
[18] Knill and Liefferink, "The Establishment of EU Environmental", 22.
[19] European Community, "Single European Act," *Official Journal of European Communities.* No L 169/1, Assented to 29 June 1987.

Maastricht, the EU's authorization also increased. The decision-making mechanism in the field of environment has developed and the legal and institutional mechanism has become consolidated through the EP, gaining strength, and the increase of subjects where the decision-making mechanism is applied by the qualified majority in Council meetings (except some environmental taxes and preference of energy source).[20]

Table 4: EU environmental action plans

Environmental Action Plans	Including Years	Content
Environmental Action plan	1973–1977	-The principles of the pollution to be payed on the source and the polluter pays -Environment to be included in the plans, raising awareness on environment -Approximation of national programmes
Environmental Action plan	1977–1981	-Preparation of regular reports -Education -Cooperation with civil society
Environmental Action plan	1982–1986	-Developing new technologies -Objective of employment creation -Producing more effective policies
Environmental Action plan	1987–1992	-Protection of environment, fundamental factor of development -Financial measures -Associating other political fields with environment
Environmental Action plan	1993–2000	-Protection from pollution and common responsibility principles -Bringing the subjects of Rio Summit to agenda -Supporting environment friendly companies -Approximation of environmental policies and creating consistency fund -Protection of life standard and constant access to natural resources

---

[20] Andrea Lenschow, "Environmental Policy," 310.

Environmental Action Plans	Including Years	Content
Environmental Action plan	2001–2010 (extended to 2012)	-Taking action on the subjects of climate change, nature and biological diversity, environment and health, sustainable usage of natural resources -Enforcements to be applied in relevant violations -Integration of energy and transportation programmes with environment
Environmental Action plan	2014–2020	-Sustainable usage of natural resources -Protection of biological diversity -Forming a resource effective Union with green and competitive low carbon economy -More investments for environment and climate change -Complete integration with other policies and increasing other information resources -A more effective Union in sustainable cities and struggle with climate change

Source: Jale Çokgezen, "Avrupa Birliği Çevre Politikası ve Türkiye," Marmara University İİBF Journal 23, 2 (2007): 93-96; Environment Action Plan to 2020, Avrupa Komisyonu, Accessed January 4, 2014, http://ec.europa.eu/environment/ pubs/pdf/ factsheets/7eap/en.pdf.

The European Environmental Agency, founded in 1994, contributed to the strenghthening of the EU environmental policy. Thus, a common observation and database setting platform was formed. With the Treaty of Maastricht, the foundations of the EU were laid and studies on more comprehensive integration began. Within this scope, the arrangements on the protection of the environment could be made from a wide perspectives. The following Treaty of Amsterdam also brought some innovations in this field. This treaty tried to overcome the problem of member states producing singular policies or their reluctance to do so with the increment of legislation authorization within the EU. Producing common environmental policy is one of the tools used to realize this purpose.[21]

Within this period, with the Fifth Environmental Action Plan including the years between 1993 and 2000, a new governance approach was adopted for environmental policy. Thereby, both in the process of decision making and the

---

[21] Knill and Liefferink, "The Establishment of EU Environmental", 26-27.

application of environmental policies, with the increase of participation, producing more flexible and sensitive policies was planned. The Sixth Environmental Action Plan called for an increase in cooperation between industries and EU citizens.[22]

According to Knill and Liefferink, unlike the acceleration in other periods, the third period of the EU environmental policy and environmental developments at the EU level was slower. Of course, in spite of the observations on the environmental standards of member states and the increase of parts referring to the environment in the EU acquis, generally a reluctance in the actions on environment at the EU level was present. The increase of unemployment after the 1990s may be indicated as the most important reason for this. The states that wanted to prevent industrial development by taking measure on environment moved more slowly and instead of creating a common policy in this period, they studied for the integration of present norms and national policies.[23]

With the Treaty of Lisbon, sustainable development became one of the main principles of the EU's foreign relations. The scope of Environmental Policy Integration (EPI) was widened and relations with different fields, such as energy, was arranged.[24,25]

As in other treaties, the jurisdiction area given to the EU with the ESA was also expanded under the Treaty of Lisbon. Civil defence, energy production and consumption were included within the EU's authorization. Although the emphasis of the EU institutions being able to take action in regional and international environmental problems does not bring out a clear judgement, it legitimizes the participation of the EU in meetings such as international climate negotiations. One of the most remarkable changes is the authorization to be given to the Commission to create de facto energy policy in order to increase energy safety and variety of energy supply. Climate change and the ongoing programmes on power market have also a big influence on this authorization.

---

[22] Andrea Lenschow, "Environmental Policy," 310.

[23] Knill and Liefferink, "The Establishment of EU Environmental", 28-29.

[24] David Benson and Camilla Adelle, "EU Environmental Policy After the Lisbon Treaty," in *Environmental Policy in the EU*, edited by. Andrew Jordan and Camilla Adelle, 3rd ed. (London: Routledge, 2013), 37.

[25] Sustainable development is one of the favourite concepts of the last thirty years. This understanding fundamentally providing economical development and developing a code of environmental respect is also one of the understandings that the EU use as an engine for development. This concept, included within the fundamental legal framework of the Union with the Treaty of Amsterdam, also became one of the main goals of the Treaty of Lisbon in 2009. The concept of Sustainable development fundamentally serves for three purposes within the Union. These are 1) Natural Source Management System serving for the purpose of the evaluation of the sources rationally, 2) Competitive positioning with the information supporting the consumers's environment friendly consumption patterns, 3) The dependency of the community wide productions and production methods to norms. see Budak, *Avrupa Birliği ve Türk* .65.

Civil Society Impact on the EU Climate Change Policy

The area of civil defence also gave the Commission the authorization of de facto legislation to increase the international co-operation in disasters influenced both by natural and human -related climate change. Natural disasters caused by climate change such as floods, droughts and storms are also evaluated under the scope of civil defence. The evaluation of the adaptation policy of climate change also seems possible under this title. The provision of solidarity that is underlined in Part 7 of the Treaty of Lisbon puts forth the obligation to act together with the European Council in terrorist attacks, and natural and human-related disasters.[26]

The area of "subsidarity" starting with the ESA is also expanded and national parliaments are given the authority to object the proposals of the Commission in case of violation of this principle. Accordingly, draft legislation processes can be sent not only to the EP and the Council, but also to national parliaments of the member states. The parliaments must send their objections on the violation of subsidiarity back to the institution responsible for the preparation of the document in 8 weeks together with the reasoned opinions. Depending on the voting of the decision, these decisions are categorized under yellow or orange card procedures. If one third or a quarter of the national parliament members object, a yellow card is used, and if more than half of the Parliament members object, an orange card is used. In any case, the objection is evaluated. However, the use of the orange card necessitates the Council and the EP to decide more quickly.[27]

The yellow card has only ever been used twice and the orange card has never been implemented. The yellow card procedure was first used by 12 parliaments representing 19 votes for the proposal suggested (Monti II) relating to the EC's offering of "freedom of establishment and the freedom to provide services". The EC withdrew the proposal in stakeholder meetings. The second time it was used by 14 parliaments corresponding to 18 votes concerning the EC's proposal of the European Public Prosecutor's Office (EPPO) in 2013. After the Commission examined the proposal and published a rescript, it was decided that it was coherent with the principle of subsidiarity and was continued.[28]

However, this method of finding a place in the text of the treaty together with the Treaty of Lisbon, creates a suitable ground to see multi-level governance on the subject of climate change. Decisions to be made concerning the environment

---

[26] Benson and Adelle, "EU Environmental Policy", 38-39.
[27] Kaisa Korhonen, "Guardians of Subsidiarity: National Parliaments Strive to Control EU Decision Making," *FIIA Briefing Paper*, no. 84 (May 2011): 4.
[28] "The Subsidiarity Control Mechanism (Protocol No. 2)," *European Commission*. Accessed June 20, 2016, http://ec.europa.eu/dgs/secretariat_general/relations/relations_other/npo/subsidiarity_en.htm.

are important because some decisions are still included in intergovernmental negotiation processes, and EU environmental policy has recently lost its dynamic compared to when it first emerged.

The Directorate General of Environment continued its studies to reach the goals determined within the Environmental Action Plans. The subject of climate change was first mentioned in the fifth plan, but became more visible in the sixth plan. Thereby, climate change was included in the EC's area of studies. The studies on carbon dioxide emission in the early 1990s also accelerated studies on climate change. Energy consumption, which can be seen as the most important reason for climate change, began to be measured from the 2000s. Although the subject of energy production from renewable resources were discussed in the 1990s, with the Directive of 2001/77/EC, the subject of electricity production from renewable energy was put forward, and with the Directive of 2009/28/EC, the promotion of the use of renewable energy was determined and it proposed to decrease greenhouse gas emissions.

European institutions

European institutions, along with their considerable contribution in forming of the climate change policy, also have permeable features. In this part, the transformation of European Institutions with their fictionalization of environmental policy within the historical process will be examined; the permeability of the institutions will be handled and considered as the influence of civil society on the decision-making mechanism.

The EC, Council, EP and ECJ are included as EU institutions. However, the Economic and Social Committee and the Committee of Regions as counselling organizations are not included here. Considering the development of climate change policy, the participation of the Economic and Social Committee in EC meetings and its presenting reports can be seen; it presents reports on directive proposals that are taken into consideration by the Council and the EP.

As each core institution of the EU has a different structuring, the way these institutions are influenced from outside also differ. While direct access through people is possible in the EC and the EP, the Council decisions are mostly influenced through national channels. Member states, before issuing of decisions in related fields, prefer being informed by their own ministries and national specialty institutions instead of obtaining information from a lobby group (including CSOs, employer organizations, industrialists and specialty institutions).

This situation is one of the most important points to be considered during the evaluation of the roles of the institutions on decision-making mechanism, because the rate of institutions' permeability is also important to measure the influence of civil society on the institution. The most important factor for the institutions is the search for "legitimacy".

The acceleration of the decision-making mechanism of the EU with the ESA and the expansion of the system of the qualified majority in the way of including more subjects, is something that increases the democratic legitimacy, especially the increase of the role of the EP parallels with the increase of democratic legitimacy.[29]

European Commission

The EC was founded in 1958 as a sui generis institution. The commissioners are seen as a kind of enterprising politician. Despite the fact that it extensively works on political fields, it resembles the government because of its special structure. The institution is also characterized as a unique hybrid by some researchers.[30]

Fundamentally, the EC has three main tasks. These are: being the Guardian of the Treaties, preparing regulations, and agenda setting.[31] The EC's obligation to prepare regulations in order to start the process of legislation indicates the supranational role of the EU. In other words, the EC can be considered as the internal motor of European integration.[32] Klüver, together with the evaluation of the opinions of Moravcsik, states that the EC provides an autonomous decision-making mechanism. Moreover, she thinks that the role of the EC in decision-making mechanism also contributes to the increase of the negotiation power of the EU on an international platform.[33]

In light of this, we can say that the EC has a key role in decision-making mechanism. The EC, especially after the reform studies in 2000, gained a more

---

[29] The problem of democratic legitimacy is one of the biggest criticisms of the EU. Within this concept the continuous changes in decision making mechanism are the studies for the EU legislations to have a democratic ground. Accordingly while studying the decision making mechanism of the EU especially in a field where industrial lobbying would request in the direct opposite direction on the issued decisions, the transformation analysis should be made quite comprehensively. For a wide criticism of the EU authorization see Bomberg, *Green Parties and Politics*, 41-42.

[30] Emmanuelle Schön Quinlivan, "The European Commission," *Environmental Policy in the EU*, edited by Andrew Jordan and Camilla Adelle (London: Routledge, 2013), 96-97.

[31] Heike Klüver, Lobbying in the European, 31.

[32] Schön Quinlivan, "The European Commission," 100.

[33] Heike Klüver, Lobbying in the European, 30.

visible outlook in planning.[34] The necessity to make plans for the next year is because it contains information of the fields that need to be studied together with the evaluation of technical data annually. Thereby, the Commission would announce its fields of study. In terms of decision makers, the situation to act earlier is thus possible. The EC is the most involved participant member of the decision-making process. Nearly at every stage, it gives its opinion more on prepared documents compared to other institutions.

In terms of its structure, the EC is the institution that has the most intense bureaucrat capacity of the EU. The Eurocrats[35] working here consist of the citizens of the candidate countries, but these citizens show loyalty to the institution rather than their own countries. The EC has the duty of preparing legal legislations within the frame of directorate generals founded in the areas determined by the member countries.

There are 44 different services that work throughout the EC. These services include horizontal and vertical services. While horizontal services provide co-ordination, vertical services are present in the stage of decision making. The service of climate is in a vertical structuring and provides information flow from other units. The commissioners working within the EC are responsible for all decision making in related fields in their directorate generals.[36]

The commissioners consist of the politician citizens of the member countries. The influence of the commissioners and their success in their working fields also enable the development of that political field. The environment commissioner, Carlo Ripa di Meana, was an important commissioner with regards of drawing the attention of public opinion to the environment in 1990. Karel van Miert who came after Di Meana was also one of the people who turned the environment into one of the most important fields in the EU.[37] In fact, where the necessity of making the EU-level decisions before the Rio Summit was urgent, the influence of an enterprising commissioner cannot be underestimated. The most important condition for the progress of the EU environmental policy can be shown as the Commission's determination in issued proposals in related fields.

The 11th Directorate General responsible for Environment, Nuclear Security and Civil Defence, founded in 1981, can be qualified as one of the most suitable

---

[34] For the related document see European Commission, *[COM(2000) 200 final] Reforming the Commission: A White Paper Part I* (Brussels: European Commission, 2000).

[35] The bureaucrats working in the EU are called *eurocrats*.

[36] Schön Quinlivan, "The European Commission," 97.

[37] Schön Quinlivan, "The European Commission," 97.

institutions on lobbying activities among all directorate generals of the Commission. Not only environmental lobbies, but lobbies active in various fields can also influence the institution. Because of this, environmental organizations – predominantly the Greens – believe that the ability of the institution to produce green policies has decreased and think that the efforts of reconciliation for finding the lowest common denominator negatively influences the role of the institution.[38]

The 11th Directorate General of the Commission is more suitable for lobbying acitivities than the others because of the greater need in technical fields and originates from the necessity of legislations prepared by the Commission in the fields that green states would support. Through the committees (comitology) formed in the process of preparation and practice, these states are able to influence the outcomes of the Commission. Another mechanism for the states to influence the Commission is the Environmental Policy Observation Committee. The reports of the Committee that are established to provide co-operation between member states and the Commission cannot be ignored by the Commission and so a kind of harmony is found. Member states find themselves in competition in this sense during the assignment of Directorate Generals. They try to influence on behalf of their own country by sending experts to the Commission.[39]

From the viewpoint that climate change policy could no longer be continued under the title of environment in 2010, the Directorate General for Climate Action was established. The main purpose of this Directorate General is to direct climate negotiations and emission trade together with providing co-ordination in the fields of environment and energy in order for the EU to meet its targets for 2020.[40]

The EC should not be seen as one of the institutions of the EU. On the contrary, despite the fact that the EC is also an institution founded by member states, it should be evaluated as a rational institution capable to act in certain measures. The EC is in need of social support to increase this capability to act and this support is given through interest groups, notably CSOs. The EC's way of policy production in the rate of social support exceeds the states' interference. As no

---

[38] Bomberg, Green Parties and Politics, 43.

[39] Duncan Liefferink and Mikael Skou Andersen, "Strategies of the 'green' member states in EU environmental policy making," *Journal of European Public Policy* 5, no. 2 (1998): 264-265.

[40] "Climate Action," *European Commission,* Accessed December 1, 2014, http://ec.europa.eu/clima/aboutus/mission/index_en.htm.

state can be an element of direct oppression on the EC, it uses this to secure its present condition.

European Council

The European Council makes its decision within the consecutive interaction of of study groups, the Committee of Permenant Representatives (COREPER), and the Council of Ministers. There is a kind of hierarchical structuring. The preparations beginning in study groups at first, are respectively directed to the COREPER and the Council. The COREPER, not being the main determinant institution, has more capability to effect the documents issued by study groups. After the convention is provided by the COREPER, the subject is passed to the Council of Ministers. On many subjects, the convention is provided in study groups and the subject is not passed to the Council as a matter of discussion.[41]

A subject of discussion which is agreed in study groups and the COREPER is not discussed in the Council and is accepted as it is. However, a subject that could not be agreed on is deeply discussed in the Council.[42] The study groups generally work depending on their area of specialty and thus the discussions are concentrated on more detailed and technical subjects, whereas the discussions in the Council of Ministers remain in a more political dimension.

For climate change, another council was not founded and it was considered to be appropriate to discuss legislation on climate change within the Environmental Council. The first Environmental Council was gathered in 1973. The second Council meeting gathered in 1977 and has gathered every year subsequently.[43]

Within the study groups, the behaviours of green states may change. For example, while Finland and Austria generally provide intense technical information within the environmental group, Denmark is more concerned with the political side of the matter. Other states follow a more pragmatist road for reconciliation.[44]

---

[41] Mikael Skou Andersen and Lise Nordvig Rasmussen, "The Making Environmental Policy in the European Council," *Journal of Common Market Studies* 36, no. 4 (December 1998): 589-590.

[42] Rüdiger K. W. Wurzel, "Member States and the Council," *Environmental Policy in the EU*, edited by. Andrew Jordan and Camilla Adelle, 3rd ed. (London: Routledge, 2013), 80.

[43] For detailed information on environmental council see Wurzel, "Member States", 85-87.

[44] Liefferink and Andersen, "Strategies of the 'green'", 261.

The presidency of the Council is handed over every six months, which affects the Council agenda. Whichever state holds presidency includes the issues that are of top priority to that state in the Council agenda.

With regards to decisions made on the environment, it can again be mentioned that the decision-making mechanism is more active in the period of presidencies of the countries that are accepted as leader. For instance, in 1993–94, compared to other countries' presidencies, Germany and Denmark took more initiatives and provided more legislations.[45]

Within the Council, decisions can be made through consensus, qualified majority vote and simple majority. Most environmental legislation is decided by the qualified majority vote, which increases the tendency of member states to cooperate.[46] Nevertheless, a considerable rate of reconciliation is needed in the issued decisions. Without the support of the green blocking minority[47] consisting of pioneer states, getting environmental legislation through is nearly impossible. Although this group is able to prevent a decision from being issued, it does not have enough influence to make the decision to be approved the way it wants it beause of the voting rate.[48]

Moreover, green states do not always share the same view and look for ways to act politically in common. However, in decisions to be made on the environment, some of the green states – while supporting the decisions that are in favor of their interests – try to prevent other decisions by stating that they are unsuitable for their domestic policies.

Apart from these, states can form groups among themselves, and by exchanging opinions can make Council decisions after these discussions, eespecially northern countries, which have important developments on this subject. Denmark, Sweden and Finland – known as the Nordic Council – are able to act as one due to their geographical location. On the review of the Basel Convention of 1995 on the Control of Transboundary Movements of Hazardous Wastes and Their Disposal, the northern countries played a key role and ran a common campaign.[49]

---

[45] Andersen and Rasmussen, "The Making Environmental Policy, 592.

[46] Andersen and Rasmussen, "The Making Environmental Policy, 593.

[47] There are 8 states that can be qualified as green blocking minority. These states are Germany, Denmark, Holland, Sweden, Finland and Austria.

[48] Liefferink and Andersen, "Strategies of the 'green'", 260-261.

[49] Liefferink and Andersen, "Strategies of the 'green'", 263.

The Nordic Council frequently come together in order to discuss environmental issues and they make this a tradition. Likewise, since the 1980s, French and German environment ministers also gather regularly and discuss their decisions.[50] Therefore, the states do not entirely leave their reconciliations to the Council but gather regularly to produce policies. This is also one of the main reasons why many important issues reach a political compromise before they reach the Council.

For example, Germany struggles for technological standards to be formed and unless it suits its own legislations, will not support an EU-level legislation. Because in states like Germany and Denmark where juridical legislations on the environment are intense, the EU's decisions that do not fit with these legislations may cause some problems in conducting and may change the competition conditions by decreasing the profits of member state industrialists.

Germany, being different from other member states, has activities on the emergence of environmental principles and environmental protection. In 1971, with the emergence of principles like tools for prevention, the polluter pays, industry-government collaboration and soon after becoming the pioneers in environmental actions, Germany distinguished itself from other states. Furthermore, because of holding a federal organization, with its political party system, policies in a combined structure should be produced. In this respect, drawing up legislation in areas that society supports and the attention of the media is drawn to, is inevitable from this point of view.[51]

Thus we can see that the behaviours of member states are regulated depending on their domestic policies, as Moravcsik points out. In the example of Germany, a strong industrialist group may affect the government at national level through lobbying, and may be the determinant factor with its behaviour in the Council. This situation is an indicator especially of the determination of the negotiation process among the member countries and that lobbying reaches the Council mostly by inside policy.

In this respect, the attitudes of Eastern European states that joined the EU at later dates may be determinant in the Council. The inside decision-making mechanisms of these states can assume a more clear attitude in the Council because of their use of traditional energy production methods and having a developed national lobby network in this field.

---

[50] Wurzel, "Member States", 76.

[51] Lyn Jaggard, *Climate Change Politics in Europe* (London: Tauris Academic Studies, 2007), 20- 28.

However, according to Liefferink and Skou Andersen, in order for the pioneer states' requests of legislations, especially on environmental policies, to be applicable at EU level, they practice certain strategies. These strategies are goal-oriented or incremental and follow two different methods, which are direct and indirect (See Table 5).

Denmark, Germany and Holland may achieve legislation such as CO_2 tax and waste water management directives by practicing these strategies.

Table 5: Strategies of influencing the EU environmental policy

Forerunner:		Purposeful	Incremental
Pusher:	Direct	Pusher-by-example	Constructive pusher
	Indirect	Defensive forerunner	Opt-outer

Source: Duncan Liefferink and Mikael Skou Andersen, "Strategies of the 'green' member states in EU environmental policy making," Journal of European Public Policy 5, no. 2. (1998): 256.[52]

European Parliament

The EP consists of 751 parliamentarians chosen according to the population of the countries. The parliamentarians are organized as political groups rather than national groups, and mostly align together when they vote. Because of the Parliament's role within the EU decision-making mechanism, the parliamentarians are heavily influenced by lobbying groups. Because of this, members of the Group of the Greens and other parliamentarians may act more sensitively while making decisions regarding the environment. Green policy can be stated to be more influencial in the EP than in the member country parliaments. In fact, the Environmental Committee can act more effectively than the Green Party parliament group.[53]

Generally, the EP has three main functions: political, legislative and budget. It consists of 26 Committees and the subjects on the area of expertise are being discussed in these committees. The majority of the EP's workload is conducted through these committees. If necessary, the EP "can establish temporary

---

[52] For the details between legislations and strategies see Liefferink and Andersen, "Strategies of the 'green'".

[53] Andrea Lenschow, "Environmental Policy in the European Union", 417.

committees and investigation committees". The EP meetings handle the related subject after the studies of these sub-committees.[54]

The most important part from the viewpoint of our subject of study is the legislative function of the EP. As it was stated in the first chapter, the EP is included in the legislative decision-making process. With the Treaty of Lisbon, the role of the EP within the decision-making mechanism became more important. The Committee of Environment, Public Health and Food Security works actively on environmental legislation. The Committee, by constantly making contact with interest groups, carries out consultation activities in order for the EP to issue a solution-focused decision.

The political functions of the EP can be seen as important in terms of the decision-making mechanism. Accordingly, EU citizens are able to ask questions to the EP through petitions and are able to deliver their complaints. The EP can ask the Commission and the Council questions in order to answer the questions posed. In 2007, one third (146) of the petitions that were transmitted by the EP to the General Secretary of Commission were about the environment.[55] The EP, while listening to the voices of the citizens, also uses its force of influence during the preparation of legislation proposals to the Commission.

The EP has more tendency to favour green policy compared to other institutions. In fact, according to Lenschow it is the greenest institution among the three groups.[56] The most important reason for this is the role of the Greens within the EP and the fact that it can be reached directly by its citizens through petitions. Moreover, with the process starting with the Treaty of Maastricht, the increase of the role of the Parliament within the decision-making mechanism with the effect of collaboration and common decision mechanisms, made it easier to adopt an understanding of representing the majority of the citizens during the process of legislation.

Parliamentarians working in the EP feel more responsible for society as they are chosen and authorized directly by the public. This means a political choice, supported by the majority of the public, being included in the legislation process indicating the institutionalization of public support for the EP.

The reports prepared by the Commission – as a technocratic institution – that are directly related to the democratic criteria and EP having more voice on the legislation proposals, result in the enterprises supported by the public to be

---

[54] Bache and George, Politics in the European Union, 295.
[55] Andrea Lenschow, "Environmental Policy," 316.
[56] Andrea Lenschow, "Environmental Policy," 315.

represented more within the complex decision-making mechanism. In decisions to be made on environmental subjects, more institutions and actors are involved in the process compared to other areas and conflicts of interests can frequently be seen. Compared to other sectors, this situation causes the result of a kind of ad-hoc decision making process to be called into question.[57]

The EP is also open to be influenced by the states. The easiest way for this is the parliamenterian to be informed on the positions and opinions of the states. However according to Liefferink and Andersen, the collaboration of the Commission and the EP is the most effective way on decision making.[58] In this situation, if the member states cannot influence these two institutions before the enacting of legislation proposals, they are to reconcile at the last degree on the legislations they want.

European Court of Justice

The European Court of Justice (ECJ) was founded by the founding treaty and is the judicial institution of the Union. The ECJ consists of 27 judges appointed with the reconciliation of the member states. The judges perform their duty for 6 years. The purpose of the ECJ is to provide the application of EU law, to protect the member states' citizens' rights and to settle any conflicts on the reconciliation of EU law and domestic law.

In this sense, the ECJ is one of the main institutions that is not actively included in the decision-making mechanism of the EU. The influence of the ECJ occurs through solving problems that emerge in the applications of the taken decisions. When generally observed, the functions of the ECJ can be gathered under two titles: to control the interpretation of the EU treaties in terms of their being suitable to the law, and to provide effective legal protection in the fields included in EU law.[59]

According to article 258 of the Treaty on the Functioning of the European Union (TFEU), the EC can take the member states to the ECJ claiming that they failed to comply with EU Treaties and secondary law. Moreover the member states, referring to article 259, can sue other member states claiming that they fail to fulfill their obligations. According to article 260 of the same treaty, the EC is given the right to sue the ECJ in case of inconsistency or low consistency of EU law and domestic law. Article 267 of the treaty legislates the national courts to

---

[57] Bomberg, Green Parties and Politics, 43.

[58] Liefferink and Andersen, "Strategies of the 'green'", 266.

[59] Ludwig Krämer, "The European Court of Justice," in *Environmental Policy in the EU,* edited by. Andrew Jordan and Camilla Adelle (London: Routledge, 2013), 113.

consult to the ECJ for fore legal decisions. This article is important for it provides the member state citizens and civil society to indirectly access the ECJ through domestic law.

The most important characteristic of the ECJ in terms of environmental policy is that it prevents the member states to make comments on acquis on their own. The ECJ, with its present interpretations, tries to ensure that the same law is applied the same way in all member states. With the decisions made on filed claims, it ensures that the environmental norms in member states are applied in the same way.

The member states generally show timidity in the subject of taking measures that will damage their economical interests. Beause of this, while passing the directives to their domestic laws, they usually make sure to include very strict rules, which results in the emergence of an asymmetry among the application practices of the states. To prevent this, national courts of member states may consult the ECJ for a preliminary ruling. When this is not possible, the EC can sue the states, claiming that they did not pass the EU law to their domestic laws as it should be and that they have deficiency in application. However, when the consultations of the EC to the ECJ are observed, we can see that it consulted in the subjects in which the Commission is most possible to win. Because of this, the ECJ does not get many chances to interpret the related articles.[60] And this situation provides a relative autonomy to the states.

In the Bottle Case, where the EC and Denmark were confronted with each other, the ECJ decided in Denmark's favor. The case is about the recycling law of Denmark and the law is a more superior legislation than the considered environmental policy of the EU. The ECJ concluded that in terms of the EU to reach its Common Environmental Goals, Denmark's laws were of first priority compared to the principle of free movement of goods.[61]

When the evolution of environmental law at the EU level is examined, it can be seen that environmental law started before the ESA but could not be placed on a legal ground. However, it showed progress within the EU law and from being a parasitic regime, became an independent regime.[62]

---

[60] Krämer, "The European Court of Justice," 117.

[61] Andrea Lenschow, "Environmental Policy," 317. For details on the case see Commission v. Denmark C-302/86 [1988] ECR 4607.

[62] Yoichiro Usui, "Evolving Environmental Norms in the European Union," *European Law Journal* 9, no. 1 (February 2003): 76.

Civil Society Impact on the EU Climate Change Policy

This change also increased the ECJ's influence. But still the problems occuring in the applications of member states cannot be prevented and the requests for judicial protection of social actors at the EU level cannot be fulfilled.[63] From this point of view, the ECJ's influence increases with the expansion of juridical ground, and the necessity of legislation on the environment to be thoroughly reconciled among the member states slows the process down.

Environmental lobbying

In the EU, in legislative decision making on a subject, there is a two-way relationship. On the one hand, decisions are taken at the EU level with input provided by member states, and on the other hand, these decisions directly influence domestic policy.[64] In accordance with Europeanization literature[65], especially in environmental and climate change, this two-way interaction can be stated to be highly effective.

Environmental lobbying is a structure including different actors; not only green actors, but also industrialists and different interest groups are included in the process and attempt to influence the decisions related to environmental policy. In this section, only the green actors will be analysed and the structuring within civil society, will be handled.

According to Bomberg, green actors can be examined under three categories. All three kinds of actors differ from each other in terms of their goals and the strategies they use to reach these goals. These three kinds of actors can also be lined up according to their organization. New Social Movements (NSMs) are of a more premature structure. They include no traditional cores and have a neutral and spontaneous structure. Pressure groups on the other hand are better organized, concentrated on the fields they have expertise, more experienced regarding pressure mechanisms and are of a structure that uses traditional methods together with untraditional methods. Green parties are of a structure that is more organized and directly articulated to politics compared to other actors. They conduct planned activities through their bases both inside and outside the parliament (See Table 6).

---

[63] Usui, "Evolving Environmental Norms", 78.
[64] Liefferink and Andersen, "Strategies of the 'green'", 255.
[65] Tanja A. Börzel, "Pace-setting, Foot-dragging and Fence-sitting: Member State Responses to Europeanization," *Journal of Common Market Studies* 40, no. 2 (2002); Simon Bulmer and Martin Burch, "The 'Europeanisation' of central government: the UK and Germany in historical institutionalist perspective" in *The Rules of Integration Institutionalist Approaches to the Study of Europe,* edited by. Gerald Schneider and Mark Aspinwall (Great Britain: Manchester University Press, 2001).

As the categorization of NSMs, pressure groups and Green parties are grouped to show the strategical differences of green actors, in a pratical sense, they cannot be used for CSO categorization. EU-wide active CSOs can generally be observed as pressure groups. With their tools of inside and outside lobbying, it can be said that, far from being spontaneous, they are more organized – for example, WWF, and Friends of the Earth (FoE), as institutions open to membership, can be evaluated in this context.[66]

New social actions consist more of actions occuring around a newly emerged problem or of citizen initiatives that have come together to make an existing problem more visible. In this sense, it seems difficult to obtain long-term political outputs without co-operating with assumably established institutions and without planning lobbying activities. Whereas Green Parties, although they are outside the scope of this book, are an important actor, especially in order for the environment to be articulated to other policy outputs. Under the name of Environmental Policy Integration (EPI), the environmental values to be taken under consideration during the decisions made in other political fields, besides the Commission's being environmental inspector, a voice from the Parliament is also a driving power in this sense. At the same time, as a result of the preferences of citizens' votes, Green Parties play an important role for environmental values to become more interiorized values within policy making.

When seen from this view, the aim of existence of CSOs can likewise be seen to force governments to make better legislation. From this perspective, CSOs mediates government practices to please and develop the community if possible. When examined specifically to the EU, the emergence of the concept of civil society in Europe also explains the reason for CSOs to be more developed and visible here today.

According to democratic theory, institutional reforms cannot produce democracy as long as they are not supported by society.[67] Seen from this perspective, civil society and public discussion are important in terms of the development of democracy. The practice of democratic governance, in this sense, expresses a bilateral relation. The influence of governance practice on the public and public discussions causing changes in governance practice are the concrete indicators of this bilateral relation.

Therefore, the claim of CSOs to influence the decision-making mechanism can be named as "participation" instead of "representation," and in order for this

---

[66] James Connelly and Graham Smith, *Politics and the Environment* (London: Routledge, 1999), 75.

[67] Beate Kohler Koch, Barbara Finke, "The Institutional Shaping of EU Society Relations: A Contribution to Democracy via Participation?" **Journal of Civil Society**, 3:3, 2007, p.206.

Civil Society Impact on the EU Climate Change Policy

participation to be encouraged, the institution must have the ability of representation.[68] Civil society organizations can obtain this ability of representation with their structuring and activities. For example, CSOs named Green 10 (G10)[69], together with their EU-wide activities, their large membership base, and their transfer of the voices of the people they represent at the right time and to the right people, can be accepted as having the ability of representation.

Table 6: Green actors: goals and strategies

	Goals	Strategies
NSMs	Social change; alternative society	Non-parliamentary; non-partisan; non-conventional (spontaneous protest and demonstrations; direct action)
Pressure groups	Policy change often concentrated on single or limited issues	Non-parliamentary; non-partisan; conventional (lobbying of media, public and government officials; direct action)
Green Parties	Fundamental societal change across a wide array of interconnected issues	Parliamentary and non-parliamentary; conventional and non-conventional; contest elections while maintaining grassroots links

Source: Elizabeth Bomberg, Green Parties and Politics in the European Union, (London, Routledge, 1998), 22.

---

[68] Beate Kohler-Koch, "Civil Society and EU Democracy: 'astroturf' representation?," *Journal of European Public Policy* 17, no. 1 (2010): 100-101.

[69] These organizations are: Birdlife Europe, CEE Bankwatch Netword, Climate Action Network Europe (CAN Europe), European Environmental Bureau (EEB), Friends of the Earth Europe (FoEE), Greenpeace European Unit, Health and Environment Alliance, Naturefriends International, Transport and Environment, WF European Policy Office. For detailed information see "About Us." *Green10.* Accessed May 12, 2014. http://www.green10.org/aboutus/.

Şekercioğlu

As one of the first and most important examples in the field of environmental lobbying, the creation of carbon tax in the beginnings of the 1990s by the Commission and subsequently the intense opposition of the industrialists and member state governments, can be shown. During this period, the proposal of carbon tax was unexpected, as until that day, the Commission generally took action when a scientifically provable thread was in question, but during the time of the creation of carbon tax, no certain scientific proof was completely visible.[70] The active lobbying role of heavy industry, in spite of the legislations enabling them to avoid responsibility in many fields, helped to prevent the formation of the carbon market.

The Commission's proposal in 1992 on CO_2 energy tax could not become a law. One of the most important reasons for this is not only the influence of industry, but also being vetoed by the UK. Although the UK works a lot on taxing itself, it suggested that supra-national taxes harm the right of independence. On the other hand, Southern European countries objected to it because of the possibility of it harming their economical progress. In Denmark, Germany and Holland, national taxation studies started.

In the course of the lobbying activities conducted during the formation of legislation possible to effect all branches of industry and right of independence not only within the EU, but also out of the Union, are rather intense and multi-component.

---

[70] Joanna Spear, "The Environment Agenda," *International Politics in Europe*, edited by. G. Wyn Rees (London: Routledge, 1993), 115.

Chapter Three
The evolution of the European Union climate change policy and organizations

Climate change, according to the Intergovernmental Panel on Climate Change (IPPC)[1], is the change of the natural variables in the climate and its components within 10 years or more, caused by human activities.[2] Although the climate has been changing throughout world history, it is possible to say that production activities increased together with Industrial Revolution, and the acceleration created by this revolution radically affected the climate actions that took place to this day.

In other words, there are two different variables affecting climate change: natural processes and antropogenic (human-related) activities. Today, what we call climate change is a fact that we have been facing for approximately 150 years.[3]

industrialization, daily life practices, increasing consumption rates, development policies, transportation and globalization, the burning of fossil

---

[1] To measure the global changes, Intergovernmental Panel on Climate Change (IPCC) regularly make measurements and regulate possible scenarios and changes caused by climate change. The main objective here is to handle a change that would effect the whole world within the scientific measurable criteria. It is also possible to say that IPCC reports also triggered the outcome of an understanding to produce solutions in a global form haldled by all states.

[2] IPCC, "Adaptation and Mitigation Options," *Fourth Assessment Report: Climate Change 2007*, Accessed March 28, 2015, https://www.ipcc.ch/publications_and_data/ar4/syr/en/spms4.html.
[3] Steven I. Dutch, *Encyclopedia of Global Warming* (USA: Salem Press, 2010), 224.

fuel, agricultural activities, carbon dioxide (CO_2), methane $(CH_4)^4$, together with industrial revolution, have caused the emission of gases that ruin the natural climate's cycle; these increasing emissions resulted in the condensation of gases, named greenhouse gases, in the atmosphere of the earth, which have increased the earth's surface temperature.[5]

Although these gases are important in terms of the protection of the earth's balance and thus have an important role, the increase in their concentrations have caused an inbalance. Solar radiation that should be reflected into space cause the temperature to rise by staying within the atmosphere, which is called the greenhouse effect, and has resulted in global warming.[6]

The world climate and the ecosystem is affected by global warming and results in unusual temperatures, floods and hurricanes. Moreover, it causes the change of balance of the flora and the fauna through temperature fluctuations and unexpected weather conditions.

As long-term outcomes, climate change and natural events related to climate change negatively affect human life, and this negativeness causes the destruction of living spaces, desertation, famine, deaths and migration. Because of these reasons, various climate change policies are being developed.[7]

There are two grounds for climate change policies: mitigation and adaptation. The policies produced on mitigation include the mitigation of greenhouse gas emmissions. Adaptation policies are the policies that, together with accepting the inevitability of the existence of climate change, aim to decrease climate change-related problems through technological developments.

Greenhouse gas emissions are directly related to economical development. Although every country has greenhouse gas emissions, the developed countries came into question to be evaluated also within the concept of their historical responsibilities. Although there are still debates on this subject, historical responsibilities are handled in the United Nations Framework Convention on

---

[4] Besides CO2 and CH4, water vapor (H2O), sulfur dioxide (SO2), nitrogen oxide (N2O) and Ozo (O3) are named as greenhouse gases.

[5] Thomas Bernauer, "Climate Change Politics," *The Annual Review of Political Science* 16, no. 13 (2013): 1.

[6] Dutch, Encyclopedia of Global Warming, 516-517.

[7] States, within the scope of the struggle with climate change, work on common grounds, in the objective of decreasing the emission such as 1987 Ozone Protocol and later on especially during the process starting with Rio, The United Nations Framework Convention on Climate Change (UNFCCC) and Kyoto Protocol. In this sense, especially the Conference of the Parties –COP organized by contracting countries every year, performs the duty of being a discussion platform. Until the Paris Agreement, although no global agreement could be made, the existence of the institution was still important.

Climate Change (UNFCCC) as common but shared responsibilities.[8] In this sense, the idea is that from the increase in world temperature, the leading countries in industrialism have responsibilities.

According to Bernauer, while developed countries prefer adaptation policies, developing countries tend to use mitigation policies more as they do not have enough capacity.[9] This differentiation is fundamentally related to the level of development. However, when the subject is evaluated at EU level, we can see that both of the policies are preferred. In this sense, it should also be stated that developed countries not only apply adaptation policies but also in parallel, apply mitigation policies.

According to the IPCC, mitigation reduces anthropogenic forcing of the climate system by human beings.[10] According to UNFCCC, the mitigation policies include measures to mitigate greenhouse gas emission and the formation of carbon sinks. For the mitigation of greenhouse gases, legislation on energy and production sectors and deforestation, airline and maritime lines can be counted. Clean Development Mechanism (CDM) and Nationally Appropriate Mitigation Actions (NAMA) are also evaluated within this context.[11]

NAMAs are applied in developing countries within the frame of sustainable development. It is prepared under the umbrella of national governments, in national or to support state policies on an individual level and the planning related to economic sector is made.[12]

CDM is the emission mitigation project created in developing countries to gain certificates of emission reduction (CER). The certificates obtained from these projects can be sold or traded by developed countries under the Kyoto Protocol mitigation objectives. While this mechanism became a tool for achieving emission mitigation in developed countries, for developing countries, it is a tool for sustainable development objectives.[13]

---

[8] Charles Kolstad et al, "Social, Economic and Ethical Concepts and Methods," Climate Change 2014: Mitigation of Climate Change (Contribution of Working Group III to the Fifth Assessment Report of the IPCC), edited by. O. Edenhofer et al. (UK: Cambridge University Press, 2014), 217.
[9] Bernauer, "Climate Change Politics," 5.
[10] IPCC. *Fourth Assessment Report Glossary E-O*, Accessed November 16, 2015, https://www.ipcc.ch/publications_and_data/ar4/wg2/en/annexessglossary-e-o.html.
[11] "Focus: Mitigation – Action on mitigation: Reducing Emissions and Enhancing Sinks," *UNFCC*, Accessed December 17, 2015, http://unfccc.int/focus/mitigation/items/7171.php.
[12] "FOCUS: Mitigation – NAMAs, Nationally Appropriate Mitigation Actions," *UNFCC*, Accessed December 17, 2015, http://unfccc.int/focus/mitigation/items/7172.php.
[13] "What is the CDM," *UNFCC*. Accessed December 17, 2015, http://cdm.unfccc.int/about/index.html.

Şekercioğlu

According to the IPCC, adaptation is the policy created as an answer to climate stimulants or to their effects. There are three types of adaptations: anticipatory adaptation, autonomous adaptation and planned adaptation. Anticipatory adaptation includes the measures taken before the observation of climate change. Autonomous adaptation is a spontaneously developing type of adaptation related to the welfare system that changes according to natural systems. And planned adaptation occurs together with negotiation processes depending on the change of conditions and awareness.[14]

Generally, adaptation policies include legislation to be made on ecological, social and economical fields in response to climate change and its effects. There are five basic components of adaptation policies: observation, assessment, planning, implementation and motoring and evaluation.[15] The main difference of this policy from mitigation policy is to produce policies to provide adaptation to climate change, moving away from the opinion that climate change is an inevitable process because of the production of new technologies.

According to the IPCC, adaptation policies, besides being able to reduce the fragility created by climate change, can also be successful with rather low-cost transformations in some sectors. However, even in this situation, its effect is pretty limited. Mitigation policies, on the other hand, can be effective in situations in which necessary political measures are taken and planning is made by removing the obstacles. Nevertheless, it is not possible that only one technology can provide mitigation policies.[16] Seen from this aspect, climate change is considered to be an example for globalization affecting the whole world in different ways.[17]

Climate change policies as a role model

The EU started producing programmes on climate change in the 1980s. Together with the inclusion of the EC in political fields, the need for the production of a policy at Union level was emphasized. In the proposal to create

---

[14] IPCC, *Fourth Assessment Report Glossary A-D*, Accessed November 16, 2015, https://www.ipcc.ch/publications_and_data/ar4/wg2/en/annexessglossary-a-d.html.
[15] "FOCUS: Adaptation," *UNFCC*, Accessed December 17, 2015, http://unfccc.int/focus/adaptation/items/6999.php.
[16] IPCC, "Adaptation and Mitigation Options," *Fourth Assessment Report: Climate Change 2007*, Accessed March 28, 2015, https://www.ipcc.ch/publications_and_data/ar4/syr/en/spms4.html.
[17] Jaggard, Climate Change Politics, 1.

the environmental Research and Development Programme of 1985, the subject of carbon dioxide emission was emphasized to be a vital problem.[18]

In the reports of 1988 and 1990, prepared by the Commission, the problem of climate change was being pointed out and proposals to take action on greenhouse gas emissions were presented.[19] In this period, one of the other reasons for climate change to be on the agenda was because of the preperations of the Rio Summit. For the legislation planned to be made on a global platform, the EU also wanted to have an active role and for this, publishing reports emphasizing the importance of climate change was essential for the agenda.

The preparation period to the Rio Summit and the UNFCCC is of critical importance for the formation of climate change policy and its course; in this period the Commission, by taking an important role, created an interservice group to provide coordination within itself. By means of this coordination, under the intense lobby of the business world, the infrastructure of the Climate Package of the Union was established.[20] Under normal circumstances, DGs, have intense conflicts with each other, but because of the decisive attitude of the Environment and Energy DGs, they all had to contribute to the creation of this package. Although every DG normally has to look after the interests of its own field, in the subject of creating a common climate policy, cooperation became inevitable. Despite the discussions on the reduction of the power of competition in EU origin products, legislation on climate change was considered to be of top priority and in order not to reduce the competition, separate measures were taken.

With these efforts, it is possible to talk about an environmental governance. For an environmental governance to be formed, it is necessary to have structural elements forming the interest union and a governance system to produce political networks. After these are ensured, the preparation and application of related legislation would be easier. Again when environmental governance is in

---

[18] The mentioned document is based on the quotations in the related article: John Birger Skjærseth, "The Climate Policy of the EC: Too Hot to Handle?," *Journal of Common Market Studies* 32, no. 1 (March 1994): 26.

[19] Skjærseth, "The Climate Policy of the EC", 26.

[20] The interservice group includes DG I (Foreign Relations), DG II (Economical Analysis), DG III (Internal Market), DG VI (Agriculture), DG VII (Transport), DG VIII (Development Aid), DG XI (Environment), DG XII (Research), DG XVII (Energy), DG XXI (Taxation). For detailed information see Skjærseth, "The Climate Policy of the EC", 27.

Şekercioğlu

question, like in the example of Rio, it is possible to talk about the simultaneous effect of global developments.[21]

As the EU aimed to be a pioneer regarding climate change, especially in the 1990s, it tried to focus on the subject that took shape around the UN. Within this scope, the Commission had studies on carbon tax, but as mentioned previously, it could not be realized because of the effects of member states (England) and industrial lobbying. Thereupon, the first national objectives for greenhouse gas emissions were suggested by Holland and Germany.[22] The legislation of these states became examples for legislation to be made at EU level.

Energy policies are also intertwined with greenhouse gas mitigation policies within the context of climate change, as 61% of greenhouse gas emissions in the world emerge as a result of energy production.[23] According to Umbach, the presidency of Germany in 2007 and the results of the presidentship on March 2007 can be considered as the most extensive action plan in the world with regards to climate change legislation and the formation of the Energy Action Plan.[24]

During the formation of the EU's environmental policy, three factors were brought forward by the Commission. Accordingly, it is important to indicate first that climate change policy evolved in the form of "learning by doing" and became more extensive during the elimination of occuring problems. Second, an integrative approach to be determined during the phases of both legal legislation and policy formation was considered to be the prior condition to produce effective policy. Third, during the formation of new policies, public consultations became one of the main principles for preparing economical and technical legislation.[25] Therefore, it can be said that climate change policy

---

[21] Andrea Lenschow, "Transformation in european environmental policy," *Transformation in European Environmental Governance*, edited by. Beate Kohler Koch and Rainer Eising (London: Routledge, 1999): 37-39.

[22] Tony Long, Liam Salter and Stephan Singer, "WWF: European and Global Climate Policy," *European Union Lobbying: Changes in the Arena,* edited by. Robin Pedler (New York: Palgrave, 2002), 90.

[23] Frank Umbach, "The EU and Germany's Policies on Climate Change," *Global Warming and Climate Change,* edited by. Antonio Marquina (Great Britain: Palgrave Macmillan, 2010), 228.

[24] Umbach, "The EU and Germany's Policies", 232.

[25] Jos Delbeke, Peter Vis, "Editors' Introduction," in *EU Climate Policy Explained*, edited by. Jos Debeke and Peter Vis (Oxon: Routledge, 2015), 1-2.
PS: Thinking that the authors of the book are senior bureaucrats of Environmental Directorate General (they work in Directorate General of Climate Change at present), the evolution of environmental policy and the climate change coming to the forefront by distinguishing itself, is because of the Commission's interior working principle to be developed in this way.

derived from environmental policy, was formed with more experience and thus made the integrated approach possible. The acceleration regarding climate change discussions that started with Rio in the 1990s evolved to be a more extensive planning process in the 2000s.[26] The negotiations of the UNFCCC had a significant influence on this process. Within this scope, firstly in the fifth Environmental Action Plan, the emphasis on climate change took place. However, climate change was seen as one of the sub-articles under the title of environment. Singularly, legislation on climate change can be found in the sixth Environmental Action Plan and in the European Climate Change Programme in 2000. Thereby the necessary planning for Kyoto Protocol was begun. Since 2005, the second programme has been valid.[27] Within the scope of the second programme, the mitigation of greenhouse gas emissions, increasing business opportunities with economical development, the mitigation of CO_2 emissions in the sectors of light-duty vehicles and aviation with carbon capture, and storage and development of adaptation policies were created.[28]

Officially, the transformation of the climate system as a result of continental areas getting warmer than the ocean and directly affecting the states, was recognized by the EU in the Summit of March 2007. Accordingly, with the necessity to regulate the increase of global warming under 2^0C, the existence of climate change was officially recognized by the EU.[29] Despite the fact that planning on climate change has long been on the agenda, the EU recognized the existence of climate change at European Council level and created a legal background for proposals of solution.

Apart from the programmes developed within the scope of struggle with climate change, various legislation was also made. These laws can generally be classified as emission trade system and energy and climate legislation. Although the process of determination of 2020 objectives occured after the Emission Trading Directive dated 2003 and extensive legal studies in 2007, this process becoming functional and together with the foundation of DG Climate, the period after 2010, is considered to be important.

The most important point here is that climate change policy becoming able to create its own field within its evolutionary process, became possible after 2010.

---

[26] Delbeke and Vis, "Editors' Introduction," 2.
[27] "European Climate Change Program," *European Commission*, Accessed December 15, 2015, http://ec.europa.eu/clima/policies/eccp/index_en.htm.
[28] "Second European Climate Programme," *European Commission*, Accessed December 5, 2015, http://ec.europa.eu/clima/policies/eccp/second/index_en.htm.
[29] Jos Delbeke, Peter Vis, "EU Climate Leadership in a Rapidly Changing World," in *EU Climate Policy Explained*, edited by. Jos Debeke and Peter Vis (Oxon: Routledge, 2015), 7.

Starting from the foundation date of the DG Climate, planning became more extensive and integrated. It can also be stated that with the idea of the Energy Union in 2014, the integration of climate change policy into other political fields gained speed.

EU climate change and energy legislation

The emergence of EU climate policy juridically starts with the ESA as a part of EU environmental policy. With the entrance to the common market, the idea of the protection of environment came forward because of the rising competition. Within this scope, environmental policy had to rise to Union level, instead of staying at national level.[30] Although the Environmental Action Plan and climate change are included in planning sessions, its presence in legal documents has developed within the process. However, it can be said that the biggest acceleration was the decision of global warming to be regulated under 2°C in the EU Summit of 2007. Thus, the visibility of climate change in legal documents increased.

When political outputs of EU are examined, a mutually complementary legal text network can be seen. In fact, while drawing the road map of EU climate policy, it can be noticed that the programmes supporting energy, transportation, agriculture and technological developments are taken as an intense reference point. We can state that climate change policy is actually a kind of inclusionary political field, because projection studies made in this field can only be possible with the functionality of plans in the fields like energy and transportation.

With the increasing importance attributed to renewable energy, creating a system by producing new technologies and being less dependent on external sources in the fields of transportation and warming, and thus decreasing greenhouse gas emissions, is a possible situation according to the EU. The activity in the field of energy of the EU's climate change policy is not only related to climate change, but also to economical developments and strategical planning.

Fundamentally, external dependence in terms of energy has an important role in the means of the Union creating new policies to decrease this dependency, and to achieve its goal of being an important actor both in regional and global platform. Within the scope of climate change, EU legislations are important in terms of measuring the influence of lobbies.

---

[30] Delbeke and Vis, "EU Climate Leadership", 11.

EU climate and energy policy: strategy documents

In this section, communications, legislative resolutions and impact assessments published by the EU will be mentioned. These documents contribute to the EU's future vision and are also seen as a substructure study during the process of the preparation of directives; the documents to be examined here are important in terms of their showing the process of policy making.

The Strategy of 2020

The Strategy of 2020 generally includes the determination of goals related to emission mitigation. However, in parallel with emission mitigation objectives, other legal documents prepared in the same period together with binding renewable energy objectives, and objectives related to the use of fuel, were also determined.

The first document related to the plans of 2020 is the Commission Communication dated 10 January 2007.[31] According to this, in the Summit of European State and Government Presidents that took place in spring 2007, it was emphasized that in order for the EU to develop a more integrated and extensive energy-climate policy, the necessary steps had to be taken. It was also mentioned that within this context, after 2012, when the first obligation period of the Kyoto Protocol ends, necessary conditions need to be formed for a new climate treaty. Although the EU supports a 30% mitigation on the ground of international treaty, it is also stated that even without a climate treaty, the promise of the EU to reduce its emissions by 20% by 2020 can also be given.

In the communication, in addition to these, it is also stated that emission mitigation would also contribute to economical development and reduction of poverty, and in order to regulate the rise of temperature under 2°C compared to the preindustrial period, developed countries could mitigate their emissions between 15% and 30% by 2020. In case of non-mitigation, it is thought that political fields such as fishing and agriculture would be affected by climate change and negative effects would occur, for example, the reduction of bio-diversity with disasters such as drought and flood; water resources would be polluted and deaths related to the heat and cold would increase.[32]

---

[31] European Commission, [COM(2007) 2 final] Communication from the Commission to the Council, The European Parliament, The European Economic and Social Committee and the Committee of the Regions Limiting Global Climate Change to 2 degrees Celsius The way ahead for 2020 and beyond, Assented to 10 January 2007.
[32] European Commission, [*COM(2007) 2 final*], 4.

With development and the increase of gross national product, the transition to a low carbon economy was also emphasized. By mentioning subjects including energy efficiency, renewable energy and energy security, efforts were made to produce extensive policy.

After the Communication of the Commission, according to the presidency results of the Brussells European Council gathered on 8 and 9 March, 2007, energy production was the primary source of greenhouse gas emission. Therefore in the document, competitiveness and the encouragement of environmental sustainability was emphasized. In the text, under the title of climate protection, the necessity of international movement in the struggle with climate change and the pioneering role of the EU was also mentioned.

Until 2020 at least 20%, or 30% mitigation to be performed by the states in case of an international treaty, was also emphasized.[33] The Energy Policy for Europe (EPE) was founded for global warming, energy security and for the competition to be planned in an integrated way.

Again in the same year, within the scope of the European Parliament Resolution on Climate Change,[34] published by the European Parliament, the necessity to limit the rise of global warming by 2°C and the necessity of the Union to mitigate the 1990 emissions at the rate of 30% by 2020 and between 60% and 80% until 2050 were emphasized. In order to apply the goal of 2020, the importance for the necessary decisions and measures to be taken were mentioned. In the resolution, UNFCCC and obligations were also emphasized and the importance of member countries to produce appropriate policies by taking the necessary measures were indicated.

The necessity to develop policies on emission mitigation related to energy production, energy efficiency, tax systems and land routes, maritime line and airline transportation with Emissione Trade System (ETS), were being dwelled on. Moreover, it was indicated that power should not be included in clean development and joint implementation (JI) programmes in order not to encourage nuclear armament and terrorism. It was emphasized that in addition to these, to mitigate greenhouse gas emission rates, public awareness needed to be raised and they needed to be encouraged to be a part of this process.

---

[33] Again the same emphasis can be seen in European Commission, [COM(2008) 30 final] Communication From The Commission To The European Parliament, The Council, The European Economic And Social Committee And The Committee Of The Regions 20 20 by 2020 Europe's climate change opportunity, Assented to 23 January 2008 and in European Commission, [COM(2009) 147 final] White Paper Adapting to climate change: Towards a European framework for action, Assented to 01 April 2009.

[34] European Parliament. [P6_TA(2007)0038] European Parliament resolution on climate change, Assented to 14 February 2007.

According to the decision taken in the European Council 2007, the Commission published a Communication to determine the steps that the Union will take against climate change. In the Communication, published by the Commission on 23 January 2008[35], global leadership, competition with climate change, energy security and economical development were handled together. The most striking part of the Communication was where the gains and losses of the EU were analysed:

> *The longer Europe waits, the higher the cost of adaptation. The earlier Europe moves, the greater the opportunity to use its skills and technology to boost innovation and growth through exploiting first mover advantage.*[36]

When this period is examined, it can be seen that the EU, being in search of leadership regarding global climate change, reflected this in all of its documents. The document mostly focused on "adaptation" policies for the mitigation of petroleum and natural gas importation, reflecting climate change policies having a parallel relationship with energy security. One of its most important emphasis was the new job opportunities created by renewable energy. It was also thought that the development of low carbon technology would contribute positively to economical growth.

The "Impact Assessment"[37] published under the Energy and Climate Package with "Directive on the promotion on the use of renewable energy", "ETS revision" and "Effort Sharing Decision". Accordingly, because of the quality of the document, subjects of economical growth, competition, ETS and sectors apart from ETS, flexibility mechanism, energy security, renewable energy, electricity production costs and consumer expenses were focused on.

In the document, a more concrete framework was drawn up compared to the others with regards to economic integration and compatibility, and climate change. Interviewee 5 commented, "the legislations on climate should increase employment and production" and for this, indicated that they constantly emphasize the competition.[38] İnterviewee 4, on the other hand, pointed out that

---

[35] European Commission, [COM(2008) 30 final] Communication From The Commission To The European Parliament, The Council, The European Economic And Social Committee And The Committee Of The Regions 20 20 by 2020 Europe's climate change opportunity, Assented to 23 January 2008.
[36] European Commission, *[COM(2008) 30 final]*, .3.
[37] European Commission, [SEC(2008) 85/3] Impact Assessment Document accompanying the Package of Implementation measures for the EU's objectives on climate change and renewable energy for 2020, Assented to 23 January 2008.
[38] Interviewee 5 (EU Commission DG Climate Consultant), interview by the author, Brussels, Setember 23, 2015.

during the preparation of the "Impact Assessment", Directorate Generals worked together and stated that the Directorate Generals of Enterprise and Industry usually created problems with the legislation. Because of this, it was mentioned that preparing more qualified and comprehensive Impact Assessment documents would make the process easier. It was also stated that economical assessments take shape within the framework of common interests and that the process would be faster if the documents are well organized.[39][40] From this point of view, it can be inferred that there is the idea that if the EU's power of competition decreases, legislation on climate change would become meaningless.[41]

The Strategy of 2030

While the predetermined strategy of 2020 is rather comprehensive, studies on the strategies of 2050 and than of 2030 began in 2011. The fundamental objective of the 2030 strategy is to provide the use of long-term investments still in the year 2020, reduce the risks of investors, clarify the determined objectives to create competitive economy and more secure energy systems, and decide on its own desired levels before the new international agreement negotiations.[42] Actually, the EU tried to negotiate the details of climate policy within the Union in order to show their ambition for a new international binding agreement (Now it is called as the Paris Agreement).

The decrease in carbon emissions of the Union took shape with the ETS, following national policies and Effort Sharing Decisions. According to the Green Paper, together with ETS, carbon trade gained functionality, but no suitable ground could be reached for long-term low carbon investments.[43] Not only carbon mitigation, but also legislation on renewable energy and energy

---

[39] Interviewee 4 (EU Commission DG Climate Consultant), interview by the author, Brussels, Setember 23, 2015.

[40] TUSIAD (Turkish Industry and Business Association) Brussels representative Bahadır Kaleağası also shares a close opinion. According to Kaleağası, EU does not prefer this as it would lose its power of competition if it acts too fast on the legislations of climate change. This situation may result in the deterioration of economy and the production to shift out. Also, it not only prevents the desired legislations but also makes it difficult to achieve the objective. Because of this, the general attitude of EU is to make 1 or 2 legislations and to provide the realization of these legislations in other states. Interviewee 8 (TUSIAD Brussels Representative), interview by the author, Brussels, September 24, 2015.

[41] As Kaleağası also emphasizes, as long as competition conditions are not created, legislations on climate change would not be accepted by the states as it would negatively influence the economy and thus would effect the future policies of the Union negatively. Therefore the output documents of the Commission to be made with reconciliation have a key importance in terms of the sustainability of the Union.

[42] European Commission, [COM(2013) 169 Final] Green Paper A 2030 framework for climate and energy policies, Assented to 27 March 2013, 2.

[43] European Commission, *[COM(2013) 169 Final]*, 4.

efficiency create a common result of the Union's energy and climate policies. Within this scope, it is possible to say that every legislation supports the other.

The numerical increase in renewable energy investments also developed in parallel with legislation. However, according to the Green Paper, many member states still need more legislation to achieve their 2020 objectives. On the subject of energy efficiency, the inadequacy of present legislation was emphasized and the need for additional legislation was indicated.[44]

In the Green Paper, the crisis of 2008 was mentioned and it was underlined that the developments related to present legislation were slowed down. It was stated that the Energy Package published in 2009 was not the only legal legislation at this point, but additionally steps on energy security were also important in terms of these policies.[45]

In the Green Paper, stakeholders on four fundamental subjects were asked their opinions. These subjects consisted of objectives, other policy tools, competition and the capacities of member countries to act. An important part of the objectives was the interaction of climate change and energy policies. The policies to be created needed to be in the direction of encouragement of long-term competition and security of supply. Acting with the information that steps taken on the subjects of renewable energy and energy efficiency could not provide security of supply and long-term competition, the importance of new planning to be made by taking these into consideration was emphasized.[46]

With regards to the objectives, the stakeholders were asked questions about what level (EU, national, sectoral) should the objectives be created and of legal dependancy. Within this scope, the objectives of 2030 and the 2050 Road Map were focused on, and in case of not reaching the objective of 40% mitigation of 2030, the costs of energy systems in long term were indicated to rise.[47]

Generally, when all the 2020 objectives are evaluated, it can be seen that member states are given roles to fulfill these objectives and they are given the opportunity to create their own legislation. It is emphasized that all legislation forming the 2020 objectives are connected with each other and every new EU legislation needs to be created by taking the applications of member states into

---

[44] European Commission, *[COM(2013) 169 Final]*, 5.
[45] European Commission, *[COM(2013) 169 Final]*, 6.
[46] European Commission, *[COM(2013) 169 Final]*, 7.
[47] European Commission, *[COM(2013) 169 Final]*, 8.

consideration, because the most important criticism made to present legislation seems to be the inconsistency between these plans.[48]

By taking all the planned legislation's influence on the economy into consideration, progress should be made on issues such as the development of internal market legislation, providing competition, employment, energy prices and thus security of energy.[49]

Within the scope of the stakeholder opinions on the Green Paper published in 2013, the Commission published a Communication and emphasized the necessity to transition to a low carbon economy, which "ensures competitive and affordable energy for all consumers, creates new opportunities for growth and jobs and provides greater security of energy supplies and reduced import dependence for the Union as a whole".[50]

The strategy of 2030, together with forming the necessary framework to fulfill 2020 objectives, also included nine new objectives:

> *- An ambitious commitment to reduce greenhouse gas emissions in line with the 2050 Roadmaps*
>
> *- Simplification of the European policy framework while improving complementarity and coherence between objectives and instruments*
>
> *-Providing flexibility for Member States to define a low carbon transition appropriate to their specific circumstances*
>
> *- Strengthening regional cooperation between Member States to help them meet common energy and climate challenges*
>
> *- Building on the momentum behind the development of renewables with a policy based on a more cost-efficient approach*
>
> *- Ensuring that the competitiveness of business and affordability of energy for consumers are central in determining the objectives of the framework and the instruments to implement it*
>
> *- Improving energy security, while delivering a low-carbon and competitive energy system*

---

[48] European Commission, *[COM(2013) 169 Final]*, 9.

[49] European Commission, *[COM(2013) 169 Final]*, 10-11.

[50] European Commission, [COM (2014) 15 Final] Communication From The Commission To The European Parliament, The Council, The European Economic And Social Committee And The Committee Of The Regions A Policy Framework for Climate and Energy in the Period from 2020 to 2030, Assented to 22 January 2014, 3.

- Enhancing investor certainty by providing clear signals now on how the policy framework will change after 2020

- Fair sharing of efforts between Member States which reflects their specific circumstances and capacities.[51]

The strategy fundamentally necessitates the objective to mitigate greenhouse gas emissions by 40% in the year 2030 in the sectors included in the ETS where energy is intensely used, or not including in ETS, compared to the rates of 1990. If the plans are fulfilled, this number is predicted to be at least 32%. In order to fulfill the objective of 40%, it was indicated that the rate of renewable energy should be 27%. According to the Commission, renewable energy and greenhouse gas emissions complete each other.[52] In addition, it was emphasized that 40% greenhouse gas mitigation would provide a 25% energy saving.[53] On October 23–24, 2014, the objective of 40% greenhouse gas domestic emission reduction was decided at the European Council. All member states will join the greenhouse gas mitigation efforts. While the objective of 27% renewable energy is bound at EU level, member states have the flexibility to determine their own objectives.[54]

The rise in energy prices directed the producers to energy efficiency.[55] Member states, while making plans according to their national preferences, should also be consistent with the Union's climate and energy objectives. The formation of a domestic energy market and the necessity of developing a structure consisting of competitive and transparent policy are emphasized. Within this context, member states will prepare plans for 2030 objectives. In the first stage, the Commission will prepare a detailed guide for the plans that the states will produce on the subjects of greenhouse gas emission, renewable energy and energy efficiency. In the second stage, regional planning with neighbor states and planning within consultations will be an iterative process. In the last stage, the plans of the member states will be assessed by the Commission and if seen as inadequate, will have to be reorganized. According to the Commission, in order for the national plans to be applied effectively, they need to be prepared before 2020.[56]

---

[51] European Commission, *[COM (2014) 15 Final]*, 3-4.
[52] European Commission, *[COM (2014) 15 Final]*, 5-6.
[53] European Commission, *[COM (2014) 15 Final]*, 8.
[54] European Council, *European Council Conclusions 23 and 24 October 2014 EUCO 169/14*, Assented to 24 October 2014, 1-5.
[55] European Council, European Council Conclusions 23 and 24 October 2014, 11.
[56] European Council, European Council Conclusions 23 and 24 October 2014, 13.

Thus, member states have not been left to prepare national plans by themselves but are required to work in harmony with the Commission and to be in constant contact with their neighbors. In other words, by integrating national plans, the plans and practices of member states are tried to be guaranteed; this situation is developing in line with CSOs' demands.

In the Communication where the objectives of 2030 were declared, the method that was used can be considered similar to an open method of coordination. The period between the declaration of the objectives of 2030 and their acceptance at Union level show that the Communication was sufficiently discussed. It can be observed that they determined a schedule to reach these objectives, and these objectives can be transformed into national objectives. Most importantly, actors other than central authority are actively involved in the process. The flexibility shown to the states on the subject of achieving the objectives is one of the most important indicators that this mechanism is being operated.[57]

Roadmap of 2050

The obligation to use the resources effectively in Europe forced the Commission to make long-term plans in the fields of transportation, energy and climate change. The transition to a low carbon economy became one of the most important fields for the EU in this sense. The Roadmap of 2050 was formed, and includes the aims of mitigating greenhouse gas emissions by 20% by 2020, which is the objective of the 2020 strategy, to increase the rate of renewable energy to 20% within energy production, and to increase the energy production at the rate of 20%.[58]

At this point it would be meaningful to mention two fundamental characteristics of the formation of climate policy. "First, given the Member States' assymmetrical interests and preferences, a high capacity to integrate these interests is needed. Second, capacity to aggregate the preferences is crucial to

---

[57] "2030 Climate and Energy Governance: Assessing an Open Method of Coordination Approach," ClientEarth. February 2015, http://www.clientearth.org/reports/2030-climate-andenergy-governance-assessing-an-omc-approach.pdf.
Open Method of Coordination was announced as a tool for Lisbon Strategy in 2000. In this process intergovernrnental negotiations were determinant whereas the role of Commission, Parliament and Court was restraint. The basis of the method is constituted by determined common objectives, indicators, comparison of the performances of EU member states and sharing the best experiences. For definition see EUR-Lex, http://eurlex. europa.eu/summary/glossary/open_method_coordination.html.

[58] European Commission, COM (2011) 112 Final] Communication From The Commission To The European Parliament, The Council, The European Economic And Social Committee And The Committee Of The Regions A Roadmap for moving to a competitive low carbon economy in 2050, Assented to 08 March 2011, 3.

avoid deadlock"[59] Legislation made within this situation created a platform for the states to discuss their own interests and also to try to provide the necessary capacity to reach reconciliation. The formation of the roadmap is important in terms of creation of this discussion platform.

To limit climate change under 2°C as the first objective, the need to make plans regarding emission mitigation until the year 2050, in light of the IPCC's data, emerged.[60] According to the reconciliation in 2011, the EU needs to provide greenhouse gas emission mitigation between 80–95% when compared to 1990 levels by 2050. A report was published on how to achieve this objective.

To achieve the objectives of mitigating greenhouse gas emission, first, energy efficiency needs to be increased and technological development needs to be encouraged. In the emissions emerging from the use of energy production, agriculture, transportation, industry, house and services and in the projections made to mitigate carbon dioxide emissions, it will be necessary to make a change between 79–82%. According to the report, it was emphasized that electrical energy would preclude carbon dioxide emissions. It was also emphasized that the productivity of energy efficiency studies would increase the importance of electricity, indicating that electricity will play a key role in transportation and heating,

The improvements on buildings' energy performances seem to be the cheapest and most effective situation. Because of this, the Directive of "Energy Performance of Buildings" issued related to the measures to be taken to increase energy efficiency and its practices, seems to be of top importance. While new buildings are obliged to obey the determined rules, member states are given the responsibility to transform old buildings and to take measures. Also on February 4, 2011 with a decision taken by the Council, public buildings of member states were given the obligation to obey precautions to be determined on the subject of energy efficiency.

In addition to this, the increase of air quality and its positive effects on health also seem important for the Commission. In other respects, the amount of investment that industry needs to spare to develop the system of carbon capture and storage is about 10 billion Euros and this creates a financial stress in the Union besides taking measures.

---

[59] John Birger Skjærseth, "The Climate Policy of the EC: Too Hot to Handle?," *Journal of Common Market Studies* 32, no. 1 (March 1994): 38.

[60] The content of the part is taken from the related document as a summary of the roadmap of 2050. See European Commission, *COM (2011) 112 Final*].

Şekercioğlu

According to the Commission, after 2020, smart grids, passive housing, carbon capture and storage, developed industrial processes, and electrification of transportation will be the main veins of transitioning to an effective and low carbon energy system.

After the public consultation made following this first document published in the process of the preparation of Roadmap of 2050, the Energy Roadmap of 2050 was published in 2011. According to this document, in order to fulfill the objectives of 2020, no sufficient planning was made. The necessary ground for the innovations on infrastructures of the sectors and long-term investments were not prepared.[61] Therefore, the main objective of the 2050 Roadmap is to make the necessary planning for long-term investments and to determine alternative ways for decarbonization.[62]

EU climate and energy policy: binding texts

Within the EU, legislation on climate change can be produced in various forms. The legislation is issued not only as regulations directly influencing member states, but also can be prepared like a directive in order to leave the methods of practice to be determined by member states.[63] Specifically to environmental policy, decisions on climate change and energy are mostly issued as directives. Although there are discussions among member states on the legislation, certain legislation is made both because of the necessity to make legislation and as a result of public pressure. The states' that determine the practical basics of the directives within their own domestic policies according to their own styles of management make their reconciliation easier.

If the Kyoto objectives and the position of member states to achieve these objectives are compared, it can be said that interstate differentiation is encouraging in creating more binding documents. That is to say, while the 15 EU members stated that with Kyoto, they will provide 8% greenhouse gas

---

[61] European Commission, [COM(2011) 885] Communication From The Commission To The European Parliament, The Council, The European Economic And Social Committee And The Committee Of The Regions Energy Roadmap 2050, Assented to 15 December 2011, 2.

[62] European Commission, *[COM(2011) 885]*, 2. The most important thing emphasized in the document is because of the difficulty to make a long term prediction, to determine the roads that will make the long terms objectives possible to achieve. Thereby the worries on the unpredictability of the process of not only the Commissions but also of the institutions involved in the consultation process caused scenarios to be organized differently. Because nobody can predict when a problem of gas or petroleum will occur.

[63] As it is stated in a research, 43 environmental policy savings approved by EU Council between the years 1993-1994 are lined up as such: 6 regulations, 18 directives, 16 decisions, 3 resolutions. Out of this 43 decisions only 36 of them could be connected with environmental policy and others were decided within the fields of common market, energy, agriculture, transportation and research policies. For detailed information see: Andersen and Nordvig Rasmussen, "The Making Environmental Policy", 585-597.

mitigation between the years 2008–2012, a rate of only 0.6% mitigation could be provided between 2004 and 2007. The reason for this is the differentiation of practices among countries. For example, while the UK and Sweden are very close to their objectives, states like Spain, Austria, Belgium, Denmark, Ireland, Italy and Portugal face difficulties in achieving their objectives.[64]

Therefore, creating a more binding Energy and Climate Package with new member states will play an encouraging role in terms of providing the mitigation objectives. As the Commission cannot function as a government, it should also use national, regional and domestic infrastructure. Because of this, the Commission depends on the management structures of member countries in the legislation it prepares.

The EU climate change regulation includes four fundamental documents. They are: the Emission Trade System (ETS), application to geological storage of carbon dioxide, application to produce energy from renewable energy resources and Effort Sharing Decision.[65]

These regulations and decision are determinant legislations in terms of climate change legislation. When seen from this perspective, all three regulations have key importance in the formation of climate change policy.

The preparations of regulations take place within different social realities and processes. For example while with ETS and renewable energy regulations, states gave approval to a new legislation process, geological storage application bears the objective to reevaluate technical legislation.[66] Therefore, it would be meaningful to consider the present conditions during the evaluation of these regulations.

Greenhouse gas emissions and Emission Trade System

The ETS is one of the fundamental anchor points of the EU's climate change policies.[67] According to the Commission, the ETS works with the logic of upper

---

[64] "In graphics: The EU and emissions," *BBC News,* last modified January 10, 2007, http://news.bbc.co.uk/2/hi/europe/6244465.stm.
[65] These texts were attained from EurLex.
[66] Interviewee 4 (EU Commission DG Climate Consultant), interview by the author, Brussels, Setember 23, 2015.
[67] The documents used in this section are as such:
European Commission, Proposal for a Directive COM(2001) 581 final; European Parliament, Legislative Resolution on the Proposal P5_TA(2002)0461; European Commission, Amended Proposal COM(2002) 680 final; Council of the European Union, Common Position (EC) No 28/2003 (2003/C 125 E/05); European Commission, Opinion of the Commission COM(2003) 463 final; European Parliament and the Council of the European Union, Directive 2003/87/EC; European Parliament and the Council of the European Union,

limit which means that there is a cap for carbon emissions. Member states allocated the allowances to the companies up to their limit determined by the Commission. Accordingly, greenhouse gas emissions, generating from the production processes of factories, energy production facilities and other production mechanisms, are limited. In case the system is functional, greenhouse gas emissions will mitigate gradually and thus important steps for the struggle with climate change will be taken.[68] Every country determines an emisssion quota for operators functioning on their own territory within the limits determined by the Commission. If operators cannot fill these quotas, they can sell the rest of their rights to another operators and therefore an emission market would be set up. The basic functioning dynamic of the system is based on this idea. This system is called "cap and trade".

The emissions of the EU are comprised of different gases. According to the numbers of 2012, 80% of the emissions consisted of CO_2, 20% of methane (CH_4), nitros oxide (N_2O) and flourinated gases (F-gases); 94% of CO_2 emerged from burning and 6% from industrial processes, 50% of methane emerged from agriculture, 31% from waste, 19% from leakage and burning activities, 81% of nitros oxide emerged from agriculture, 5% from industrial processes and solvent, 10% from burning, and 4% from wastes; 100% of flourinated gases emerged as a result of industrial processes.[69] The general logic of emission trading is to place a limit on these gases and to control this process through an EU-level market.

According to the second Annex of Emission Trade Directive, greenhouse gases consist of carbondioxide (CO_2), methane (CH_4), nitrous oxide (N_2O), hydrofluorocarbon (HFCs), perfluorokarbon (PFCs) and sulphur hexafluoride (SF6). The EU ETS on the other hand, is only focused on carbon dioxide. The limitation of the anthropogenic emissions of these greenhouse gases is the main goal of the Directive.

The ETS first came into focus to solve the problem of acid rain in the 1980s in North America and Europe.[70] The EU is the first organization throughout the world to accept the application of this system on the climate within the scope of

---

Directive 2009/29/EC; European Parliament and the Council of the European Union, Directive 2004/101/EC; European Parliament and the Council of the European Union, Directive 2008/101/EC; European Parliament and the Council of the European Union, Regulation (EC) No 219/2009.

[68] "The EU Emission Trading System," *European Commission*, Accessed December 12, 2014, http://ec.europa.eu/clima/policies/ets/index_en.htm.

[69] Jos Delbeke and Peter Vis, "EU Climate Leadership in a Rapidly Changing World", 16-17.

[70] Michele Betsill and Matthew J. Hoffmann, "The Contours of "Cap and Trade": The Evolution of Emissions Trading Systems for Greenhouse Gases," *Review of Policy Research* 28, no. 1 (2011): 84.

the Kyoto obligations. The Directive, published in 2003, was put into practice in 2005 with amendments of 2004[71] and after the legislation on aviation in 2008, it was broadened. Then in 2009, it took its final shape with a new Regulation and Directive. Therefore, the final text of the ETS was formed after four different changes.[72] The ETS can be examined in three different periods: 2005–2007, 2008–2012 and 2013 onwards. The fundamental logic of ETS is to mitigate the emissions predicted in Kyoto Protocol for the states.

The first step of the Emission Trade Directive is the Council Directive published in 1996[73] under the title "Integrated Pollution Prevention and Control". To fulfill the obligations of the sixth Environmental Action Plan published in 2002 and the obligations of the Kyoto Protocol that came into effect with the approval of the Council in 2002, the Commission tried to form the fundamental legal base of the ETS by suggesting a change to the Directive of 96.

The Commission saw the ETS as the most effective solution for emission mitigation and the Emission Cap and Trade system under the ETS provides more mitigation. When the EU ETS is taken into consideration, it contains 31 countries and it affects more than 500 million people, around 12000 industrial plants and aircraft operators. Although there was a downfall in 2012 in the market numbers together with the allocation problems rising from the cap system, with the binding and applicable rules, it is stated that the system can work.[74]

The allowances are carbon market units and take place in an electronic form. All the actors of the system are recorded in this system and from 2012, all the records of carbon units within the Union Registry and the ETS have been recorded. As everyone can make carbon allowance trade, energy firms and intermediary institutions are the most active participants.[75]

---

[71] European Parliament and the Council, [Directive 2004/101/EC] DIRECTIVE 2004/101/EC amending Directive 2003/87/EC establishing a scheme for greenhouse gas emission allowance trading within the Community, in respect of the Kyoto Protocol's project mechanisms, Assented to 27 October 2004.

[72] The consolidated version of the directive went in effect on 25.06.2009. To reach the consolidated version of the directive see
http://eurlex.europa.eu/LexUriServ/LexUriServ.do?uri=CONSLEG:2003L0087:20090625:en:PDF.

[73] Council of the European Union, [Council Directive 96/61/EC] concerning integrated pollution prevention and control, Assented to 24 September 1996.

[74] Damien Meadows, Yvon Slingenberg and Peter Zapfel, "EU ETS: pricing carbon to drive cost effective reductions across Europe," *EU Climate Policy Explained*, edited by. Jos Delbeke and Peter Vis, (Oxon: Routledge, 2015), 29-33.

[75] Meadows, Slingenberg and Zapfel, "EU ETS: pricing carbon", 44-48.

Within this framework, the Directive of 2003/87/EC[76] fundamentally draws the frame of the legislations to be made by the Union for the mitigation of greenhouse gas emission rates. First, it was guaranteed by the Union that compared to the rates in 1990, greenhouse gas emissions between 2008 and 2012 were to be mitigated at the rate of 8% and in the long-term it was emphasized that a mitigation at the rate of 70% was necessary. According to the decision made on March 2007 in the European Summit, it was aimed to mitigate emissions by 20% in the year 2020 compared to the rates in 1990.[77]

The Directive, aiming to create an effective European Market in the allowance of greenhouse gas emission, also underlines the roles of the member states within this process. The member states, both during the distribution of the allowances and in the process after the distribution, should observe the operators and in case of a violation, should make sure they get punished. It is also emphasized that in order for the process to function transparently, the public should also be able to follow this process.

In the preamble of the Directive, in the first proposal of the Commission, while greenhouse gas emission trade was emphasized[78], this emphasis was changed as greenhouse gas emission allowance trade in Common Position,[79] and was reflected as such in the last text published in 2003.

Again in the preamble, while the guarantees of the member states on greenhouse gas emissions related to Kyoto Protocol were emphasized[80], this was changed in the Parliament's proposal with the emphasis that Kyoto Protocol was accepted with an overwhelming majority in the European Parliament upon the proposal of the Council and that the member states should fulfill their obligations.[81]

In return, the Commission, in the amended proposal that it prepared, the expression that the addition of the approval of the European Union and also that

---

[76] European Parliament and the Council, [*Directive 2003/87/EC*].

[77] In the preface of the directive dated 2009, the 2007 Council outputs and COP negotiations were mentioned.

[78] European Commission, [COM(2001) 581 final] Proposal for a Directive of the European Parliament and of the Council establishing a scheme for greenhouse gas emission allowance trading within the Community and amending Council Directive 96/61/EC, Assented to 23 October 2001.

[79] European Council. *[(2003/C 125 E/05)] Common Position (EC) No 28/2003*, Assented to 18 March 2003.

[80] European Commission, *[COM(2001) 581 final]*.

[81] European Parliament, [P5_TA(2002)0461] Legislative resolution on the proposal for a European Parliament and Council directive establishing a scheme for greenhouse gas emission allowance trading within the Community and amending Council Directive 96/61/EC (COM(2001) 581 – C5-0578/2001 – 2001/0245(COD)), Assented to 10 October 2002.

the obligations of the states originating from Kyoto Protocol should be achieved by using the resources they see appropriate, is emphasized not to be acceptable, as the countries would be able to act in defiance of the Union law.[82] In accordance with the Common Position and by referencing the allowance of greenhouse gas emission and economical development, it was stated that it aims to contribute to member states to fulfill their obligations.[83]

Another important discussion that attracted attention in the Directive was on the subject of legislation, on emissions to be made at member states level or Union level. In the Parliament's proposal, it was emphasized to solve the problem of emissions at EU level, instead of member states level[84]; but the Commission rejected this change emphasizing that an EU approach would not be able to solve the problem.[85] However, in the final text, this adding of the Parliament did not take any place. It can be said that the insistence of the Parliament on this subject was related with information flow provided by civil society organizations and lobby activities.

It was also emphasized that member states would be able to prepare their own national plans on the subject of the practice of their own applications and would be able to determine their own national trade programmes in the fields staying out of Annex 1.[86] Accordingly, the first plans to be prepared by the member states within the context of "National Allocation Plans" would firstly include a three-year period starting from 2005 and second, plans would be prepared for a five-year period after 2008.

While in the ninth amendment of the preamble, the Parliament suggested that not only the energy intense industry sector and energy sector, but also other sectors should be emphasized and a flexible mechanism should be applied. The Commission suggested that a flexible mechanism would strengthen the "volunteering" approach and thus could not be accepted and that this approach would decrease the economical productivity of the Document. The 19th amendment, emphasizing the production of policies and measure in all sectors of the EU economy for emission mitigation, was accepted by the Commission.

---

[82] European Commission, [COM(2002) 680 final] Amended proposal for a Directive of the European Parliament and of the Council establishing a scheme for greenhouse gas emission allowance trading within the Community and amending Council Directive 96/61/EC, Assented to 27 November 2002..
[83] European Council, *[(2003/C 125 E/05)] Common Position (EC) No 28/2003*, Assented to 18 March 2003.
[84] European Parliament, *[P5_TA(2002)0461]*.
[85] European Commission, *[COM(2002) 680 final]*.
[86] Annex 1 sorted the activities causing greenhouse gas emission that are within the scope of the directive. According to this energy production, iron steel industry, mineral industry (including cement, glass and ceramic industries) and paper industry are within the context of the directive.

In the final shape of the document dated 2003, it was emphasized that member states could use the mechanisms of Clean Development and Joint Implementation within the scope of project flexibility mechanisms.[87] Moreover, member states would be able to apply their administrative and financial policies for the application.

In the 13th amendment, the Parliament's proposal on the development of other strategies, along with emission trade, was accepted by the Commission. The Commission stated that it did not think that the emission trade was the only way to follow.

One of the fundamental sources of the problems to be faced after the preparation of the ETS in 2003 was the distribution of emission allowances. Accordingly, while 95% of the emissions in the first period between 2005 and 2007 would be distributed free of charge, in the second period including 2008–2012, 90% of the emissions would be distributed free of charge. The businesses were expected to make emissions in accordance with the emission allowance for the year. Within this period, any businesses exceeding the rate of emissions assigned to them paid a penalty of 40 Euros per ton in the first period and 100 Euros per ton in the second. Operators with extra emission could transfer the unused amount via a bank system or could sell it to other operators.

When the amendments on the articles that the Parliament is eager to make are examined, it can be stated that the Parliament expected to have a more general quality in terms of the sectors included and greenhouse gas types. The Parliament also presented a contradictory text to detail the legislation, to suggest the voluntary basis and at the same time with its emphasis on the techniques to be applied. Within this context, the Commission found 55 proposals of the Parliament unacceptable, 7 requests for amended proposals acceptable and 11 requests for amended proposals partially acceptable.[88]

After the Directive was published in 2003, the first amendment in 2004 was on the CDM and JI mechanisms. The amendments started with the addition of the definitions of CDM and JI. The amendments included the subject of allowance

---

[87] While project infexibility mechanisms did not take any place in the first draft of the Directive prepared by the Commission, after the reconciliation with the Commission following the publishment of the document of Joint Implemantation of the Parliament and the Council, it was added to the Directive. Likewise it was emphasized that more effective technologies were supported including Combined Heat and Power-CHP. While the Parliament insists that it was to be acted with the help of guidelines prepared by the Commission on the subjects of Combined Heat and Power and waste fuels, the Commission insists that the member states should decide themselves on the allowance of CHP. Thus the final document took its form as the Commission demanded. Here the influence of civil society in the Parliament can be seen.

[88] See European Commission, [*COM(2002) 680 final*].

in article 11, the subject of competent authority in article 18, the subject of member state reports in article 21 and the subject of evaluation process in article 30.[89] Although it was not a very extensive legislation, as observed in the civil society reports in the proceeding period, the addition of the CDM and JI mechanisms was important.

The amendment of 2008 added five chapters to the Directive. With the amendment in article 2, there were changes in the scope of the Directive, in article 3 in definitions, in article 11 in allowances and in article 12 in transfer, release and cancels. In articles 14, 15, 16 and 18, amendments in observation, verification, penalties and competent authority were made. In addition to these, there were changes in articles 23 including the Commission, and in articles 25, 28 and 30 mentioning the connection with other emission trade programmes.[90]

The first amendment that took place in 2009 with a regulation. The main purpose in these amendments was to add the necessary provisions that were needed for the application of article 11 and to add the necessary information for preparing the observation process guidelines. Amendments in the registry system (article 19), amendments to Annex III (article 22), committees (article 23), unilateral inclusion (articles 24), and article 25 mentioning the link with other greenhouse gas emission trading shemes as well as amendments in Annex 4 were made.[91]

Finally in 2009, the need for new legislation overcome the cap problems was emerged. Within this scope, the ETS Directive, Renewable Energy Directive and Geological Storage Directive were published April 23, 2009. The legislation made in the Climate and Energy Package fundamentally aimed to create integrated policies. The ETS Directive is the directive that most attracted the attention of CSOs.

The Directive made many additions to its 2003 version and tried to overcome the problems and criticisms originating from other annexes. Amendments were made In all articles except articles 8, 17, 18, 20, 26, 30 and 31. The articles without any amendments were concerning coordination, access to information,

---

[89] European Parliament and the Council, [*Directive 2004/101/EC*].

[90] European Parliament and the Council, [Directive 2008/101/EC] amending Directive 2003/87/EC so as to include aviation activities in the scheme for greenhouse gas emission allowance trading within the Community, Assented to 19 November 2008.

[91] European Parliament and the Council, [Regulation (EC) No 219/2009] adapting a number of instruments subject to the procedure referred to in Article 251 of the Treaty to Council Decision 1999/468/EC with regard to the regulatory procedure with scrutiny, Assented to 11 March 2009.

competent authority, central administrator, amendment directive number 96/61/EC, review and implementation.

As it is stated in Directive 2009, starting from 2013, every year at the rate of 1.74%, allowances were to be made in the assigned amounts in line with the period 2008–2012 (article 9) and together with this, Annex 1 was enhanced and new categories of activities were applied to the system.[92] All the allowances that were not distributed free of charge from the year 2013 will be distributed by auction – 88% of the allowances within the member states' own rates will be distributed by auction. A rate of 10% will be assigned to some countries to increase the solidarity of the Union and a rate of 2% will be assigned to states with greenhouse gas emissions below 20% (article 10).

Member states can decide how they will utilize their revenues gained from the auction. However, at least 50% of these revenues have to be used in fields determined by article 10. They are to report these utilizations to the Commission, and member states should inform the Commission once again for the auction for transparency, open access, price formation and technical subjects. The Commission will prepare annual reports by following the operation of carbon markets (article 10). Also within the scope of the Directive, legislation was made on to whom the free allowances will be given and on the allowances of operators newly entered into the system.

In the same article, legislation related to carbon leakage in energy intense industries and subtitles on how the allowances will be organized within the scope of modernization of electric production systems was included. In the Directive, Certified Emission Reductions (CERs), together with Emission Reduction Units (ERUs), were handled in article 11 within the context of National Implementation Measures.[93]

When the amendments and additions of Directive 2003 are examined generally, a constant change can be seen in article 3 including the definitions, and articles 10 and 11 in which allowances are organized. Within the context of the reorganization of the ETS, these amendments took place to overcome the issues encountered in the first period and to protect the framework of the Directive.

---

[92] Within this context energy producing centrals by burning fuels, mineral oil refineries, coke production, metal ore burning and moulding, pig iron production, production of metals, aluminium production, cement and brick production, lime, glass, ceramic, mineral wool, gypsum stone productions, pulp, paper, carbon black, nitric acid, adipic acid, glyoxal ammoniac, organic chemicals, hydrogen, sodium oxide productions, greenhouse gases caught during transportation and geological storage, emissions related to the Treaty are included in the Directive.

[93] Apart from these legislations there are many addings in the directive, but only the most important ones and the ones connected to civil society reaction is tried to be summarized.

Civil Society Impact on the EU Climate Change Policy

The most important criticism on the ETS is the market mechanism being unable to operate because of the higher allowance in the first period. In the second period, the flexible legislation became stricter. The third period also differs from the first and second period. According to official data, the third period includes an EU-wide limitation instead of a national one. The allowances would not be free of charge, and every year the part included within the auction would increase; free of charge distributions will be dependent on performance and more sectors and gas directives are included in the directive and a 300 million Euro allowance will be allocated for the new entries into the system.[94]

In the interviews carried out on the subject of legislation on the ETS with the objective of analysing the influence of civil society on these legislations, Interviewee 4 emphasized that the preparation process of the ETS had taken a long time and involved meetings with CSOs as consensus was tried to be reached at every stage after 2000. The Interviewee also stated that the Green Paper published in 2003 and the reports of impact assessment influenced the preparation process of the directive and that the negotiation process was managed in this way.[95]

Interviewee 5 on the other hand emphasized that for ETS legislation, the Kyoto Protocol and even the Chicago Protocol from the 1960s should have been taken into consideration.[96] The negotiations during this process formed the base of the ETS. Interviewee 9 indicated that climate change was the driving power in this process and ETS legislation proceeded in parallel with climate change developments.[97]

The EU also published Effort Sharing Decision numbered 406/2009/EC[98] with the ETS Directive. The Effort Sharing Decision is one of the most important documents on the greenhouse gases to be brought under control. The decision includes the mitigations of the Union between the years 2013–2020. The greenhouse gas emissions of member states are limited at a certain rate based on 2005 levels. The document is binding for the states. In accordance with the

---

[94] "The EU Emission Trading System." *European Commission*. Accessed December 12, 2014. http://ec.europa.eu/clima/policies/ets/index_en.htm.

[95] Interviewee 4 (EU Commission DG Climate consultant), interview by the author, Brussels, September 23, 2015.

[96] Interviewee 5 (EU Commission DG Climate consultant), interview by the author, Brussels, September 23, 2015.

[97] Interviewee 9 (EU Commission DG Climate consultant), interview by the author, Brussels, September 25, 2015.

[98] European Parliament and the Council, [Decision No 406/2009/EC] on the effort of Member States to reduce their greenhouse gas emissions to meet the Community's greenhouse gas emission reduction commitments up to 2020, Assented to 23 April 2009.

Decision, the emissions of the member states in 2020 cannot be higher than the rates indicated in the second Annex of the decision.

The Decision includes the sectors of transportation (except aviation and maritime shipping), buildings, agriculture and waste that are not included in the ETS.[99] The aim is to provide mitigation in the fields that are not included in emission trade, to achieve the goal of limiting global warming by 2°C and at the same time to encourage emission mitigation in all sectors.

The EU Commission, under the title number 10, in the preamble of the Effort Sharing Decision states that in order to achieve the EU level emission allocation rates, member states can transfer their own emission allocations to other states. Under the title 11 it emphasizes that CDM credit's usage should be improved but only to be used in conditions that do not create negative environmental effects. In proportion to CSOs' views, it also states that the usage of the credits should be limited. Under the title number 12, it is emphasized that the flexibility mechanism that member states apply to fulfill their obligations, should be used in a way to support sustainable development in third countries.

Under the proceeding titles in relation to CDM projects, credits and flexibility mechanisms, decisions related to Joint Implementation projects are indicated. In case of not coming to an agreement on the subject of climate change, it is emphasized that after the year 2012 Joint Implementation projects will not continue.[100]

Of course when considered that CSOs are mostly of the opinion not to use these credits, the idea to limit the usage by the EU should be seen as a positive development. By emphasizing multi-level governance, it can be said that not only central authorities of member states, but also local and regional authorities have important roles in this process.[101]

To organize the allocation of emission allowances within the scope of the ETS, a Commission decision was published in 2011 titled 2011/278/EU.[102] The main purpose of the text was to draw the fundamental frame of allowances to be distributed free of charge in the period after 2013. The related decision was sued

---

[99] "Why did greenhouse gas emissions decrease in the EU between 1990 and 2012?," *European Environment Agency*. Accessed May 23, 2016, http://www.eea.europa.eu/publications/why-did-ghgemissions-decrease, 15.
[100] "Why did greenhouse gas emissions decrease", *European Environment Agency*, Title 15, 3.
[101] "Why did greenhouse gas emissions decrease", *European Environment Agency*, Title 28, 5.
[102] European Commission, [2011/278/EU] Commission Decision determining transitional Union-wide rules for harmonised free allocation of emission allowances pursuant to Article 10a of Directive 2003/87/EC of the European Parliament and of the Council, Assented to 27 April 2011.

by Poland, but the CJEU considered the Commission to be rightful in this legislation. In 2013, in addition to this decision, the Commission decision number 2013/162/EU[103] determining the free allocations of member states was published.

The developments on the ETS form the most important keystone of the EU'S current policies on climate and energy. After 2009, with the effect of global crisis, carbon prices per unit decreased immensely. To overcome these issues that could possibly ruin the function of emission trade mechanism, the methods of "backloading" as a short-term measure and "Market Stability Reserve" as a long-term measure were suggested.[104]

The basis of the backloading method was formed by the postponement of the auction of 900 million tons of allowances to the period 2019–2020. In this context, a mitigation of 400 million tons in 2014, 300 million tons in 2015, and 200 million tons in 2016 was foreseen. The market stability reserve will be formed by making a reform in the ETS starting from 2018. The reserves will be organized to develop the elasticity of the system against big shocks of surplus allowances to be distributed by auction.[105]

The basic logic of this transfer process is the prediction that economical conditions will be more appropriate at the mentioned period of time. Although the suggestion of backloading was highly disputed, it was approved by the Parliament and the Council.[106]

Energy dimension of climate change policy and renewable energy legislations

Energy, especially because of the use of fossil resources during its production, is the relative component of environment and thus of climate change. Except fossil resources, environmental disasters that can be caused by nuclear energy usage and nuclear power plant waste, necessitates environment and energy evaluation during policy making. Because of this, the EU, by founding the DG

---

[103] European Commission, [2013/162/EU)] Commission Decision on determining Member States' annual emission allocations for the period from 2013 to 2020 pursuant to Decision No 406/2009/EC of the European Parliament and of the Council, Assented to 26 March 2013.
[104] İlge Kıvılcım, *İKV Değerlendirme Notu AB'nin En Büyük Sınavlarından Biri "AB ETS" Olacak*. Last modified October 2014,
http://www.ikv.org.tr/images/files/AB_nin_En_Buyuk_Sinavlar%C4%B0ndan_Biri_AB_ETS_Olacak.pdf.
[105] "Structural Reform of the European Carbon Market," *European Commission*, Accessed March 25, 2015, http://ec.europa.eu/clima/policies/ets/reform/index_en.htm.
[106] Meadows, Slingenberg and Zapfel, "EU ETS: pricing carbon", 50.

Şekercioğlu

Climate Action, tried to provide different units to merge their potential for make climate legislation more easily and comprehensively.

Although in previous years there have been studies on limiting carbon dioxide emission, the first extensive climate change package was created in 2000. The energy related legislations in the 1990s made the formation of climate change package easier. Within this package, the subjects of renewable energy, efficiency, carbon and energy tax were mentioned. As climate policy cannot be considered independent from energy, this kind of legislation is meaningful.

During the formation of the climate and energy package that was agreed on March 2007, there was cooperation with the Environmental Council as well as with Energy and Finance ministers.[107] The climate and energy package focuses predominantly on energy. One of its greatest driving power is energy supply security. The dependency on Rusia for natural gas and the issues of gas interruptions with Ukraine, increase the necessity of the Union to take measures. This necessity goes together with the development of necessary technologies to mitigate greenhouse gas emissions, to support clean energy and the productive usage of energy.

The integration of environmental policies with other political fields is very important. To measure the integration of environmental policies with other political fields, the Environment Policy Integration (EPI) research field was developed. The studies in this field were transformed into the formulation of Climate Policy Integration (CPI).

In EPI studies, there are two different views on the subject of the degree of integration. According to this, the understanding that supports the integration in other political fields, primarily environmental, indicates "Strong EPI", the understanding that supports only the consideration of environment in other political fields indicates "Weak EPI".[108] In directly related fields like energy, while strong integration is in question, in fields indirectly related with environment, weak integration may be in question. In the analysis of this effect especially during the formation of the climate and energy package, it is meaningful to find experts from different fields.

The most important reason for environment policy is because of the environment being directly influenced from implementations carried out in

---

[107] Wurzel, "Member States and the Council," 88.

[108] Claire Dupont, "Combating Climate Complexity in Integration of EU Climate and Energy Policies," in *Energy and Environment in Europe: Asssessing a Complex Relationship, European Integration Online Papers (EIoP)*, edited by. Jale Tosun and Israel Solorio, Special Mini-Issue 1 15, no. 8 (2011):4.

different fields. Especially as 80% of emissions causing climate change originate from energy, it is important to create an integrated policy. In this sense, energy and climate change policies present an integrated structure and a common legislation in both of the fields makes sense. While analysing the influence of CPI on other political fields, energy policy is also included in this process. As legislation on environment is directly related to decisions made on the field of energy, climate change legislation cannot be taken into consideration independently from energy.

The increase in renewable energy usage is directly related to energy efficiency, steps to be taken in energy security of supply, decreasing emission rates and the development of mechanisms to compete with environmental problems originating from the usage of fossil fuels are the fundamental components of energy policy. And this relation shows the necessity to make decisions to be made in the context of the struggle with climate change and legislation to be applied all together.

The integration of political fields form upon the requests of states on this subject. Although the Commission is in charge of proposing law, states being the last to decide at the last stage indicate that the process also functions intergovernmentally. According to this, Dupont also approves as Moravcsik's and Schimmelfenning's claim that every political field's evolution and integration with each other is a part of the intergovernmental negotiation process.[109]

As a result of the negotiation process and changes in Union Treaty, legislation determined the way of policy that the Union will follow. On the one hand, the importance of intergovernmental reconciliation is the deteminant of current policy, on the other hand the importance given to community involvement to close the deficit in democracy of the Union emphasized the importance of a multi-graded, layered involvement in determining the limits of the political field.

The first step for legal legislation on renewable energy was the Green Paper, published in 2006. The main purpose was to determine the necessary criteria and policy priorities to form the EU's long-term energy policy and to qualify the objectives more extensively.[110]

---

[109] Dupont, "Combating Climate Complexity", 6.

[110] European Commission, [COM(2006) 105 final] Green Paper A European Strategy for Sustainable, Competitive and Secure Energy, Assented to 8 March 2006.

In the Green Paper, while there is the emphasis that new measures need to be taken on energy security, economical stabilization and action against climate change, there is also the emphasis that within objectives such as competitiveness and internal energy market, diversification of the energy mix, solidarity, sustainable development, innovation and technology, external policy can be reshaped and renewable energy can be one of the main factors of this.[111]

The Commission states in the Green Paper that it will prepare both the Renewable Energy Roadmap and Strategic Energy Review.[112] In the EU Summit on March 2006, this subject was discussed inclusively. To provide energy security of supply, competitiveness and environmental sustainability, the need of an energy policy was also emphasized here.

According to the Council, the Energy Policy for Europe (EPE) should be created with shared evaluations, taking the needs and present policies of member states into consideration in relation to long-term supply and demand balances.[113] By mentioning the consistency with the ETS, it is emphasized that certain principle objectives need to be taken into consideration during the formation of the policy:

- *Ensure transparency and non-discrimination on markets*
- *Be consistent with competition rules*
- *Be consistent with public service obligations*
- *Fully respect Member States' sovereignty over primary energy sources and choice of energy-mix*[114]

One of the most important demands of the Summit is while it agreed with the Commission's request to prepare Strategic Energy Review, it demanded the Commission and the Council to prepare timetables along with an action plan until the Spring Summit of 2007.[115]

After the Summit, "The Renewable Energy Roadmap" prepared by the Commission was also published in 2007. It stated that climate change and energy dependency made EU economies vulnerable and to prevent this, the use

---

[111] European Commission, *[COM(2006) 105 final]*, 4,5,10,11.

[112] European Commission, *[COM(2006) 105 final]*, 11.

[113] Council of the European Union, *Brussels European Council Presidency Conclusions 23/24 March 2006 (7775/1/06)*, Assented to 8 July 2006, 14.

[114] Council of the European Union, Brussels European Council Presidency Conclusions 23/24 March, 16

[115] Council of the European Union, Brussels European Council Presidency Conclusions 23/24 March, 16.

of renewable energy had to be increased and greenhouse gas emissions had to be mitigated.[116]

Another interesting condition indicated in the Roadmap was that the rate of renewable energy determined in 1997 failed to achieve its objective and therefore it was necessary to have binding objectives. Energy consumption rates increased more than expected and the member states had insufficient policies, which could not encourage energy resources to be used at the demanded rate.[117] In this sense, it can be stated that renewable energy policy was created after 1997.

Renewable energy was not mentioned alone again in this text; on the contrary it was qualified as a tool and a "spring board" both for providing energy security and for greenhouse gas emission mitigation. In the newly prepared renewable energy directive, the subjects that should take place are organized as such:

> *Be based on long term mandatory targets and stability of the policy framework*
>
> *Include increased flexibility in target setting across sectors*
>
> *Be comprehensive, notably encompassing heating and cooling*
>
> *Provide for continued efforts to remove unwarranted barriers to renewable energies deployment*
>
> *Take into consideration environmental and social aspects*
>
> *Ensure cost-effectiveness of policies*
>
> *Be compatible with the internal energy market*[118]

The issue specifically indicated here is that this directive needs to create a structure so that member states can have the flexibility for their own special conditions in a way to cause long-term stability. Because when seen in terms of cost, the mitigation of approximately 600–900 Mt CO_2 to achieve the objective of 20%, will provide a profit of approximately 150–200 billion Euros. In renewable energy investments, when the decrease of the costs are taken into

---

[116] European Commission, [COM(2006) 848 final] Communication from the Commission to the Council and the European Parliament Renewable Energy Road Map Renewable energies in the 21st century: building a more sustainable future, Assented to 10 January 2007, 3.

[117] European Commission, *[COM(2006) 848 final]*, 4-5. Besides; In the directive number 2001/77/EC published in 2001 that only nine states could come close to objectives determined for the usage of the produced energy of renewable energy resources: Denmark, Germany, Finland, Hungary, Ireland, Spain, Sweden and Holland.

[118] European Commission, *[COM(2006) 848 final]*, 9.

consideration, it can be evaluated that it is possible for an advantageous condition to emerge in terms of Union.[119]

The European Parliament announced two different resolutions related to climate change on February 14, 2007[120] and to renewable energy on September 25, 2007[121]. In the March 2007 Summit[122] the Commission was invited to prepare a directive on the subject of renewable energy. Here for the first time it was dwelled on that in case of an International Treaty by the Council, the Union could make 30% emission mitigation compared to 1990 levels, until 2020. The directive proposal prepared by the Commission consisted of a Directive on the promotion of electricity produced from renewable energy sources 2001/77/EC and the Directive on the promotion of the use of biofuels or other renewable fuels for transport, numbered 2003/30/EC.[123]

In addition to the expressions in Green Paper, it was indicated in the directive proposal that renewable energy would provide employment, and also by contributing to economical growth and rural development, would decrease the vulnerability of economy. And together with greenhouse gas mitigation, pollution would decrease. In the text, greenhouse gas mitigation and energy security of supply are dual objectives that should be handled together with renewable energy. According to the Commission, the ETS Directive and the Renewable Energy Directive possess mutually complementary qualification and make it easier for each other to achieve their objectives.[124]

The Renewable Energy Directive, ETS Directive and greenhouse gas reduction targets, with the discount in sectors not included in the ETS and national obligations regulation are seen as "interlinked". It is emphasized that for export and import of renewable energy, no restrictions should be in question. It is pointed out that the Union should leave a movement area for all renewable energy producers both inside and outside, the proposal should be conducted by putting objectives for member states and industry, and that relations with third countries should be conducted within this legal framework.[125]

---

[119] European Commission, *[COM(2006) 848 final]*, 10-18.

[120] European Parliament, *[P6_TA(2007)0038]*

[121] European Parliament, [P6_TA(2007)0406] European Parliament resolution of 25 September 2007 on the Road Map for Renewable Energy in Europe, Assented to 25 September 2007.

[122] Council of the European Union, Brussels European Council Presidency Conclusions 8/9 March 2007 (7224/07), 9 March 2007.

[123] European Commission, [COM(2008) 19 final] Proposal for a Directive of the European Parliament and of the Council on the promotion of the use of energy from renewable sources, Assented to 23 January 2008.

[124] European Commission, *[COM(2008) 19 final]*, 2-4.

[125] European Commission, *[COM(2008) 19 final]*, 4.

Civil Society Impact on the EU Climate Change Policy

The most important discussion on the impact assessment during the preparation of the directive proposal, was on the subject with which units the renewable energy objectives would be expressed. Finally it was decided that instead of primary energy consumption, the use of final energy consumption would be appropriate. The reason for this is that it will enable the objectives to focus more on thermal and nuclear energy in terms of primary energy consumption.[126]

On the subject of how the objective of 20% will be distributed among member states, it is emphasized to look at the resource potentials of member states and that the distribution should be done according to GNP. In the report, answers for questions such as how to encourage cross-border renewable energy among member states, administrative obstacles preventing the development of renewable energy, the way to remove the Market obstacles, and which criteria should be developed to form a biofuel sustainable regime were being searched. In the proposal, three sectors were focused on: electricity, heating and cooling, and transportation. In achieving the national objectives, the member states were advised to make a plan including these three sectors. One of the other objectives of the directive is to reach the use of biofuel to 10% in the transportation sector by the year 2020.[127]

While the sectors of heating and cooling were not included in previous legislation, it can be stated that the lack of legislation in these fields slowed down the development of the political field. Therefore, the addition of heating and cooling into this directive, together with electricity and biofuel legislation, by putting together all three renewable energy sectors, helped to overcome administration obstacles and to form a more integrated energy policy.[128]

The Renewable Energy Directive was accepted after the first reading of the Council and of the Parliament.[129] In the preamble of the Directive, primarily the emission mitigation emerging from Kyoto Protocol, energy efficiency, the use of renewable energy and the national benefits to be obtained together with economical growth and the development of employment were mentioned.

The Directive (Directive 2009/28/EC) on energy production from renewable energy resources, generally mentions subjects such as renewable energy resources, smart grids, energy production and transparency. Accordingly not

---

[126] European Commission, [*COM(2008) 19 final*], 6-7.

[127] European Commission, [*COM(2008) 19 final*], 7-8.

[128] European Commission, [*COM(2008) 19 final*], 10.

[129] European Parliament and the Council, [Directive 2009/28/EC] on the promotion of the use of energy from renewable sources and amending and subsequently repealing Directives 2001/77/EC and 2003/30/EC, Assented to 23 April 2009.

only renewable energy consumption, but also the increase in energy production will result in greenhouse gas mitigation of the Union.

The binding decisions for member states were taken with the claim of the Commission, Council and the Parliament and their main objectives were to provide improvements for investors and to encourage the development of technology to produce energy from renewable energy resources. Although the objective of 20% is the desired objective for all member states, taking the countries' own conditions and GNP, it was determined as 20% in total. On the contrary, the 10% objective of renewable energy consumption in transportation is valid for every member state at the same rate. The 10% share here not only includes biofuels but also all the renewable energy resources.[130]

To fulfill the necessities of the Directive, member states should prepare a National Renewable Energy Action Plan including the sectoral objectives and with this purpose they are to develop support mechanisms to provide finance to Research and Development (R&D) projects of renewable energy technologies.[131]

In the Directive, the necessity for these plans to be prepared until June 30, 2010 is stated.[132] It is especially emphasized that this Directive and the environmental law of the Union should be consistent. While new renewable energy investments of member states were made, in every stage of the process, the Union is to consider the compatibility of environmental acquis.[133]

Between the articles 52 and 56, in the preamble of the Directive, there is the document of "guarantees of origin", which is not included in the proposal. Here it is emphasized that the obtained documents can only be used once. In other words for the same electricity from the producer to final consumer, one single document should be prepared.[134] Guarantees of origin is the document in which information about the source of electricity is given.

In the Directive, in order to provide public participation, these important expressions were also included: "The implementation of this Directive should reflect, where relevant, the provisions of the Convention on Access to Information, Public Participation in Decision-Making and Access to Justice in Environmental Matters, in particular as implemented through Directive

---

[130] European Parliament and the Council, *[Directive 2009/28/EC]*, Preamble, title: 13-18, 17-18; a.3.

[131] European Parliament and the Council, *[Directive 2009/28/EC]*, Preamble, title: 19, 22, 25.

[132] European Parliament and the Council, *[Directive 2009/28/EC]*, a. 4.

[133] European Parliament and the Council, *[Directive 2009/28/EC]*, Preamble, title: 44

[134] European Parliament and the Council, *[Directive 2009/28/EC]*, Preamble, title: 52

2003/4/EC."[135] Also in the Directive, the transfer of energy obtained from renewable energy resources among member states prepared an infrastructure in terms of making joint projects both among themselves and with the third countries.[136]

As distinct from the proposal prepared by the Commission, in the final text, there is an article about the administration of the process and the procedures.[137] Thereby to the aspects indicated in the Directive, the infrastructure that is needed to be obeyed by the member states is also provided. On the subject of guarantees of origin there were additions at the first reading of the Parliament in the proposal and in the final text, these additions were included.[138] Also in the Directive, the subject of sustainable fuels were mainly handled.[139] Finally, there are articles on the subjects of member states reporting the Commission's observation and processes and transparency.[140]

The Renewable Energy Directive was settled with a co-decision procedure and the DG Ennergy had a lot of influence during its formation. It was observed that experts of both climate and environment participated in the process.

Behind the promotion of the use of renewable energy there are concerns about climate change and energy security. However the Union, taking steps on the ETS and the legislation of climate change within the framework of a seperate Directorate General, show the importance given by the Union to environment and energy relation. In this sense, by decreasing traditional energy production facilities and orienting to renewable resources are considered to be an effective solution for the two important issues.

The preparation phase of the renewable energy directorate operated differently from the ETS. The presence of the previously made legislations on the subject of energy prevented the emergence of a long-term platform similar to ETS. According to Interviewee 9, the decision to create a renewable energy directive was a political decision and the States worked on that to overcome the worries

---

[135] European Parliament and the Council, *[Directive 2009/28/EC]*, Preamble, title: 90

[136] European Parliament and the Council, *[Directive 2009/28/EC]*, a. 6-11.

[137] European Parliament and the Council, *[Directive 2009/28/EC]*, a. 13.

[138] European Parliament and the Council, [Directive 2009/28/EC], a. 16; European Parliament, [EP-PE_TC1-COD(2008)0016] Position of the European Parliament adopted at first reading on 17 December 2008 with a view to the adoption of Directive 2009/.../EC of the European Parliament and of the Council on the promotion of the use of energy from renewable sources and amending and subsequently repealing Directives 2001/77/EC and 2003/30/EC (EP-PE_TC1- COD(2008)0016), Assented to 17 December 2008, 67.

[139] European Parliament and the Council, *[Directive 2009/28/EC]*, a. 17-19.

[140] European Parliament and the Council, *[Directive 2009/28/EC]*, a. 22-24.

of security of energy supply.[141] Similarly other Commission representatives indicated that renewable energy directive was discussed for a shorter period.

At this point the remarks of İnterviewee 4 are highly interesting. As renewable energy has already been under active development for about 20 years, it was emphasized that prior to the preparation of the Directive, no impact assessment report, green paper or programme were prepared and only before and after the preparation of the draft, Council meetings took place. Thereby it should be indicated that CSOs did not participate much in the process.[142] Although Interviewee 4 states that there has been a wide range of parties supporting renewable energy since 1990, they also indicated that there were lobbies trying to prevent the process at the time of the first emergence of legislation, with the argument that it was expensive.[143]

Climate change struggle policy: geological storage legislation

The Directive for geological storage of carbon dioxide (Directive 2009/31/EC)[144] is a legislation covering all the processes within the Union, from the removement of CO_2 to its storage. The process of storage to be carried out in full security is emphasized in this legislation. Storage, seen as an important factor to develop effective solutions for climate change, was published in the form of a directive in order to prevent the chaos to be created by different legislations.

Carbon capture and storage is a solution produced for the mitigation of CO_2 gas emerging during the production of thermal power plants. According to the EU:

> *"Carbon capture and storage (CCS) is a set of technologies aimed at capturing, transporting, and storing CO_2 emitted from power plants and industrial facilities. The goal of CCS is to prevent CO_2 from reaching the atmosphere by storing it in suitable underground geological formations."*[145][146]

---

[141] Interviewee 9 (EU Commission DG Climate consultant), interview by the author, Brussels, September 25, 2015.
[142] Interviewee 4 (EU Commission DG Climate consultant), interview by the author, Brussels, September 23, 2015.
[143] Interviewee 5 (EU Commission DG Climate consultant), interview by the author, Brussels, September 23, 2015.
[144] Dupont, "Combating Climate Complexity", 12.
[145] "Carbon Capture and Storage," *European Commission*, Accessed May 20, 2015, http://ec.europa.eu/energy/en/topics/oil-gas-andcoal/carbon-capture-and-storage.
[146] Accordingly in carbon capture and storage system, the most used and preferred trading methods are the methods of wet scrubbing with aqueous amine solutions and pre-combustion capture of CO2. John Gibbins and Hannah Chalmers, "Carbon Capture and Storage," *Energy Policy*, 36 (2008): 4318.

The methods in this context fundamentally aim to store carbon dioxide by decontaminating it from other chemicals and thus to prevent the gas from spreading to the atmosphere. Considering that dependency on fossil fuels cannot be overcome within a short period of time, the technological development, aiming to reduce the emission of carbon dioxide gas, is designed to be used with the present reserves, such as coal.[147]

The Communication prepared by the Commission was the first step taken on the subject of CCS. This Communication was prepared by taking the views of Second European Climate Change Programme (ECCPII) into consideration, by paying attention to the studies of the Executive Office of Energy and Environmental Affairs, to the preparations of the seventh Framework Programme and to the studies of Zero Emission Fossil Fuel Power Plants Technology Platform and prior to this an impact assessment was made: SEC (2006) 1743.[148] According to the Communication, in the production of coal energy, the fuel that is mostly used is fossil fuel and developing countries will continue using this. Also the existence of coal fields brings out the necessity to develop new technologies for its use. With the idea that coal will provide 25% of energy need in the future, the EU feels the need to make new legislation taking its sustainability objectives into consideration in order to decrease CO_2 emission originating from this by 20%.[149]

It is important that CCS integrates with big investments instead of small sectors that are being currently used to move to sustainable fossil fuels. And for this, the Commission will determine the most appropriate construction and operation mechanisms. The Commission believes that if coal is not being viewed from a perspective that is applicable in terms of long term and trade, electricity operators will be reluctant to use new technology. For this, it determines the need to support integrated risk assessments for research and development

---

[147] The international visibility of carbon capture and storage systems especially increased after IPCC report published in 2005. International Energy Agency (IEA) attracts the attention of energy focused institutions like OPEC and International Energy Forum (IEF). Besides, G8 countries also determined objectives on the subject of creating energy power plants where this technology is used. Except Canada, Australia and America, EU also determined objectives and created various funds to achieve these objectives. However these developments do not make a lot of noise in the eyes of UN Development Programme and UN Commission on Sustainable Development (CSD). Heleen de Conninck and Karin Bäckstrand, "An International Relations Perspective on the Global Politics of Carbon Dioxide Capture and Storage," *Global Environmental Change*, No. 21 (2011): 369.

[148] European Commission, [COM(2006) 843 final] Communication from the Commission to the Council and the European Parliament Sustainable power generation from fossil fuels: aiming for near-zero emissions from coal after 2020, Assented to 10 January 2007, 3.

[149] European Commission, *[COM(2006) 843 final]*, 4.

studies and CO_2 sink. It is indicated that CCS, by coming under flexibility mechanisms like CDM, can be a part of international climate treaty and that the supports on this subject may trigger the transformation in traditional thermal plants. The first proposal of the Commission is that all plants within the EU to be built with CCS starting from 2020 and the other existing thermal plants to gradually transform to the use of CCS technology.[150]

In the Summit of March 2007, the Council also called for the encouragement of the use of CCS especially within the scope of R&D and for the reach to the technologically developed and environmental safe power plants until 2020.[151] In the Summit of March 2008[152] an administrative framework to be formed for CCS was called for and in the Summit of June 2008[153] that the technological developments to be encouraged by the Commission.

In the Commission proposal for the geological storage directive of carbon dioxide, it is assumed that within 10 years, the energy consumption and demand of China, India, Brazil, South Africa and Mexico will increasingly be provided from fossil fuels. Within this context, it is considered that in order for the EU to decrease CO_2 emissions at the rate of 50% in 2050 compared to 1990 levels, CCS is necessary and that it is necessary to draw a legal frame of CCS as an option of an appropriate mitigation.[154]

In order to do this, a study group was formed on CCS within the European Climate Change Programme II (ECCP II) as the first step. This group indicated that there is a need both to develop policy and to form administrative framework. In the proposal, four directives that were already in effect were changed. These directives were 96/61/EC (on CO_2 capture risk), 85/337/EEC (on CO_2 capture, pipeline transportation and on environmental risks of storage), 2004/35/EC (local environment damage originating from CCS), and 2003/87/EC (on carbon leakage).[155]

---

[150] European Commission, *[COM(2006) 843 final]*, 5-10.

[151] Council of the European Union, Brussels European Council Presidency Conclusions 8-9 March 2007 (7224/1/07) REV 1, 2 May 2007, 22.

[152] Council of the European Union, Brussels European Council Presidency Conclusions 13/14 March 2008 (7652/1/08) REV 1, 20 May 2008, 13.

[153] Council of the European Union, Brussels European Council Presidency Conclusions 19/20 June 2008 (11018/1/08) REV 1, 17 June 2008, 12.

[154] European Commission, [COM(2008) 18 final] Proposal for a Directive of the European Parliament and of the Council on Geological Storage of Carbon Dioxide and Amending Council Directives 85/337/EEC, 96/61/EC, Directives 2000/60/EC, 2001/80/EC, 2004/35/EC, 2006/12/EC and Regulation (EC) No 1013/2006, Assented to 23 January 2008, 2.

[155] European Commission, *[COM(2008) 18 final]*, 2.

As it is indicated in the text, a conservative approach was adopted on the subject of CO_2 capture and transportation. While the existing framework is to be used in transportation, the subject of CCS, is left to the carbon market within the framework of ETS. It was decided that CSS is not to be mandatory at this stage as obligation will bring extra cost and when it is cost-effective, its settlement will be easier.[156]

The scope of the CCS Directive includes the transportation of CO_2 emissions from industrial institutions of the existing technology, to a secure storage space.[157] In addition to this, in a later expanded preamble which was not in the Directive proposal pepared by the Commission, it was emphasized that the use of this technology should not encourage the increase of plants using fossil fuel and that it should not slow down the development in energy efficiency, renewable energy and sustainable low carbon technologies.[158]

As it is stated in the directive proposal, in the report published in June 2006 by the study group formed within the scope of European Climate Change Programme II, it was emphasized that it was advised to develop both policy and regulatory frameworks on the subject of CCS. It was mentioned that the existence of a regulatory framework was important for site selection, the prevention of possible leakage and in case of damages, for the recovery to be handled quickly.[159]

In the preamble in which the subject of security of storage areas, which is the biggest worry of stakeholders, were also mentioned, it was indicated that carbon dioxide storage should be safe to the environment safe, the public should be informed and the development of technology should be supported.[160]

The directive should include member states' borders, exclusive economical territory and continental shelf. The member states have the right to decide which territories within their borders will be chosen for storage, the option of not to allow storage areas and to decide according to their own energy security strategies. Countries that allowed storage areas to be built within their own borders should evaluate the capacity and the Commission should provide the

---

[156] European Commission, [COM(2008) 18 final], 3.

[157] European Parliament and the Council, [Directive 2009/31/EC] on the geological storage of carbon dioxide and amending Council Directive 85/337/EEC, European Parliament and Council Directives 2000/60/EC, 2001/80/EC, 2004/35/EC, 2008/1/EC and Regulation (EC) No 1013/2006, Assented to 23 April 2009.

[158] European Parliament and the Council, [Directive 2009/31/EC], Preamble, title 4.

[159] European Parliament and the Council, [Directive 2009/31/EC], Preamble, title 6-7.

[160] European Parliament and the Council, [Directive 2009/31/EC], Preamble, title 11.

international information exchange.[161] As the choosing of storage areas are seen as especially important in terms of environmental security, it takes up a wide space in the preamble of the Directive.

When the articles of the Directive are examined, it can be seen that primarily exploration and storage permissions and the related conditions are arranged.[162] On the subjects of the close of carbon sink and storage areas, the measures to be taken afterwards, rules to be followed and the transfer of the responsibility, there have been changes and new additions to the Directive.[163] In the Directive there is also legislation on financial mechanisms and on dispute resolution.[164]

When looked from a realistic perspective, it can be stated that steps in the field of CCS were mostly taken by states intensively using fossil fuels and who are more sensitive on the subject of national sovereignty rights. The use of CCS in this sense is not just a technological necessity but also a subject directly evaluated by the states upon their sovereignty rights. Therefore when looked at from an EU perspective, the attitudes of states supporting the use of coal and owning reserves like Poland should be handled within this framework.[165]

At this point in the intergovernmental negotiation process, the subject of the usage of coal, seen as a direct national interest, corresponds to Moravcsik's prediction that it can be used with CCS technology. Although CSOs do not lean towards the use of this technology on the subject of climate change and struggle, when national interests are in question, the Council should come to terms with it. Thus the use of this technology to be seen as a solution in the EU, should be handled from a realistic perspective.

The Directive on the Geological Storage is the most technical legislation that all the Commission representatives agreed on.[166] Therefore CSOs participation was less during this legislation process, compared to other legislation. Interviewee 5 indicated that institutions with expertise were more involved in

---

[161] European Parliament and the Council, *[Directive 2009/31/EC]*, Preamble, title 18-22.
[162] European Parliament and the Council, *[Directive 2009/31/EC]*, a. 5-10.
[163] European Parliament and the Council, *[Directive 2009/31/EC]*, a. 16-18.
[164] European Parliament and the Council, *[Directive 2009/31/EC]*, a. 19-22.
[165] EU, together with European Energy Programme for Recovery and NER 300, created funds to encourage developments in CSS technology. However it is not possible to say that these funds were successful. To discuss this situation, European Commission organized a public consultation in 2013 for a situation assessment. "Carbon Capture and Storage." *European Commission*, Accessed May 20, 2015, http://ec.europa.eu/energy/en/topics/oil-gas-andcoal/carbon-capture-and-storage.
[166] Interviewee 4 (EU Commission DG Climate consultant), interview by the author, Brussels, September 23, 2015; Interviewee 5 (EU Commission DG Climate consultant), interview by the author, Brussels, September 23, 2015; Interviewee 9 (EU Commission DG Climate consultant), interview by the author, Brussels, September 25, 2015.

this process and that especially Bellona was rather active during this process.[167] Interviewee 4 pointed out that in the directive on geological storage, the discussions on labelling were effective and that the subject of carbon capture and storage emerged from necessity, although it was arguable.[168]

When the directive is generally analysed, it can be mentioned that in parallel to the opinions of the interviewees, the directive did not undergo big changes. A proposal of an amendment including 114 articles given by the European Parliament Committee on Environment, Public Health and Food Safety were designed not to effect the content to a large extent, for example word changing.[169]

EU Wide Civil Society Organizations

Civil society originally comes from the English term "civics". In the meaning that we use it today, according to Belge, it has been used since Rousseau and has been handled as a term formed by the citizens.[170]

When seen this way, it is possible to handle civil society as a community formed by the citizens in which social and political involvement is aimed. This wide definition and the general use of civil society caused an ambiguity.[171] The fundamental reason for this is that civil society is rather general. Nevertheless, despite the ambiguity caused by the use of the term, it can be evaluated as the most extensive and suitable term consisting citizens and aiming to influence the official decision-making mechanism. When looking at the literature, it can be seen that apart from civil society, non-governmental organizations, non-profit institutions, pressure groups, interest groups are also present. The main reason of the differentiation here is closely related to the attitudes, the structuring and the strategy these groups follow.

---

[167] Interviewee 5 (EU Commission DG Climate consultant), interview by the author, Brussels, September 23, 2015.

[168] Interviewee 4 (EU Commission DG Climate consultant), interview by the author, Brussels, September 23, 2015.

[169] European Parliament Committee on the Environment, Public Health and Food Safety, Report on the proposal for a directive of the European Parliament and of the Council on the geological storage of carbon dioxide and amending Council Directives 85/337/EEC, 96/61/EC, Directives 2000/60/EC, 2001/80/EC, 2004/35/EC, 2006/12/EC and Regulation (EC) No 1013/2006 (COM(2008) 0018 – C6-0040/2008 – 2008/0015 (COD)), Assented to 16 October 2008.

[170] Murat Belge, "Sivil Toplum Nedir?," in *Sivil Toplum ve Demokrasi Konferans Yazıları,* edited by. Nurhan Yentürk and Arzu Karamani, no:1, 2003, http://stk.bilgi.edu.tr/media/uploads/2015/02/01/belge_s td_1.pdf, 2-6.

[171] Hande Paker, "Çevre Rejimleri ve Türkiye'de Sivil Toplum Örgütlerinin Rolü: Akdeniz'de Sürdürülebilirlik," *Marmara Avrupa Araştırmaları Dergisi* 20, no 1 (2012): 153.

When the development process of the concept of civil society is examined, it can be seen that generally in tradional studies it is included in an autonomous area, whereas in current studies, by getting seperated from this definition beyond the prediction of traditional studies, it can be stated that it plays a role in relation to political actors and policy-making processes. Civil society has normative, organizational and public space dimensions.[172]

When looked at from this perspective, while the aim of existence of civil society is to influence the decision-making mechanism[173], pressure groups can be characterized as groups aiming to influence not only the state, but also social sections in accordance with their own ideas. Pressure groups in this sense also hold a more emotional association.[174] While interest groups are expressed as social groups that come together around certain common objectives and interests, the groups that demand their requests directly through government institutions gain the characteristic of being political interest group.[175]

Within this study, interest groups, as discussed in Klüver's study, include all the organizational structures with a certain organizational structure aiming to influence political decisions and not bearing the characteristic of being a public institution. In this sense, it includes not only civil society organizations, but also all the formations bearing the same criteria, such as employee and employer unions, companies and professional unions.[176]

According to Truman, every group showing common attitudes has the quality of being an interest group.[177] Therefore, not only civil society organizations formed by citizens but also different representation mechanisms like trade associations or industrial unions can be characterized as interest groups. The most important reason why these groups are included in civil society is explained by Alemdar: "The aim of civil society organizations is not to be useful to their own members, but to be useful to society."[178] Thus it is possible to separate institutions aiming to be useful to their own members, from the definition of civil society. On the other hand because of the EU's distinctive situation, some studies analysing EU-wide civil society organizations indicate

---

[172] Hande Paker, "Çevre Rejimleri ve Türkiye'de Sivil", 154.

[173] Zeynep Alemdar, "Baskı Grupları ve Sivil Toplum," in *Karşılaştırmalı Siyaset*, edited by Sabri Sayarı and Hasret Dikici Bilgin, 3rd ed. (İstanbul: İletişim Publishing, 2015), 170.

[174] David Truman, *The Governmental Process* (USA: Greenwood Press, 1981), 38.

[175] Truman, The Governmental Process, 37.

[176] Klüver, Lobbying in the European Union, 6.

[177] Klüver, Lobbying in the European Union, 33.

[178] Alemdar, "Baskı Grupları ve Sivil Toplum," 179.

that organizations formed to be useful to their own members and to society, can be characterized as CSOs.[179]

Generally, it is difficult to separate the concepts of pressure groups and interest groups. The reason for this difficulty is that groups organizing their requests within a certain plan, and are organized in a way to gain interest, obtained the specialty to be a pressure group. Hence, Connelly and Smith also indicated that ECSOs within the EU are to be defined as pressure organizations.[180] However, in the EU literature, the definition of interest group is more used instead of pressure group. The main reason for this preference is thought to be the concern of including EU-wide institutions and institutions conducting lobby studies.

Based on these definitions, it is not possible to use the concepts of pressure groups and interest group to be used for the organizations to be analysed within this book. While organizations in the business world represented by the likes of Business Europe are defined as interest group, most of the time they stand against civil society organizations focused on the environment with these roles.

Nevertheless this definition is sometimes mentioned here, as it is used within the scope of lobbying activities. Interest groups, as indicated in the first chapter, in accordance with Klüver's definition includes all the possible formations except government institutions. But use of such a broad concept in lobbying studies is because of the fact that lobbying activities can be carried out by various organisations. It can either be a CSO or a business organisation that want a decision to be made in a certain direction; and all these institutions come together under the umbrella term of interest groups.

According to Kohler-Koch, civil society organizations can be differentiated from other political groups by their six characteristics: "They are nongovernmental, not-for-profit, and voluntary associations which peacefully and publicly operate for implementation of their goals and do not run for office".[181] While CSOs express a more general framework, non-governmental institutions are mostly used in a much narrow sense.

These organizations, although they possess non-governmental characteristics as they are accepted generally, the fact that they conduct their activities by receiving funds from the EU mean that they have a certain connection with the EU. And this situation is one of the points mostly criticized by Greenpeace,

---

[179] Beate Kohler Koch, "Civil Society and Democracy in the EU: High Expectations under Empirical Scrutiny," *De-Mystification of Participatory Democracy*, edited by. Beate Kohler-Koch et al. (Great Britain: Oxford University Press, 2013), 5.
[180] Connelly and Smith, Politics and the Environment, 75.
[181] Kohler Koch, "Civil Society and Democracy in the EU", 5.

which does not receive any funds and is free to determine the contents of their campaigns and activities.

Greenpeace generally does not accept and ask for any funds from companies or political parties. It also does not accept or look for any donations that would destroy its objectives and integrity.[182] The continuity of the actions of Greenpeace are through member donations and independent funds.

When looking specifically at the EU, interest groups are divided into EU-wide active groups and national interest groups. EU interest groups are generally formed by national unities coming together. In this sense as EU interest groups possess more technical information, they tend to influence EU institutions with know-how. However, it is pointed out that these groups' financial resources are less compared to national organizations. Still, their most important function is their mission to bring national unities together and create a common ground.[183]

Umbrella organizations include many different institutions in respect of their structure. Because of this, the decisions to be made by umbrella organizations mostly emerge with a negotiation process within their own dynamics.

Civil society organizations that are not in umbrella organizations have a different decision-making dynamic. Warleigh, in one of his studies, came to the conclusion that decision makers of civil society organizations might prefer to find ad hoc allies for their strategical needs instead of permanent allies.[184] And this preference can form different partnerships on the basis of activity as well, as it can also cause inconveniency in creating a permanent civil society. Thereby, the formation of partnerships on some subjects that are hard to be observed normally, are theoretically possible.

The classification of these organizations is made according to their institutional structures; whereas generally civil society is classified according to its activities. Accordingly civil society can be classified in three different ways: aimed at creating information, at creating agenda and carrying out activities.[185]

In this book the selection of the CSOs in EU, active in the fields of climate change and energy, are based upon the classificiation of Rudiger K. W. Wurzell and James Connelly in their study (See Table 7). To make these analysis, first,

---

[182] Sally Eden, "Greenpeace," *New Political Economy* 9, no.4 (2004): 601.

[183] Rainer Eising and Sonja Lehringer, "Interest Groups and the European Union," in *European Union Politics*, edited by. Michele Cini and Nieves Pérez Solórzano Borrogán, 3rd ed. (Oxford: Oxford University Press, 2010), 198.

[184] Alex Warleigh, "Europeanizing' Civil Society", 630.

[185] Alemdar, "Baskı Grupları ve Sivil Toplum," 180.

the organizations are classified and in the context of the study only some of these organizations are handled. There are many civil society organizations working in EU on climate change and energy. Under this wide umbrella, it is highly difficult to classify these organizations.

Within this scope, it is aimed to determine the organizations around five different criteria. The first criterion is the organization to have within its principle aims, the studies on climate change and energy. The second criterion is the organization to be active in the activities influencing EU policies. The third criterion is the organization to be active during the time period or in the most part of the time period determined by the study. The fourth criterion is the organization to have influence on the member countries for being organized in EU in general or for its organizational structure. The fifth and the most important criterion is the organization to be part of Green 10 groups.

Within the study, five organizations complying with these criteria are analysed. These organizations can be classified under two main topics and categorization. Under the first topic umbrella organizations housing many different institutions under its roof are examined. According to this, it was decided to analyse European Environment Bureau being an Environmental Civil Society Organization network trying to influence the environmental policy actively starting from the first period to 2000s and CAN Europe an umbrella organization playing a more active role compared to EEB after 2000.

Under the second title, globally working individual organizations playing an active role in EU that are Greenpeace, World Wild Foundation (WWF) and Friends of the Earth (FoE) are tried to be examined.

The examined five organizations are the ones considered to be influential in the EU policies of climate change and energy.[186] The other four organizations besides EEB, for being organized world wide, are more widely recognized. However with the help of the wide network of EEB, it can be accepted as the voice of civil society organizations active in EU. From this aspect, the difference between the organizations active in differents parts of the world and itself can be seen during the research.

On the other hand it is possible to say that every other organization other than Greenpeace, receive fund from EU for their study. Therefore also at this point a differentiation can be made between the organizations supported by EU and non-supported ones and their activities. Thus, the methods of the organization

---

[186] Anne Therese Gullberg, "Rational Lobbying and EU Climate Policy," *International Environmental Agreements: Politics, Law and Economics*, 8, (2008a): 167.

that is used to influence the Union and whether these methods achieve success or not, are also possible to be analysed.

Table 7: Brussels-Based European NGOs, Think Tanks and Research Institutes Active on EU Climate Change Issues

ENGOs active in EU climate change policy issues:
G4:   EEB, FoE, Greenpeace and WWF   G10:   BirdLife International, CAN Europe, Central and Eastern Europe (CEE) Bankwatch Network, EEB, HEAL, FoE, Greenpeace, Friends of Nature International (NFI), T&E, and WWF   Four most active large ENGOs in the EU climate change policy: CAN, FoE, Greenpeace and WWF   Large European ENGO umbrella groups active in EU climate issues level: CAN Europe   HEAL   T&E   Large European ENGO networks groups active on EU climate issues: EEB   FoE   Greenpeace   WWF   Small ENGOs active on specific EU climate issues: Belona   Client Earth   E3G
NGOs other than ENGOs active on EU climate change policy issues:
Aprodev   Christian Aid   Oxfam
Think tanks and/or research Institutes:
Centre for European Policy Studies (CEPS)   Ecologic   Institute for European Environmental Policy (IEEP)   Öko Institut   The Centre
Foundations which fund NGO lobbying activities on EU climate policy:
European Climate Foundation   Oak Foundation

Environmental Foundation Bellona
Wider civil society platforms: Civil Society Platform   Agora   Concord

Source: Rudiger K. W. Wurzel, James Connelly, "Environmental NGOs," The European Union As a Leader in International Climate Change Politics, edited by. Rudiger K. W. Wurzel and James Connelly (New York: Routledge, 2011), 219.

Umbrella organizations

An umbrella organization is an association of organizations having found a common objective or having the same objectives on a certain subject. The European Environmental Bureau (EEB) and Climate Action Network Europe (CAN Europe) are two institutions that have an active role in EU climate studies. Generally, national organizations that cannot reach the EU decision-making mechanism and organizations that believe that working around the same aim would give better solutions, came together.

Since the 1980s, Brussels-based environmental organizations have conducted studies to influence EU climate change policy. EEB, Friends of the Earth (FoE), Greenpeace and the Worldwide Fund for nature (WWF) are the most active and long-established organizations. These organizations are also referred to as the Gang of Four.[187] After the foundation of the EEB in 1974, Greenpeace, WWF and FoE opened headquarters in Brussels. The most important reason for this expansion can be shown as the EU's increasing environmental acquis and the addition of the environmental section to the ESA.[188] Apart from these organizations, in the 1990s, together with new organizations, a strong environmental lobby called Green 10 (G10) was also formed.

While the EEB represents 15 million citizens on its own, G10 countries represent 20 million citizens in total. Besides, in the surveys of Eurobarometer about the EU environmental policy, it is possible to observe that European citizens intensely support environmental organizations.[189] Therefore, a Commission taking the subject of democratic representation seriously and

---

[187] Wurzel and Connelly, "Environmental NGOs," 214.

[188] Camilla Adelle and Jason Anderson, "Lobby Groups," in *Environmental Policy in the EU*, edited by. Andrew Jordan and Camilla Adelle, 3rd ed. (London: Routledge, 2013), 154.

[189] Adelle and Anderson, "Lobby Groups," 164.

publishing transparent directives should pay attention to establishments with such representation skills.

Umbrella organizations not only bring national organizations together, but also tend to be a more effective driving power by developing cooperations with other organizations active in Brussels.

There are four reasons for Brussels-based ECSOs to provide coordination. First, they do not have enough financial resources and employees. Second, they can establish coalitions easily as they possess similar objectives. Third, they are in less competition compared to national CSOs. And finally, these ECSOs are aware that they have more chance to influence the EU's political structure if they come together, as they represent a lot of countries.[190]

European Environmental Bureau

The European Environmental Bureau (EEB), founded in 1974, is the largest federation of Europe representing 145 member organizations today. They claim to be the voice of 15 million citizens. For environmental policies to develop, experts work in coordination with scientists and members. The Brussels office, by making connections with member national organizations, conduct EU based activities. Besides, global politics and sustainability unit also conduct coordinated studies with international coalitions like G10 and the Spring Alliance.[191]

Apart from being the first environmental lobby organization founded in Brussels, it also regularly uses legal consultation process and informal communication channels.[192] Although the EEB conducts EU-wide activities, as it has a limited number of employees on the subject of climate change, it has not continued to possess the importance it had in the first period compared to CAN Europe, which is an umbrella organization. The reason for this is that although it organizes many activities related to eco taxes, it has not been successful in using it.[193]

The reason for the foundation of the EEB is the organization of the EU's first environmental plan. Today, the EEB is the most extensive establishment in the EU in terms of representation. The EEB, in 2004, provided 52% of its financial

---

[190] Wurzel and Connelly, "Environmental NGOs," 215.
[191] "European Environmental Bureau." *EEB official web page*. Accessed May 25, 2015. http://www.eeb.org/index.cfm/about-eeb/.
[192] Adelle and Anderson, "Lobby Groups," 153-156.
[193] Wurzel and Connelly, "Environmental NGOs," 215, 224.

resources from the EU.[194] When looking at the 2015 budget, the EEB receives €1,333,579 of its total €3,266,046 budget from Environmental Commissariat.[195] If generally evaluated, it is possible to say that financial resources from EU can possibly decrease the organisation's ability to act freel, and also every year the EEB receives an increase in funds from the EU.

In the interview the author conducted with an EEB respresentative, it was indicated that decision-making mechanisms within the organization were democratic and that they focused on energy efficiency with biomass instead of ETS or renewable energy. They try to increase public awareness on the subject of sustainable biomass. It was also indicated that the EEB was the most institutionalized CSO within the G10. In addition, the resprestentative emphasized that the Commission and Environmental Council generally met with G10 members and that the dialogues with these institutions tend to develop this way.[196]

Therefore, although the EEB does not study specific to climate, it can be mentioned that it carries out the criteria of creating a common position for civil society.[197]

The EEB gave its opinions on public consultations within the scope of the 2030 Strategy, emphasizing the IPCC report while mentioning the inadequacy of greenhouse gas mitigation objectives. It also indicated that mitigation could be observed in other sectors outside of the ETS's extent and that in the Effort Sharing Decision, only 10% mitigation was predicted. Apart from that it was pointed out that the use of biomass could result negatively in terms of biodiversity and climate and that it is not sustainable.[198]

Regarding 2030 objectives, it underlined that renewable energy, energy efficiency and emission trade systems are to be consistent with each other. It also emphasized that objectives should be binding at country level and it is indicated that the mechanisms to follow this should be developed. The reason for this, is the prediction that ETS and renewable energy objectives are adapted

---

[194] Eising and Lehringer, "Interest Groups and the European Union," 200-201.

[195] European Environmental Bureau Transparency Register, *European Commission Transparency Register page*, Accessed June 1, 2015,
http://ec.europa.eu/transparencyregister/public/consultation/displaylobbyist.do?id=06798511314-27.

[196] Interviewee 1 (EEB Representative), interview by the author, Brussels, September 22, 2015.

[197] Here the conceptualization of "mission to create a common position" was taken from Rainer Eising.

[198] European Environmental Bureau, The EEB's Response to the European Commission's Consultation on a 2030 Framework for Climate and Energy Policies, Transparency Register Number: 06798511314-27, 01/07/2013, 2.

as they are mandatory and that energy efficiency objectives are not adapted as they are not.

The EEB claims that 80% emission mitigation rate in 2030 is consistent with the facts. However, in the EEB text, at least 60% mitigation is seen as appropriate, because a 40% mitigation indicated in the 2030 objectives is predicted to prevent reaching the 2050 objectives. Therefore, the year 2050 is not to be the last date for emission mitigation and the process to continue after this year, is seen as appropriate. On the subject of the financial burden of the process, the EEB mentions the importance of Effort Sharing Models and indicates that it is possible to reduce the cost of mitigation at EU level with a mechanism functioning from bottom to top.[199]

The EEB determined that in present legislation, the sustainability criteria on biofuel and liquid biofuels, biomass for electricity and sustainability criteria for heating and cooling are inadequate.[200] The EEB text also mentions the importance of determining objectives at EU level on renewable energy and the development of support mechanisms such as feed-in tariffs for the mechanisms providing the member states to form their own energy profiles as they want to function.[201]

The EEB commented on costs in the text and that by adding a monitoring mechanism to the energy products market, it is possible to make observation easier. Thus it is stated that by giving up subventions harming the economy, it is possible to remove the obstacles preventing the development of energy efficiency and renewable energy. Because of this, it is thought that by removing fossil fuel subsidies, the use of alternative methods like environmental designs can be encouraged and that it is possible to achieve objectives with enforcement.[202] With regards to shale gas, the EEB considers it to be a risky and nonsecure resource.[203]

Climate Action Network Europe

CAN Europe is an umbrella organization founded in 1989 and today includes 135 organizations that are active in 30 European countries. The reason for its foundation is to avoid dangerous consequences of climate change and to support

---

[199] European Environmental Bureau, *The EEB's Response*, 3-5.
[200] European Environmental Bureau, *The EEB's Response*, 6.
[201] European Environmental Bureau, *The EEB's Response*, 7.
[202] European Environmental Bureau, *The EEB's Response*, 8-9.
[203] European Environmental Bureau, *The EEB's Response*, 12.

the formation of sustainable climate and energy policies in Europe.[204] At the present time, it represents 44 million EU citizens.[205] CAN Europe, while coordinating member institutions, is also engaged in subject based lobbying activities. It does not like general lobbying and participates in international debates.[206]

CAN Europe is an establishment that conducted active studies in the 1990s. The "isolate and embarrass" strategy developed by CAN during the first Conference of Parties (COP 1) in March 1995 against the positions of the USA and the EU, influenced the EU's attitude. The success of this strategy is expressed with the efforts of EU trying to form an alliance with the Group of 77 (G77) countries. By forming the Berlin Mandate, it was tried to avoid USA, Russia and Organization of Petroleum Exporting Countries (OPEC) to sabotage the negotiations and the creation of a ground for agreement. This temporary relative 'green' group made negotiations on how developed countries, under the UNFCCC, should develop policies and measures.[207]

As most of ECSOs have a loose management, CAN Europe has become a leading association on the subjects of climate change. Within this scope, it forms a common strategy with other ECSOs and develops task sharing in this context. However some ECSOs like WWF, try to make their own priorities more visible and of top priority. The common goal of ECSOs is to provide binding legislation to be developed in both national and supra-national levels.[208]

While the general budget of CAN Europe in 2015 was €1,240,655, the funding it received from the EU was €406,947[209] and this funding almost doubled within 2 years. When these rates are analysed, it can be said that CAN Europe received less funds than the EEB. Because of this, it has resource inadequacies in lobbying activities, so to cover this, by determining priorities, they conduct lobbying in several political fields, interoperating with other organizations.[210]

---

[204] "About Us," *CAN Europe*, Accessed June 2, 2015, http://www.caneurope.org/about-us.
[205] "Members," *CAN Europe*, Accessed July 22, 2016, http://www.caneurope.org/membership/index.php?option=com_civicrm&task=civicrm/profile&gid=50&reset=1&force=1&search=0.
[206] Gullberg, "Rational Lobbying and EU Climate Policy," 169.
[207] Long, Salter and Singer, "WWF: European and Global", 95.
[208] Wurzel and Connelly, "Environmental NGOs," 220-223.
[209] "CAN Europe Transparency Register," *European Commission Transparency Register page*, Accessed June 3, 2015, http://ec.europa.eu/transparencyregister/public/consultation/displaylobbyist.do?id=55888811123-49.
[210] Gullberg, "Rational Lobbying and EU Climate Policy," 173-175.

Şekercioğlu

In the interview conducted with the CAN Europe representative, it was stated that in-house decisions were made with member organizations with consensus. As each member was concerned with different fields, when an opinion was asked, everyone gave their opinion. It was also stated that it was the only organization focused solely on climate change within G10 and that there were still objections within the organization against the carbon market. It was also expressed that in their relations with EU institutions, they tended to pursue both proactive and reactive policy and that in this context, they had more chance to negotiate more with the Commission. The most important point here is that it is easier for national CSOs to reach the Parliament and the Council. The role of CAN Europe at this point is to ensure coordination. To do this, both inside and outside lobbying are applied.[211]

CAN Europe, in the public consultation opened for 2030 Strategy, mentions the determination of reconciliation between emission trade, renewable energy and energy efficiency and it emphasized that these goals support each other. In the example given on this subject, it was shown that if the objectives of renewable energy and energy efficiency could be achieved, this situation would also provide 24% emission mitigation. The decrease in carbon prices and its being an obstacle for technological development were criticized and therefore it was emphasized that the use of equalizing credits that are used at present, were to be reviewed. They indicated the main criticism points as such:

> *Lacking coherence between the three targets (renewable energy, energy savings and emission reductions)*
>
> *Weak ambition in the emission reduction target and ETS (includes energy efficiency measures)*
>
> *Lack of sustainability guarantees*
>
> *International carbon credit should no longer count towards the EU GHG emission reduction target*
>
> *Lack of binding commitments on the EU's share and delivery of international climate finance.*[212]

According to CAN Europe, the EU, by recognizing its historical responsibilities, should increase its greenhouse mitigation objectives. A mitigation of 55% until the year 2030 is necessary for 2050 objectives to be

---

[211] İnterviewee 2 (CAN Europe Representative), interview by the author, Brussels, September 22, 2015.
[212] CAN Europe. CAN Europe's Response to the European Commission's Greenpaper Consultation on a 2030 Climate and Energy Framework. Transparency Register Number: 55888811123-49, Accessed 26 June 2013, 3-4.

achieved. In this context, an objective of 40% could be qualified as a deviation to decrease the process. Moreover, by indicating that the objective determined for 2020 was actually under the potential of EU, it was emphasized that the objectives should be higher for renewable energy technologies to develop. It was underlined that the 18.3% mitigation objective for the year 2011 showed that the objectives were low. When it is examined extensively, it is predicted that three objective strategies including emission trade, energy efficiency and renewable energy give the most successful result.[213]

The CAN Europe text also emphasized that international credits, by dragging down their emission prices, result in a slowing down of the process. It indicated that subsidies applied to fossil fuels by states should be removed and its economical and environmental effects should carefully be analysed by bringing forward the transparency in this process. When only renewable energy is considered to have an effective role within present technologies in the struggle with climate change, the importance of the development of renewable energy with support mechanisms is emphasized.[214]

Moreover, the costs of health problems caused by fossil fuels and environmental degradation resulting in the use of biofuels are indicated to be other important points to be considered while forming long-term policies.[215]

Global organizations

Greenpeace, WWF and FoE may differentiate from each other with their activities other than their qualification of being global. In accordance with the approach where lobby groups are named generally as light green and dark green, WWF is named as light green, as it is in a position to give information to decision makers with its specialized scientific research, and it is indicated that it uses inside lobbying activities. Whereas Greenpeace, uses outside lobbying activities more, and so is dark green.[216]

While Greenpeace does not receive any funds from the EU, WWF Europe and FoE do receive funds. Thus it can be pointed out that similar to umbrella organizations, the difference of their lobbying activities originate from different factors such as the resources they possess or their finance mechanisms.

---

[213] CAN Europe, *CAN Europe's Response*, 5-6.
[214] CAN Europe, *CAN Europe's Response*, 6-9.
[215] CAN Europe, *CAN Europe's Response*, 7-8.
[216] Adelle and Anderson, "Lobby Groups," 158.

Greenpeace

Greenpeace, unlike other organizations, emerged as an action group and continues to exist this way. According to Sally Eden:

> *"Greenpeace originally emerged in 1969 from an anti-nuclear splinter group of the Sierra Club in Canada, focusing upon American nuclear weapons tests and called the 'Don't Make a Wave' committee."*[217]

When Greenpeace's headquarters in Canada had financial problems, Vancouver's debt was paid by its European office in Holland and it was decided that the global organization called Greenpeace International was to be Holland based. The North American and European groups were united under one single umbrella. This structure still exists today.[218]

Greenpeace is an organization with a strict and hierarchical structure. Its campaigns are conducted by professional activists, and other members gather donations. The country-based organization of Greenpeace also transfers funds to its international office, and its action planning is attached to the international office. The organization focused on toxins and pollution in the 1970s, and acid rain and air pollution in the 1980–1990s; considering that its influence was not adequate in 1992 in the UN Environment and Development Conference, it became more institutionalized. The more strategically organized climate policy still continues, and for this continuity to be provided, it was necessary for the establishment to move away from its radical appearance.[219]

The Greenpeace European Office, on the other hand, is mostly active in the fields of energy and emission. It has a voice in fields such as renewable energy and ETS.[220] The Greenpeace European Office intensified its lobby activities on ECCP and ETS. At the same time, it carries out lobbying in international climate negotiations.[221] Greenpeace Europe had a total budget of €1,655,727 in 2015, which came from donations.[222]

---

[217] Eden, "Greenpeace," 595.
[218] Eden, "Greenpeace," 596.
[219] Eden, "Greenpeace," 595-605.
[220] Wurzel and Connelly, "Environmental NGOs," 221.
[221] Gullberg, "Rational Lobbying and EU Climate Policy," 169.
[222] "Greenpeace European Unit Transparency Register," *European Commission Transparency Register page*. Accessed June 3, 2015,
http://ec.europa.eu/transparencyregister/public/consultation/displaylobbyist.do?id=9832909575-41.

Civil Society Impact on the EU Climate Change Policy

In an interview carried out with a former employee of Greenpeace, it was indicated that there were only 10 organizations in Brussels studying both climate and energy. It was evaluated that Greenpeace, WWF and CAN Europe were the most important ones among them. It was stated that lobbying necessitates professionalism, that every way was being tried by CSOs, a good network was important and the recognizability of CSOs was a positive factor. As they are chosen democratically within EU institutions, it was emphasized that it was easier to influence the Parliament and it was tried to be effective through CSOs in member states in political subjects.[223]

Greenpeace, after participating in the public consultation on CCS[224], opposed to the use of CCS. Greenpeace knew the influence of energy usage on climate change and believed that the usage of CCS technology would increase the use of fossil fuel. It also thought that CCS technology was new and had not yet been tested sufficiently. Therefore, it was of the opinion that the use of this technology would influence the use of renewable energy and energy efficiency negatively and for this reason it indicated that CCS was not presenting any solutions on the struggle with climate change.

Greenpeace, believing that nuclear energy is no better solution than CCS, stated that renewable energy and energy efficiency are secure and sustainable solutions. CCS on the other hand is still on trial and even if it is of any use, it will take years to know exactly how useful it could be.

Greenpeace participated in the 2030 Strategy Public Consultation, with an extensive report that was more extensive than other CSOs. Greenpeace not only approachs on only one side of climate and energy policy, but approachs each at the same level, unlike other organizations.

Greenpeace lines up the lessons learned from 2020 Framework as such:

> *Greenhouse gas reduction targets should be in line with the upper end of the EU's 2050 emission reduction goal.*
>
> **Targets must be legally binding**. *The energy savings target for 2020 proves non-binding targets do not work.*
>
> *The EU should continue a multiple target approach.*

---

[223] İnterviewee 10 (Greenpeace former employee), internet interview by the author, April 25, 2016.

[224] The public consultation texts written for CCS have not yet been published. Only the report of the colsultation was published. The documents were tried to be obtained from EU Commission. On the documents the name of the establishments that contributed were erased and only the answers of Greenpeace could be reached. Because of this, only the answers of Greenpeace is given place within the book.

Şekercioğlu

> *For 2030, the EU must agree a set of targets irrespective of action in third countries. Instead, the conditionality has created unnecessarily uncertainity for investors within Europe.*
>
> *Free allocation under the EU's Emission Trading Scheme (ETS) led to untargeted financial support for energy-intensive industries, undermining the incentive for cost-efficient emission reductions and investments in clean and efficient industrial technologies.*
>
> *The use of offset credits under the ETS has contributed to the oversupply of ETS emission allowances, undermining the credibility and effectiveness of the scheme. The EU should therefore prohibit the use of offset credits after 2020.*
>
> *The promotion of bioenergy under the 2020 Climate and Energy Package without qualitative limits comes with a risk of serious socio-environmental costs. The level of cap should be fixed on the basis of the EU's maximum sustainable potential of domestic biomass supply.*[225]

Objectives including energy security, competition and mitigation in health costs are directly related to energy and climate policies. Therefore, while determining the objectives of climate and energy policy, the importance of bindingness for member states increases. When looked at from a long-term investments point of view, if there is no clearness in the process, the investments decrease as their costs will increase. To prevent this uncertainty, the importance of determination of binding objectives is one of the key points that Greenpeace dwells on.[226]

The objectives determined for 2020 are not seen enough and it is stated that an objective of 55% greenhouse gas mitigation should be determined, including sectors mentioned in the Effort Sharing Decision for 2030. The objective model called "trias energetica" should be continued and in addition to this, it is underlined that by using supportive mechanisms like carbon tax, clean energy should be aimed at more. Also subsector legislations, especially the usage of biofuels in transportation sector should be supported and in return, it is advised to focus on efficiency in transportation with technological developments. The

---

[225] Greenpeace, Submission to the European Commission Public Consultation on a 2030 Framework for Climate and Energy Policies, Transparency Register number: 9832909575-41, 3-4.
[226] Greenpeace, Submission to the European Commission, 5-6.

idea to support new technologies until they become economic. Thus the 45% renewable energy share proposed for 2030 will be fulfilled.[227]

On the subject of carbon leakage, Greenpeace expresses that industrialists make an exaggerated risk definition and that their assertive 2030 objectives, despite the fact that it can expose some sectors to carbon leakage effects, underlines that many braches of industry are in position to be able to reduce their costs without falling behind competition. Upon the subject of shale gas, they are in the opinion that there is more environmental risk than assumed and moreover, it possesses more carbon footprint than traditional gas and that the decrease in dependency on importation is doubtful.[228]

Greenpeace, attending the public consultation related to the EU's 2050 Road Map[229], emphasized that models and data systems to be used to reach the objectives should be transparent and instead of traditional energy profile, in long-term objectives, the development in energy sector should be considered. According to Greenpeace, the EU should be in international cooperation on the subject of climate along with global developments and should support the development of renewable energy.

Greenpeace believes that the EU should use its sustainable energy resources to have a strong line of course and should create a system in which together with local energy production, local needs like waste management are also taken into consideration. It emphasized that the carbon pricing of the EU's energy policy should include the fields of energy efficiency and renewable energy. It is also indicated that in order to achieve 80–95% greenhouse gas mitigation in 2050, the transition to 100% renewable energy is at a critical period and the objective of energy efficiency should be binding and moreoever after reviewing 2020 objectives that greenhouse gas mitigation should at least be 30%. As main factors to influence energy profile in the future, global fossil fuel prices, international cooperation that can be developed on the subject of climate and EU climate policy were determined.

In addition, by reviewing strategical preferences that would decrease the system cost, it should be recognized by the EU that nuclear and CCS will be much more expensive than renewable energy. In conducted researches, it is stated that

---

[227] Greenpeace, Submission to the European Commission, 7-12.
[228] Greenpeace, Submission to the European Commission, 16-21.
[229] The texts of Public Consultation for 2050 Road Map are not open to the public yet. It was obtained from the Commission, after the interviews made with EU.

energy efficiency and 100% renewable energy usage will save up 800 billion Euros until 2050.

World Wide Fund for Nature

For approximately 50 years, the World Wide Fund for Nature (WWF) has been seen as one of the establishments with the most powerful institutional representation in Europe, with projects produced with more than 100 countries. In 1989, the institution opened an office in Brussels with only one person to carry out lobbying. In the proceeding period, it widened and increased its activities within EU. During this process, believing that the subject of environment affects not only wildlife but also many different sectors; different policy fields such as agriculture, rural development and energy and climate change policies were also included in the organization's area of interest.[230]

"By 2012, WWF entered the scene of the international as well as the national climate change debates as a visible player. Two years earlier, WWF had become a member of the global 'Climate Action Network' (CAN) representing more than 250 NGO's worldwide."[231]

The WWF, while showing a more marginal attitude in the Rio Summit and UNFCCC meetings, conducted more professional studies in the following COPs. From this perspective, its evolution process resembles Greenpeace. It can be commented that these studies are more effective on media when evaluated together with communication developed with decision makers.

The WWF, just like Greenpeace, is an establishment with a hierarchical structure and professional employees. However, what separates it from Greenpeace is that is conducts its activities around scientific studies. In order to provide this, they work with highly qualified people.[232] From this perspective, WWF has the chance to conduct more privileged lobbying studies together with the technical data it owns, compared to other CSOs.[233]

The WWF is one of the CSOs with many employees. It focuses on general lobbying activities, and compared to other organizations, it is more at the forefront of EU institutions. On the subject of climate policy, it conducts studies

---

[230] Long, Salter and Singer, "WWF: European and Global", 87-88.
[231] Long, Salter and Singer, "WWF: European and Global", 94.
[232] Wurzel and Connelly, "Environmental NGOs," 217.
[233] Adelle and Anderson, "Lobby Groups," 161.

on nearly all fields, including ECCP, CCS, the carbon market and Kyoto objectives.[234]

When the 2015 budget of the WWF is examined, it can be seen that it has a relatively larger budget than other establishments – WWF Europe had a budget of €3,642,316 in total, in 2015; €588,127 of its budget came from the European Commission.[235] It can be said that the funds it receives from the EU decreased.

In the interview carried out with a former employee of the WWF, it was stated that the WWF is an organization based on protection, and that while the European sector is mostly focused on climate, the USA sector mostly studied on protection. The WWF is evaluated to be one of the largest civil society organizations. The former employee indicated that relations with the EU institutions constantly continue and that at every stage, even before the preparation of the proposal, they lobby. Here, the nature of strategy becomes important. With a reasonable budget from the establishment, the experts are asked to prepare reports and information, and a common position is tried to be provided. The interviewee mentioned that influencing the Parliament was much easier, but talking to influencial people in the Commission also showed good results. Here, building a trusting relationship with the institutions also has a determining role.[236]

The WWF prepared an assessment text within the scope of the energy and climate package, the 2030 Strategy, the 2050 Road Map and CCS consultations organized in 2013.

The WWF published a report in 2008 related to the energy and climate package.[237] The 20% greenhouse gas mitigation objective determined by the EU was not low. Moreover, to achieve this objective, the purchase of emission mitigation credits outside EU is against international commitments. It is also claimed that it is not contributing to developing countries' economies getting decarburised. The WWF proposal on this subject is a 30% greenhouse gas mitigation until 2020 within the EU and in addition for adaptation and emission

---

[234] Gullberg, "Rational Lobbying and EU", 170.

[235] "WWF European Policy Programme Transparency Register," *European Commission Transparency Register page*, Accessed June 3, 2015, http://ec.europa.eu/transparencyregister/public/consultation/displaylobbyist.do?id=1414929419-24.

[236] İnterviewee 7 (WWF former employee), interview by the author, Brussels, September 23, 2015.

[237] "Freezing Climate Change WWF Position Statement EU Climate and Energy Package," *WWF*, Accessed May 24, 2016, http://awsassets.panda.org/downloads/effort_sharing.pdf.

mitigation activities, financial investments to developing countries and corresponding to 15% mitigation.[238]

Similar to the ETS, with the Effort Sharing Decision, a 30% mitigation is also encouraged in the sectors outside the ETS. The need for the encouragement of member states for mitigation is emphasized. In addition it is thought that the objective of 20% energy efficiency should be binding, that renewable energy directive should come into effect at once and the objectives determined for the transportations to mitigate CO2 emission should be strengthened.[239]

In the document prepared by the WWF including its views, opinions on five different legal texts emerged at the mentioned period, were summarized.[240] The advice of the WWF on the ETS Directive was:

> *Set the cap on emissions to a 36% EU emission reduction target based on 2005 values and amend the year on year linear reduction percentage accordingly.*
>
> *Full auctioning of emission permits for all sectors – meaning all polluters must buy permits, and cleaner companies can benefit.*
>
> *All auctioning revenues earmarked for climate protection measures; at least 50% invested in decarbonisation and adaptation in developing countries; the rest in the EU.*
>
> *Ensure the EU ETS sectors deliver a fair proportion of the financial equivalent of an additional 15% emission reduction in investing in adaptation and emission reduction in developing countries.*
>
> *Close loophole for industry to off-set EU emissions via external credits in developing countries under the overall 30% EU reduction target.*
>
> *Only approve external credits from the Clean Development Mechanism (CDM) projects which meet the 'Gold Standard' or equivalent quality criteria for the additional 15% reduction effort.*
>
> *Exclude Domestic Offset Projects, surface transport, land use, land change and forestry (LULUCF) and the buildings sector from the EU*

---

[238] "Freezing Climate Change", *WWF*, 1.

[239] "Freezing Climate Change", *WWF*, 2.

[240] "WWF summary position paper on EU Climate and Energy Package poposals," *WWF*, Accessed November 25, 2015, http://www.wwf.se/source.php?id=1185063.

ETS as they will undermine the effectiveness of the system and hamper overall emission reduction activities.[241]

Related to the Effort Sharing Decision where the legislation was made in relation to sectors outside ETS, the criteria below were determined:

30% domestic reduction target by 2020 - from the start (not only in case of international agreement in UN).

Financial equivalent of an additional 15% emission reductions as EU's share of support for developing countries' emission reduction and adaptation measures.

External credits based on environmental and additionality criteria – equivalent to "CDM Gold Standard", on top of EU 30% reductions.

Introduce strong monitoring and reconciliation regime with automatic penalties for MS.

Ensure the adoption of stringent EU-wide policies and measures to ensure the non-ETS sectors deliver results in a coherent and non-distortionary manner.[242]

It continues its advices on the subject of renewable energy as such:

Ensure adoption of the 20% target with truly sustainable renewables.

Strengthen certification system for biofuels to ensure solid social and environmental criteria.

Expand certification to all bio-energies.

Fast financial support for creation of a large network of offshore wind power in the Atlantic.

Establish harmonized load and grid management across EU borders to compensate for some variable power fluxes.[243]

Finally its views on CCS are summarized as below:

Mandatory 'in time' and real monitoring for all storage sides to ensure geological safety and binding remediation plans in case of leakage.

---

[241] "WWF summary position paper", *WWF*, 3.
[242] "WWF summary position paper", *WWF*, 4.
[243] "WWF summary position paper", *WWF*, 5.

> *Set emission ceilings for all new, and later all existing, power plants at 350g CO_2/kWh.*
>
> *Mandatory assessment, before building any new power plant, of potential for other ways to meet energy needs - via demand side measures, supply efficiency (such as Combined heat and Power) and renewable energy.*
>
> *Public funding for safe storage site evaluation.[244]*

Hans Verolme, responsible for the global campaigns of the WWF, indicated that they expected the climate and energy package to be more powerful, a step taken on this subject was to be evaluated positively, and that they would encourage member states' governments in this direction. He also underlined the necessity to bring a legislation for car industry.[245]

The WWF, in its report published within the scope of the 2030 Strategy, predicts that if a suitable mechanism was not put into action, in 7 years emissions would increase and expresses that European leaders would have to make a choice. According to the WWF, the 2030 objectives should be 55% in the ETS, 40% in energy efficiency and 45% in renewable energy. For the ETS, internal market should be completed and research and development studies should be focused on and to make sure that all member states' domestic emission mitigations are through energy efficiency and renewable energy, the framework of effort sharing should be renewed.[246]

While forming mitigation objectives, limiting global warming under 2°C should be at the forefront and on subjects related to climate change such as occupations, stable economy and health security, measures should be taken. Otherwise other countries will benefit from low prices emerging as a result from the EU's efforts and will reduce their costs and will gain interest. The WWF gives importance to renewable energy and it defends that in 2050, it is possible for the EU to achieve 100% renewable energy share.[247]

It is stated that energy efficiency, greenhouse gas mitigation and innovator low carbon technologies being together, provide effective results. It is emphasized that in order for the ETS to function properly, it is necessary to follow a

---

[244] "WWF summary position paper", *WWF,* 6.
[245] Richard Black, "EU's energy plans – how revolutionary?," *BBC News,* Last modified January 10, 2007, http://news.bbc.co.uk/2/hi/science/nature/6247723.stm.
[246] WWF, *Response to the European Commission Public Consultation on a 2030 Climate and Energy Package*, Transparency Register Number: 1414929419-24, 3.
[247] WWF, Response to the European Commission, 4-8.

coordinated policy among member states by evaluating the ETS and the Effort Sharing Decision used for greenhouse gas mitigation, together. At this point it is pointed out that instead of seeming to make more mitigation than its present objective, it is necessary to make effective/enough effort with a higher mitigation objective. Besides the idea that the ETS has fallen down, while emphasizing the importance of having strict emission mitigation objectives and an effective carbon pricing, the prohibition of emission equalizing is demanded.[248]

Related to the 2050 objectives, it is stated that with the acceptance of the use of CCS and nuclear energy, polluted technologies are built cheaply, and as ETS cannot seperate these energy production mechanisms from the network alone, the Commission should evaluate renewable energy and energy efficiency technologies. The opinion that the decrease in energy prices of energy intense industries would slow down climate and energy policy is not shared by the WWF. It is indicated that lowering high prices to make the usage of fossil fuels easier is wrong and moreover, alternatives like shale gas are dangerous. According to the WWF, a huge amount of fossil fules should be left underground.[249]

When the WWF's opinions of the 2050[250] Road Map are evaluated, the emphasis that modellings should be prepared by looking at the costs, attracts attention. Together with the learning process of EU nuclear and of CCS which is slow, but fast in renewable energy, it is stated that this transition to be provided safely is possible through the development of 10-year strategies. Related to global developments in the EU 2050 Road Map, it is emphasized that energy efficiency, renewable energy and developments in fossil fuel markets should be paid attention to.

It is pointed out that for the EU to have a stronger line, it has to have an energy infrastructure providing high performance, has to consider the high rate of electricity and has to use sustainable energy resources. Fundamental features that should be given place in the 2050 perspective should be an infrastructure to support energy efficiency, renewable energy and 100% renewable energy together with emission performance standards.

On the subject of 2020 objectives, it is indicated that energy efficiency objective should be binding and 30% greenhouse gas mitigation should be provided. In

---

[248] WWF, Response to the European Commission, 10-12.

[249] WWF, Response to the European Commission, 14-15.

[250] The texts of Public Consultation for 2050 road map have not yet become open to the public. It was obtained from the Commission after interviews made with EU.

addition to these, it is emphasized that 95% greenhouse gas mitigation, as far as possible 100% renewable energy usage, and development of infrastructure and energy efficiency to be provided at 50% compared to the levels of 2005 should be provided. And in order to achieve these objectives by determining temporal objectives for 2030 and 2040, it is stated that it would be possible for the energy sector to become zero carbon in 2050.

While forming the EU energy policy, it is stated that global fossil fuels, member states' political decisions and the EU climate policy are effective. It is expected from the new road map new to be formed, to be designed as sustainable as possible, cost-effective and in a way to present future vision of secure energy. In order to provide this, it is pointed out that development of infrastructure besides renewable energy, greenhouse gas and energy efficiency objectives should be provided and it should be avoided to use divergent resources and should be focused on factors causing environmental effect other than CO_2.

Among the CSOs, only the WWF gave feedback related to the CCS Communication in 2013. The WWF, after the publication of Communication on the future of carbon capture and storage on March 27, 2013, published an evaluation text on July 2, 2013.

The text generally tends to oppose the use of CCS. Firstly it is considered that technological developments progress slowly and at the same time the use of this technology will not contribute to the mitigation of fossil fuels. Also, it is stated that renewable energy objective is more realistic and in terms of cost, it will not be more expensive than CCS. In return, while it is indicated that it is acceptable to use CCS technology in the industrial sector where decarbonization is not possible, it is pointed out that storage spaces are not as much as they are thought and that in this sense public support cannot be provided and it is emphasized that funds created for technological development should be reduced.[251]

Friends of the Earth

The international organization of Friends of the Earth (FoE) was founded in 1971 by four organizations that are French, Swedish, English and American. FoE, in the proceeding periods including many civil society organizations, today consists of 75 member organizations and is in the position to be the environmental network with the largest grassroot organization of the world. In 1985, European CSOs included in FoE in Brussels, founded the European office

---

[251] "WWF Reaction to the European Commission's 'Consultative Communications on the Future of Carbon Capture and Storage in Europe'," *WWF.* Accessed May 20, 2015, http://ec.europa.eu/energy/en/topics/oil-gas-andcoal/carbon-capture-and-storage.

to provide regional cooperation on the European continent.[252] The foundation of the European office coincides with the signing of the European Single Act. In this context, they indicate that they make an effort for the environment to play a bigger role in EU policies. Their basic fields of activity are subjects that can cause an influence in the EU generally, such as biotechnology, supporting environmental actions in Middle and East European countries, providing sustainable development in EU, climate change and emission mitigations within this scope.[253] The European office coordinates 33 organizations at present.[254]

They are more engaged in grassroot organization rather than lobbying activities.[255] When the 2014 budget of FoE Europe is analysed, it is possible to say that it is €4,830,196 and €2,610,891 of this budget was received from EU funds.[256]

Within the context of the 2030 Strategy, FoE, in the report it published, considers the 40% objective to be inadequate. The result of the reseach that FoE had Stockholm Environment Institute carry out, is that the EU, having a minimum of 60% mitigation in 2020 and 80% in 2030 are necessary objectives to limit global warming under 2°C. FoE also emphasizes that including the energy efficiency that failed to succeed in 2030 and 2020 objectives, all three legislations should be consistent with each other and should be organized as high and binding objectives. It is also predicted that the preparation of renewable energy draft with collective ownership will strengthen local initiatives.[257]

FoE supports the binding objectives for all three sectors. Accordingly, greenhouse gas levels should be 80% mitigated with respect to 1990 levels and energy efficiency should be increased 50% with respect to 2005 rates. It is not believed that without determining the objectives, the development of energy efficiency and renewable energy can be enough provided. Also it is indicated that solutions like nuclear energy, natural gas, bioenergy and CCS cannot provide long-term emission mitigation and that they are technologies

---

[252] "History," *Friends of the Earth International,* Accessed April 12, 2016, http://www.foei.org/about-foei/history.

[253] "Our History," *Friends of the Earth Europe*, Accessed April 12, 2016, https://www.foeeurope.org/about/history.

[254] Interviewee 11 (FoE representative), internet interview by the author, June 21, 2016.

[255] Gullberg, "Rational Lobbying and EU", 169.

[256] "Friends of the Earth Europe Transparency Register," *European Commission Transparency Register Page,* Accessed April 15, 2016, http://ec.europa.eu/transparencyregister/public/consultation/displaylobbyist.do?id=9825553393-31.

[257] "Submission on the European Commission's Green Paper on a 2030 framework for climate and energy policies," *Friends of the Earth.* Transparency register number: 9825553393-31, 07/2013, 2-4.

endangering the environment. Traditional fossil fuels like shale gas and coal cause health problems along with air and water pollution. It is claimed that CCS is actually a platform where big energy companies try to keep the present technology alive.[258]

It is stated that objectives should be determined in sub-sectors and especially the objective of transportation is very objectionable in that it would encourage the use of bio fuels. The EU's equalization policy is also being questioned because of the social and ecological problems it can cause. It is suggested that 2030 legislation should possess the approach that would overcome the structural failures of ETS. It is also emphasized that developing networks among member states is important.[259]

It is pointed out that upon the subject of carbon leakage, the industry makes exaggerated predictions and that it does not coincide with the data of International Energy Agency. Moreover, it is stated that it is positioned to provide the minimum change to be made in the studies of industrial unions like BusinessEurope, on this subject. According to FoE, more delays in determining the measures to be taken will make the harmful results of global warming inevitable to avoid.[260]

FoE stated its opinion in the context of the 2050 Road Map within the framework of Public Consultations. It seems possible to summarize its opinions as such: FoE emphasized that energy efficiency objectives of 2020 should be binding, that in order to limit global warming under 2°C, 40% of mitigation until 2020 is necessary and it is important that public awareness should be raised in this context.

FoE points out that international cooperation is needed on the subject of climate related to global developments, development of energy efficiency should be followed and by decreasing fossil fuel subsidies gradually, it is necessary to postpone the development of non-traditional fossil fuels. To strengthen the line of course of the EU, it is stated that projects on the increase of the rate of electricity in energy usage, the usage of sustainable and publicly accepted energy resources, renewable energy, and energy efficiency should be provided with more appropriate credits, and energy costs should be reduced.

In the 2050 objectives, it is thought that binding energy efficiency objectives, transportation policy and renewable energy should be included. For the

---

[258] "Submission on the European Commission's", *Friends of the Earth*, 4-6.
[259] "Submission on the European Commission's", *Friends of the Earth*, 7-9.
[260] "Submission on the European Commission's", *Friends of the Earth*, 11.

transition to low carbon energy systems, a 80–95% greenhouse gas mitigation objective in 2050 is needed and in the energy sector, mitigations should nearly be zeroed. In this context, access to energy efficiency and renewable energy objectives will contribute to the energy security of supply, competition and employment.

While forming future energy profiles, factors such as the global fossil fuel prices, EU climate policy and 2020–2050 objectives being binding are indicated to be effective. In addition to this, it is emphasized that both nuclear and CCS technologies should not be supported.

While forming the 2020 vision of the Union, determining the objective of 20% instead of 30% is accepted as an indication of political reluctancy by FoE.[261]

---

[261] "EU reveals energy plan of action," *BBC News,* last modified January 23, 2008, http://news.bbc.co.uk/2/hi/science/nature/7203514.st m.

Chapter Four

The influence capacity of the EU wide civil society organizations within the Union

International literature on environment generally examine the influence of CSOs from different perspectives. When designing the methodology of this study, the works of Michele M. Betsill and Elizabeth Corell have been of a great influence.[1] Although the authors generally tackle the role of CSOs on international treaties, in this book, the influence of CSOs on decision making mechanism of EU can also be tackled using the same frame (See Table 8). Besides, the methodology of influence analysis by Andreas Dür and the influence of interest groups on EU decision making processes have been used to strengthen the methodology.

When studies on influence are examined, it can be seen that these studies usually focus on individual sources like lobbying activities and access and they do not discuss the conceptualization of influence.[2] Influence can be taken as a soft power. Irina Michalowits suggests that it would be meaningful to look at the three components to define the power. Accordingly, the level of conflict between the decision makers and the actors, the structural conditions of

---

[1] Michele M. Betsill and Elizabeth Corell, "NGO Influence in International Environmental Negotiations: A Framework for Analysis," *Global Environmental Politics* 1, no. 4 (November 2001): 65-85.; Elizabeth Corell and Michele M. Betsill, "A Comparative Look at NGO Influence in International Environmental Negotiations: Desertification and Climate Change," *Global Environmental Politics* 1, no. 4 (November 2001): 86-107.

[2] Irina Michalowitz, "What determines influence? Assessing conditions for decision-making influence of interest groups in the EU," *Journal of European Public Policy* 14, no. 1. (2007): 134.

influence and the type of influence need to be looked at. The lobby alliances established within the level of conflict should especially be considered.[3]

According to this explanation it is possible to state that the actors follow an active or passive strategy depending on the related subject within EU. Moreover, through lobby coalitions, it can be considered that these actors are influential in the final decision making. Here, points like the situation during the decision making or cooperation between the institutions gain importance. It would make sense to look at the type of the subject and the stage at which legislation of the lobbying activities occur.

In the works of Betsill and Corell, the concepts of power and influence are separated and the concept of "influence" is used to reach a conceptual clearness while measuring the role of CSOs during the process of International Treaties. As the CSOs do not use the qualifications of the power that the national state generally uses, they may still have influence on the states. For this, influence should be conceptualized. Influence can generally be qualified as a type of relation between the actors emerging during the political process.[4]

The word influence, as well as being a word broad in scope, is taken as "the ability of an actor to shape a political decision in line with his preferences"[5] especially when examined in the scope of EU studies, as Klüver uses in her analysis. Both definitions of influence, because of their structure, aim to test the influence of the connection between the actors and visibility of this connection in the final decisions.

At this point, in order for a lobbying activity to successfully cause influence, a few conditions need to be formed. According to these conditions, influence in lobbying activities usually come into question in the stage of agenda setting and in cases when there is not a lot of conflict on the subject or when there is a weak opposition. The unsuccessful cases of influence can generally be lined up as the existence of a strong opposition and a non-transparent decision-making mechanism.[6]

In this context, influence should be taken in the frames of both transmission of data and the attitude of reaction to data. There are three criteria suggested by Betsill and Corell to measure the influences of CSOs, which are activities,

---

[3] Michalowitz, "What determines influence?", 134.
[4] Betsill and Corell, "NGO Influence in International", 73.
[5] Heike Klüver, *Lobbying in the European Union* (Great Britain: Oxford University Press, 2013a), 7.
[6] Michalowitz, "What determines influence", 137.

access to negotiations, and resources.[7] From the opportunities to participate in related interviews to their technical and financial sources, a wide range of examinations can be done by looking at the activities of CSOs. Therefore, not only the achieved result, but also the activities carried out to achieve that result is important.

Table 8: Framework for Analysing NGO Influence in International Environmental Negotiations

Research Task: Gather Evidence of NGO Influence (2 Dimensions)		
Triangulation by:	1) Intentional Transmission of Information	2) Behaviour of Other Actors
Data Type	NGO Participation	Goal Attainment
	Activities: What did NGOs do to transmit information to decision makers? Access: What opportunities did NGOs have to transmit information? Resources: What sources of leverage did NGOs use to transmit information?	Outcome: Does the final agreement contain text drafted by NGOs? Does the final agreement reflect NGO goals and principles? Process: Did negotiators discuss issues proposed by NGOs (or cease to discuss issues opposed by NGOs)? Did NGOs coin terms that became part of the negotiating jargon?
Data Source	*Primary texts* (e.g. draft decisions, country position statements, the final agreement, NGO lobbying materials) *Secondary texts* (e.g. ECO, Earth Negotiations Bulletin, media reports, press releases) *Interviews* (government delegates, observers and NGOs) Researcher *observations* during the negotiations	

---

[7] Corell and Betsill, "A Comparative Look at NGO", 87.

Research Task: Analyse Evidence of NGO Influence		
Methodology	Process Tracing	Counterfactual Analysis
	What were the causal mechanisms linking NGO participation in international environmental negotiations with their influence?	What would have happened if NGOs had not participated in the negotiations?

Source: Michele M. Betsill and Elizabeth Corell, "NGO Influence in International Environmental Negotiations: A Framework for Analysis," *Global Environmental Politics* 1, no. 4 (November 2001): 79.

The most important problem encountered during general lobbying studies is the analysis of the level of "influence". There are three different examination methods that Andreas Dür put forward to measure the influence level, in the form well accepted in literature.

The capacities of interest groups to influence decisions can be examined by using process tracing, assessing attributed influence and gauging the degree of preference. Accordingly, process tracing expresses the preferences, reports and activities of the groups to be examined by different variables. Assessing attributed influence expresses the use of surveys. Gauging the degree of preference reaches the result mostly by interviews.[8] Accordingly, the influence capacities of CSOs chosen based on the determined criteria analysed in the third chapter will be focused in this chapter.

When seen specifically to lobbying activities, the ability of the CSO's influence on EU policies seems lower than the ability of professional lobbyists' influence working under consultation companies. To handle CSOs as a whole becomes difficult in this sense. The difficulty of civil society to create an integrated EU civil society results fundamentally from not sufficiently democratic management practices within their own inner structures.[9] However, it can be

---

[8] Andreas Dür, "How Much Influence Do Interest Groups Have in the EU? Some Methodological Considerations," *Opening EU Governance to Civil Society Gains and Challenges*, edited. by. Beate Kohler Koch, Dirk De Bièvre and William Maloney (Mannheim. CONNEX Report Series no. 5, February 2008): 45-68.

[9] Alex Warleigh, "Europeanizing' Civil Society: NGOs as Agents of Political Socialization," *Journal of Common Market Studies*, 39 no. 4 (November 2001): 623.

Civil Society Impact on the EU Climate Change Policy

said that this theoretical view has started to change lately. Accordingly, CSOs have also started to become professional lobbyists.

Including in the 1990s having a more radical attitude and being against the idea of carbon markets, CSOs, after the White Paper in 2001, started to get more involved with the EU decision mechanism. After 2009, the relations of EU institutions and civil society organizations (or it can be called interest group to represent the whole of conducted academic studies) evolved in a way to show continuity. This evolution process made EU institutions and civil society come closer. The continuity of these close relations resulted with the transformation of radical features of CSOs and by taking an agreeable attitude, came to function professionally in Brussels.

In this respect it would be meaningful to show a perspective that analyses the developing events based on the change of CSOs. When lobbying activities are examined, it can be seen that two types of preferences come to the forefront by interest groups. In accordance with this, while some interest groups conduct lobbying activities with decision-makers closer to themselves, others try to change the attitudes of decision-makers that are against them.[10] Thus it is possible to make an evaluation not only in terms of institutional lobbying/ lobbying of CSO perspective, but also in terms of the characteristics of lobbying activities.

Another perspective developed on this subject is formed by lobbying strategies. Accordingly, general lobbying or singular/subject based lobbying studies can be conducted.[11] To influence Commission proposals, beforehand, interest groups practice general lobbying strategies. According to studies, it is considered that lobbying activities carried out when the first stage of the draft is prepared, are more successful.[12]

When we look at the process in general, it can be indicated that in order for ECSOs to increase their influence and their ability to create a civil society in the EU level can be handled with some variables. As it can be seen in Table 9, the existence of an EU-level civil society is measured with variables like cooperation on CSOs, their financial independency, internal management structure, their producing political view and ability to criticise themselves.

---

[10] Anne Therese Gullberg, "Lobbying friends and foes in climate policy: The case of business and environmental interest group in the European Union," *Energy Policy*, 36 (2008b): 2964.

[11] Gullberg, "Lobbying friends and foes", 2968.

[12] Gullberg, "Lobbying friends and foes", 2968-2969.

These variables are important to show the spots where institutions differentiate from each other. When we look at the five CSOs analysed in the book, we can say that other organizations except the EEB tend to cooperate based on the subject. At this point it can be stated that under CAN Europe, of which they are a member, they build some sort of a coalition. On the subject of financial independency on the other hand, only Greenpeace preferred to stay out of the EU system. Therefore the intensity observed in its activities compared to others is because of this reason.

Table 1: NGOs and Civil Society Construction

Key variable	Indicator in EU context
Collaboration with other NGOs and like-minded actors	Ability to construct policy coalitions
Independence	Reliance on non-official sources of funding (either EU or national)
Democratic internal governance	Participation in decision-making by supporters
Cognitive impact on supporters	Increased awareness of, and engagement with, EU decision-making
Concentration on politicization rather than service delivery	Privileging advocacy role
Ability to be self-critical	Officer-supporter dialogue; internal review
Ability to draw on existing political socialization	Large base of supporters willing to participate in decision-making

Source: "Europeanizing' Civil Society: NGOs as Agents of Political Socialization," Journal of Common Market Studies 39, no. 4 (November 2001): 628.

On the subject of democratic internal management, all organizations exhibit differences. Although most of the interviewees say that there is in-house democratic decision-making, when considered especially in umbrella organizations that each organization does not have the same knowledge, it can be pointed out that democratic structure cannot be provided completely. Greenpeace on the other hand, as a difference from the others, having already professionalized its management structure, adopted the concept of democratic inner management exceedingly.

When the institutions' dependency with EU decision-making mechanism is being looked at, it can be said that although they receive EU funds, they mostly criticise Commission drafts. But the relations they developed with EU institutions within time are a kind of a life form. And this life form brings both civil society and EU institutions together and makes them dependent on each other which can be explained via intertwined asymmetrical relationship. Thus, these organizations actually gain a privilege in terms of access to EU and they become usual members of decision-making mechanism. Nevertheless their own inner structure and way of actions are what makes them different.

ECSOs not only make the effort to influence EU policies but also try to mould public opinion in a broad sense and raise awareness. ECSOs play an important role in the determination of the framework of the subject in public discussions regarding the environment.[13] The relations between target group and decision-makers seem like a relation of knowledge change. If the CSOs provide the public support with their specialized knowledge, this situation may create the result of political decision's control by the CSOs. Therefore, here the CSOs conducting lobby activities may have the ability to influence decisions in order to serve their knowledge to the decision maker who has a limited knowledge. Because if the people who will be influenced by political decision unite against the political decision, this situation creates a pressure that decision makers cannot exclude.[14]

As it is frequently mentioned while analysing influence, criteria such as whether there is cooperation or not, the quality of the management, institution's inner structure and financial resources are important. In this respect, organizations with the ability to create public discussion and the ability to determine the direction of this discussion can be called "more influential" organizations.

One of the most important examples of this is Greenpeace. Greenpeace generally shoots its own videos and distributes them to television stations itself. Because of time-consuming editing processes, such as montage, Greenpeace tries to eliminate any possibility of the news not being broadcasted. It produces knowledge and distributes it.[15] In a sense it tries to control the process of knowledge transmission to increase its visibility and to provide its actions to be understood by everyone in the same way.

While analysing influence, another point that needs to be taken into consideration is that CSOs in time may change their ideas. The most important indication of this is while in 1990, CSOs were against the ETS because of its flexible structure, in the 2000s with the increase of the studies made for

---

[13] Wurzel and Connelly, "Environmental NGOs," 215.
[14] Skodvin, Gullberg and Aakre, "Target group influence", 856.
[15] Eden, "Greenpeace," 603.

legislations like ETS, they had to accept this situation and by integrating into the process, they tried to create a stricter mechanism – CAN and WWF played a key role in these legislations.[16]

In general, it would be meaningful to look if CSO coalitions were formed or not, rather than looking at certain CSOs singularly. As mentioned in the first chapter, CSO representatives may exaggerate the CSOs influence on decisions more than it is. In this sense it should be kept in mind that on some subjects, there are singular reactions, and on some subjects, there are the reactions of coalitions. And in this direction, it is nearly impossible to make counterfactual analysis on the field of environmental lobbying.[17]

According to Adelle and Anderson, CSOs are generally able to form coalitions more easily as there is no competition between them and they are able to have a higher rate of public support.[18] However, in lobbying studies it can generally be seen that there are benefit and cost calculations. If the costs are higher than the benefit, lobbying is generally avoided. Lobbying studies are based on three factors in this sense. These are: the "probability (P) of gaining influence when lobbying on the policy decision; the benefits (B) of a favourable policy decision; and the costs (C) of lobbying"[19]. As lobbying on only one subject requires specialties like knowledge and expertise, it is much more costly and hard to guess its benefit at the beginning.[20] Because of this, CSOs conducts lobbying studies extremely strategically.

As resources are very limited, it would be meaningful for the organizations to calculate the lobbying cost, and then to conduct their activities with the lowest cost. The pressure created by this situation enabled the employees of civil society organization to become professional lobbyists. These professionals, even though they do not adopt the values defended by the organization they work for as much as a volunteer, transfer the defended ideas to institutions. Even if these people change the organizations they work for, their work does not change. This progress in professionalism caused the organizations to review their employment policies and thus to recruit more employees. And this situation makes it difficult for the organizations to conduct lobbying activities unless their budgets are raised. At this point, umbrella organizations take over

---

[16] Wurzel and Connelly, "Environmental NGOs," 225.

[17] This method of analysis was designed to make inferences moving from the idea that how the situation would be if there were no lobbies. Adelle and Anderson, "Lobby Groups," 160.

[18] Adelle and Anderson, "Lobby Groups," 160.

[19] Gullberg, "Rational Lobbying and EU", 165.

[20] Gullberg, "Rational Lobbying and EU", 171.

the duty and although they do not have a high budget, they can conduct this lobbying as they are only focused on one subject.

CSO reports and analysis

When the Commission is going to create legislation on one subject, it generally forms a Green Paper at first. The reason for this is to create a basis on how the legislation will be and to review different alternatives. Then the prepared White Paper presents the Commission proposal in more clear lines and different opinions are expected by the Commission from different sides related to the proposal.[21]

With the publication of the Green Paper, CSOs also starts to share its opinion on the subject and thereby a public discussion platform is formed. The legal texts to be examined within this section will be the comments of CSOs, CSOs reports and views in the areas where the EU was opened to consultation through its web site.

The declaration of 2020 objectives pleased the civil society organizations. Although there will be a need for binding legal texts, the first step to be taken created excitement in CSOs. In this context, while FoE organized a walk in Brussels, Greenpeace qualified the 2020 framework as the best step since Kyoto. The WWF, on the other hand, indicated that one of the best reasons for celebrations was nuclear energy being a part of green energy objectives.[22]

Within the framework of the ongoing CSO meetings before the Emission Trading Directive in 2009, CAN Europe published a report together with the Greenpeace European Unit, WWF Europe and FoE Europe. Most of the people interviewed for this book think that the reason why the names of these other organizations, even though they are a member of CAN Europe, are in the report, is because CAN Europe is not well known and that other organizations are better known by the public.[23]

In the reports, the general principles ask that the ETS should not only be active environmentally, but also economically and that in order to create both short- and long-term carbon pricing, the upper limit of the ETS should be determined.

---

[21] A. Aslı Bilgin, "Avrupa Komisyonu," in *Avrupa Birliği – Tarihçe, Kurumlar ve Politikalar*, edited by. Belgin Akçay and İlke Göçmen (Ankara: Seçkin Publishing, 2012), 189.

[22] "Green groups upbeat over EU energy/climate package", *Euronews*, Last modified July 9, 2007, http://www.euronews.com/2007/03/09/green-groupsupbeat-over-eu-energyclimate-package/.

[23] İnterviewee 2 (CAN Europe Representative), interview by the author, Brussels, September 22, 2015; İnterviewee 7 (WWF former employee), interview by the author, Brussels, September 23, 2015; İnterviewee 10 (Greenpeace former employee), internet interview by the author, April 25, 2016.

It is indicated that in the ETS's design and application, a simple allowance method should be used and that a wide range of public support, transparency and public participation at every stage is necessary.[24]

For the period after 2012, the improvements that should be made in the ETS's design are indicated as such by civil society organizations: the greenhouse gas mitigation of 2020 should at least be 30%; the limit in the ETS should be determined at EU level and all the emissions starting from 2013 should be distributed by the method of auction. Also, the incomes obtained from the auction should again be used related to climate change and the usage of CDM/JI credits should be limited. The ETS to expand by means of containing other greenhouse gases except CO_2 should carefully be examined, Land Use, Land Use Change and Forestry (LULUCF) and road transport should stay outside the ETS and the inclusion of aviation should be seen as the first stage. Finally, the ideas that offset projects in EU countries that damage the environment and JI credits should not take place in the ETS, are defended.[25]

The ETS, which includes 40% of the total emissions of 27 member countries, is considered to be very important in terms of providing greenhouse gas mitigation in EU. It is mentioned in the directive prepared in 2013 that over allowance reduced the carbon prices and that this situation should be changed. Moreover, it is indicated that the limits determined on a national level create non-transparent, partial and ineffective applications.

It is dwelled on that the determination process of emission upper limit should be coherent and simple and carbon pricing should be directive for more clean and effective technological investments. Also, as each sector has different needs within the scope of climate change, it is pointed out that there is not one single method suitable for everyone and that the ETS is only one of these methods. Here again it is underlined that meeting the commitments by supporting the projects outside the EU with credit support provides the improvement of existing technologies but also does not support research and development.[26]

It is mentioned that this system created by EU attracts the attention of the world and that the ETS will be a tool both in the struggle with climate change and long-term decarbonization.[27] On the subject of emission mitigation, a mitigation

---

[24] "ECCP EU ETS Review Process: Written Comments CAN-Europe, Friends of the Earth Europe Greenpeace and WWF," *CAN Europe, Friends of the Earth Europe, Greenpeace, WWF,* June 2007, http://ec.europa.eu/clima/events/docs/0065/caneurope_ngo_en.pdf.
[25] "ECCP EU ETS Review Process", CAN Europe, Friends of the Earth Europe, Greenpeace, WWF, 4.
[26] "ECCP EU ETS Review Process", CAN Europe, Friends of the Earth Europe, Greenpeace, WWF, 6-7.
[27] "ECCP EU ETS Review Process", CAN Europe, Friends of the Earth Europe, Greenpeace, WWF, 7.

of 30% in 2020 and 80% until 2050 is seen as necessary. In this context, the necessity of forming concrete policies is emphasized because possible delays will cause more costs to emerge. It is pointed out that trade periods in the ETS should be longer than 5 years otherwise it would not be possible to achieve the desired objectives. The fundamental point here that the CSOs come to terms with and dwell on, is that each member country prepares its own allocation of allowances. They defend the idea that this situation will create a partial application and there will be no consistency by the removal of transparency. They indicate that when the period between 2008 and 2012 is examined, the countries gave their own industry and energy sectors more allowances by being generous. This situation of states in both the first and second period also damaged subsidiarity according to CSOs.[28]

It is assumed that the determination of allowances by emission cap and the method of auction will solve the problems occured before the 2009 amendment with an application at EU level. And to be sure of that, the allowances after 2012 should be determined at EU level and this should reflect the total amount of member states' allowances.[29] It is also indicated that open allowances is also against the polluter pays principle. In addition to this, although developing benchmarks may be good in theory, when considered within the scope of the EU ETS, it is pointed out that determining an open, enduring and transparent benchmark is difficult. It is thought that developing technical norms would not provide the best application, but would provide the common lowest share and thus the method of auction is seen as the best method for the distribution of the allowances.[30]

One other subject that the CSOs dwell on is the subject of CDM/JI credits. CSOs find the usage of these credits unfavorable and they indicate that within the period from 2003 to 2007, this became a necessity. Because the projects taken place outside the EU weaken the functioning of ETS within the Union and emission rates on the territory of the EU cannot be decreased. Beyond this, in the meetings, the opinions of specialists are also given place, and it is pointed out that nearly 50% of CDM credits does not provide real mitigation and that it contradicts the Kyoto Protocol. With the credits provided to projects like big hydroelectric power plants created the position that is not compatible with the

---

[28] "ECCP EU ETS Review Process", CAN Europe, Friends of the Earth Europe, Greenpeace, WWF, 8-10.
[29] "ECCP EU ETS Review Process", CAN Europe, Friends of the Earth Europe, Greenpeace, WWF, 10.
[30] "ECCP EU ETS Review Process", CAN Europe, Friends of the Earth Europe, Greenpeace, WWF, 11-12.

principle of sustainable development. It is stated that only CDM projects which have golden standard can support sustainable development aims.[31]

The subject of CCS on the other hand is a subject where not many CSOs have detailed information and the expertise. However, the CCS system commercialized with the European Commission's push to a large extent. At the same time, the increase of the media visibility of the CCS technology positively affected its recognition among people. Also the carbon dioxide Capture and Storage Report published in 2005 indicated that the CCS will be able to contribute 15 to 55% cumulative of the carbon mitigation objective worldwide. And the predictions of this report caused CCS also to be taken into consideration in the greenhouse gas mitigation of European Commission.[32] Hasson and Bryngelsson emphasize in their research that there is still not enough knowledge on CCS and that while these uncertainties are present, it is too early to use it in energy production. Interestingly, they indicate that the determination of the CCS was used for nuclear power plants in previous years.[33]

Greenpeace also claimed that although it does not have much experience on this subject, a technology yet to be on trial will not provide the expected benefit. The WWF, participating in the consultation in 2013, also emphasized technological developments, and that renewable energy costs much less. The point on which the two organizations agreed with is the possible harmful results of CCS. Generally it can be said that these organizations are against providing public support to CCS both by the Union and the states.

In the Public Consultation prepared within the framework of 2030, five CSOs, were also included. Although all organizations generally have a common opinion, each of their political fields they mainly handle are different from each other. In accordance with this, while the EEB concentrates on energy efficiency, the WWF mostly emphasizes renewable energy. CAN Europe on the other hand, while claiming that Climate and Energy Package is not assertive enough, also underlines the necessity of a more extensive plan. FoE and Greenpeace acknowledge that all three objectives to be planned with consistent articulation is the prerequisite for a successful policy. All five organizations share this view fundamentally, but they may think differently in terms of the subject that should play the most important part in this process.

---

[31] "ECCP EU ETS Review Process", CAN Europe, Friends of the Earth Europe, Greenpeace, WWF, 14-16.

[32] Anders Hasson and Mårten Bryngelsson, "Expert Opinions on Carbon Capture and Storage – A Framing of Uncertainties and Possibilities," *Energy Policy* 37 (2009): 2273.

[33] Hasson and Bryngelsson, "Expert Opinions on Carbon, 2273- 2275.

On the subject of 2030 greenhouse gas emission objectives, the EEB predicts 40% until 2030, CAN Europe, Greenpeace and the WWF 55%, and FoE predicts 80% mitigation. In addition, Greenpeace and WWF indicated that a 45% renewable energy rate is necessary. The WWF emphasized the importance of having a share of 40%, and FoE 50% of energy efficiency.

Here the differentiation in objectives determined by the organizations are related to their access to scientific data, their efforts in creating applicable alternatives and their institutional claims. The EEB, by being the establishment with the lowest objective, shows the importance it gives to reconciliation with EU institutions. This situation can be the indicator of a state of thinking like a decision maker. CAN Europe, Greenpeace and the WWF on the other hand see the situation technically, as they obtain similar scientific data and at the same time, as they also carry out studies on the obligations resulting from the Kyoto Protocol, determine objectives that are more suitable to international obligations.

When the 2050 objectives are examined, it can be metioned that all the organizations see the objectives as inadequate. Accordingly the EEB and CAN Europe indicate that the process should be limited with 2050. While Greenpeace defend the idea that greenhouse gas rates in 2050 should be mitigated between 80 and 95%, the WWF on the other hand emphasizes that it should be 95%. Both organizations point out that in 2050, 100% renewable energy should be used and WWF also states that achieving 50% energy efficiency should be on the agenda.

In this context, it would be meaningful to indicate that 2050 evaluations would be focused on renewable energy and energy efficiency and the follow-up of global developments. The most important point agreed on both for 2030 and 2050 documents, is the necessity of the energy efficiency objectives to be binding. The increase in energy efficiency and development in renewable energy will also provide a fast decrease in greenhouse gas rates. Greenpeace's statement that in this sense with the transition to 100% renewable energy, €800 billion savings will be provided, can be evaluated in this context. By developing support mechanisms, it will both be possible to reduce the costs of renewable energy technologies and to provide economical development.

CSOs, in their reports, adopt a highly agreeable and problem-solving attitude. When the general characteristic of the reports are examined, they are written in a way to create an alternative to law proposals, but that it is commented according to the titles these proposals include. For example, the objectives of the directives are considered to be low. Or the emission upper limit in trading directives is requested to be reduced every year and in distributions only the method of auction is requested to be used. And these proposals are taken into consideration by the institutions.

This advice, already included in civil society reports, also reflect the problems encountered during the application of the directives. It can also be said that generally in the texts there is an agreement that biofuels are not sustainable. In this sense, it can be stated that during the determination of objectives it should not be acted against the understanding of sustainability. Another notable issue is the creation of an opinion that the technological developments to be supported and in this context economy to be prevented from deterioration.

Although Greenpeace seems dark green on the scale in this sense, in its reports it emphasizes that in order for the EU not to be able to catch up the world, technological developments should be supported. This emphasis is for the economy not to be deteriorated and for the long-term investments to be possible with binding objectives. From this perspective, it is interesting for an organization like Greenpeace to publish a report with such an agreeable language. Moreover Greenpeace prepares a detailed report on nearly every new legislation. Thus, it can be commented that Greenpeace aims to be an agenda setter or to be one step ahead of the other CSOs.

The means of participation of the organizations to the process of decision making

The participation process of the organizations are an interactive process. Within this process, organizations with the same objectives make benefit-cost analysis, either transparently or not, and determine in what circumstances they will communicate with the other organizations. These organizations generally have a certain level of cooperation to influence the final decisions they desire. Private or public institutions involved in the process are interconnected within the framework of needs,[34] because the formation of the knowledge that is necessary to be provided to the estalishments for finally accessing the EU can only be possible as a result of intense resource usage.

In the process of the formulation of an interest, if there are a lot of parties interested in the subject, there is a need for a more extensive legislation.[35] Here there are groups that can handle the different aspects of the subject, and the

---

[34] Pieter Bouwen, "Corporate Lobbying in the European Union: the Logic of Access," *Journal of European Public Policy* 9, no. 3 (2002): 368

[35] Bouwen, "Corporate Lobbying in the European", 370.

participation of professional organizations with excellent representation skills are also important in terms of providing expertise.

According to Gullberg, the point that is agreed in lobbying literature is that the lobbying process is generally the transfer of information from the informed interest group to the uninformed decision-maker. These studies can be named as informative lobbying. Finally, by providing the information transfer that target decision-maker needs, the importance of the subject is emphasized. As decision-makers and interest groups cannot be expected to come to an agreement at every subject, interest groups can also give deficient information to decision-maker.[36] Because of this, decision-makers, being aware of the deficient information, conduct their meetings accordingly.[37]

The Commission tried to establish its first step in 1992 by "An Opened Structured Dialogue" to provide more official communication pathways with CSOs and to form a more trasparent mechanism.[38] With the publication of the White Paper on Governance in 2001, it was aimed to institutionalize this dialogue. Afterwards the Commission also signed treaties with the European Economic and Social Committee and Committee of Regions. Thus, it shows that by enabling interest groups to be included earlier in the decision-making mechanism, the Commission attributes to these institutions a conciliatory role to play between the EU and CSOs.

The European Transparency Initiative, published in 2005, is a result of EU citizens' lack of confidence in the system. The legal basis of this process was formed by the Green Paper on the European Transparency Initiative, published in 2006. An online Register of Interest Representatives web base providing the CSOs to be included into the system was created. The improved state of this system by integrating with European Parliament register system was reorganized under the name of the Transparency Register on June 2011.[39]

In 2015 under the name of "Better Regulation," the "Regulatory Fitness and Performance Programme-REFIT" was put forward for EU law to be used more effectively.[40] The common reason of these developments was to make the stakeholders a part of the decision-making process by making them participate effectively especially to the decision-making mechanism. These ongoing efforts

---

[36] Anne Therese Gullberg, "Lobbying friends and foes in climate", 2965.

[37] Interviewee 12 (EP former parliamentary), internet interview by the author, June 28 2016.

[38] Eising and Lehringer, "Interest Groups and the European Union," 194.

[39] Adelle and Anderson, "Lobby Groups," 162-163.

[40] "Better Regulation," *European Commission*, Accessed November 3, 2015, http://ec.europa.eu/smart-regulation/index_en.htm.

also provide the lobbying studies on EU institutions to be more institutionalized. The institutions conducting lobbying activities through these means join meetings by becoming accredited to the system and can use official ways to announce their own arguments.

All civil society employees who were interviewed for this book affirm that they use these official channels and all EU institution employers affirm that CSOs reach them within this determined framework. Another common point that CSO interviewees made is that they are trying every way to influence the EU and they are trying to reach every actor. In order to provide this influence, they emphasize the importance of taking action as soon as possible.

This is because if the lobbying carried out at the first stage is successful, CSOs will also have the quality of being an agenda setter. In this case, the proposal of the Commission is more close to the demands of CSOs. As the legislation of a prepared text is discussed extensively in the Parliament, it becomes more influenced by more lobbyists. And this may decrease the chance of success. The important thing is that the views of the CSOs are reflected in the final outcome. Public consultations, from which official opinion is taken, does not seem to provide much influence.

In this context, the idea of an EEB representative seems rather interesting. As the representative, the EU Commission itself prepares the texts of public consultations. Therefore, for the CSOs participating in the consultation is not a particularly productive. The Commission is criticized for asking questions while already knowing the answers.[41] Thereby, the view that official mechanisms do not meet the CSOs' expectations, was put forward. Here the creation of a platform that is seen as democratic and where CSOs is given permission to raise its voice, can also be evaluated as the attempt of the Commission to increase the legitimacy of its own actions.

On the other hand, a former WWF employer indicated that it is possible for everyone to talk to the Commision because of the democratic deficit and that it is enough to only have information on the subject. The interviewee emphasized that Commissioners play an important role in this process, stating that once ECSOs acted harshly to a Commissioner, and that he/she did not forget this in the next process.[42]

At this point it would be meaningful to look at the eight-stage programme developed by the WWF. According to this, first the timing of lobbying activities

---

[41] İnterviewee 1 (EEB Representative), interview by the author, Brussels, September 22, 2015.
[42] İnterviewee 7 (WWF former employee), interview by the author, Brussels, September 23, 2015.

are decided. As a proactive study programme was formed, term presidencies and the date of the related decision to reach the Council are being determined. Second, a technique is determined in the lobbying studies that are carried out in a certain field, to whom will the correct and understandable message should be transmitted and how this message will be transmitted. And then the content of the message is developed by different participants. Third, in order for the subject to be on the agenda, previously determined representatives are being reached. As generally the target group knows the organization from earlier studies, here, when it is not possible to meet with the targeted person, national offices are attempted to be reached by using personal contacts.

The fourth stage is the consolidation stage. At this stage the visibility of the subject is increased by trying to reach all the stakeholders related to the subject such as key people, problematical countries and non-governmental organizations of these countries. Thus the message, that the subject is not included within the interest of one organization but is included within the interest of a large mass, is given. The fifth stage is the stage in which alliances and opponents are determined. For example by associating the studies conducted by the WWF, with the CSOs represented by CAN Europe, a kind of CSO cooperation platform is being created. With the effect of the consolidation stage, CSOs try to create a more extensive effect by using the same discourse. In response to this positive list, a counter lobby is formed as their attitudes become clearer.

The sixth stage is the increase of visibility in the media. But as the subject, being very detailed, would make it difficult to find a place in media, influence can also be made by using different subjects. For example, an effort was made to reach larger masses with the CDM mechanism, used after nuclear discussions. The seventh stage is the stage of collecting results. Although the organizations cannot always make their plans be accepted, on some subjects they can make a decision to be issued on their behalf. Therefore, it is possible to handle success not as a reflection of the whole report, but as a similitude on the basis of subtitles. The last stage is the stage of learned lessons. Accordingly, the outcomes of the WWF on the subject of CDM are as such: it is not difficult to reach the key person and the process should constantly continue. Within the complex functioning of the EU, it is necessary to reach all parties. National prejudices should be avoided. It is important to reach EU term presidency. Timing is very important and the result is unpredictable.[43]

---

[43] Information related to the stages were summarized from the article of Long, Salter and Singer, "WWF: European and Global", 97-103.

When the process is analysed, during the stage of determination of 2020 objectives, the WWF believes that despite the fact that the text includes some uncertain articles, it being accepted, will make an important change in global warming and thinks that the continuity of this acceleration in the EU, by creating successive effects, will be influential in Japan, New Zealand, Norway, Switzerland and even in the USA.[44] In short, it both lobbies within the EU and tries to influence the public by emphasizing its importance globally.

While determining the renewable energy objectives, British firms conducted lobbying studies for the aviation industry to be removed from the legislations. However, according to the parliamentarian Claude Turmes, with the removal of aviation industry, only 18.5% of the renewable energy objective will be able to be achieved. Besides, Turmes thinks that also because of the pressure of nuclear and coal plants is why Britain wanted the objectives to be changed. On this subject, Britain made one of the most important oppositions. According to the director of Greenpeace, removing the aviation industry from the treaty will decrease the investment made on clean technologies. Therefore, renewable energy objectives will not be realistic.[45] Again at this point it is observed that lobbies with opposite opinions are in conflict with each other and that they try the subject to evolve in the way they want it.

Interestingly, in Gullberg's article it is mentioned that after the determination of renewable energy objectives, there had not been many discussions related to the subject and that the situation was very favorable in determining the renewable energy objectives. According to this data obtained from the interviews made with the stakeholders of the subject, a "window of opportunity" is opened.[46]

Also while forming the 2030 Strategy, the states had difficulties to reconcile on the subject of binding objectives. Britain and Poland indicated that binding objectives will create pressure on the public. Similarly, France and Spain made the effort to remove the objectives from the strategy. In this process, FoE stated that the Climate Commissioner Connie Hedegaard had not achieved any success in the last 4 years.[47] Greenpeace representative Joris Den Blanken claimed that the investments of the EU for clean energy in 15 years would regress. Trying to

---

[44] Stephen Mulvey, "Summit to test EU climate resolve," *BBC News,* Last modified March 7, 2007, http://news.bbc.co.uk/2/hi/europe/6427015.stm.

[45] Roger Harrabin, "UK opposes green aviation target," *BBC News,* Last modified September 26, 2008, http://news.bbc.co.uk/2/hi/science/nature/7636780.stm.

[46] Anne Therese Gullberg, "Pressure or Information? Lobbying for Binding Renewable Energy Targets in the European Union," *Review of Policy Research* 30, no. 6 (2013): 620.

[47] Matt McGrath, "Burnt ou' EU likely to curb climate goals," *BBC News,* Last modified January 21, 2014, http://www.bbc.com/news/science-environment-25828181.

include shale gas within the package to reduce the cost of the industry also draws the reaction of environmental organizations.[48]

The Commission, within the scope of 2030 objectives, proposed that greenhouse gas emission should be 40% and the renewable energy share should be 27%. These objections could not please the environmentalists. When it comes to member states, as Germany has its own energy transformation, it supported the binding objectives. Other countries like Poland, Spain, and Britain insisted on forming energy profiles as they desire.[49]

Generally, it can be said that in the articulation of organizations to the decision-making process, the conjuncture of the period is also important. No matter how good the strategies are developed, the decision will not be as desired if there is no suitable platform. The states, by putting their own interests at top priority, will want the intergovernmental discussions to be the determinent in the Council. By being the blocking minority, they will try to prevent more strict legislations being accepted.

The levels of influence of the organizations to the process of decision making

European Commission

To analyse the rate of influence, it would be meaningful to first mention the Commission's present structure and decision-making mechanism. In this sense it is possible to observe the point where the influence capacity of CSOs step in. In general terms, within the Commission there are both Commissariats that are dominated by political will and General Directorates that function as administrative unit.

The Commisioners are assigned with the proposal of member states and the approval of the EP. Determining the number of the Commisioners and setting the agenda is under the authority and responsibility of the Commission President. Although Commission members are chosen by member countries, they cannot come closer with any political formation during their period of office. Otherwise this would be against the legislation in article 17/3 of the European Union Treaty.[50]

---

[48] "Environmentalists criticise new EU climate goals," *Euronews*, last modified January 23, 2014, http://www.euronews.com/2014/01/23/environmentalists-criticise-new-eu-climate-goals/.
[49] Matt McGrath, "EU outlines 2030 cimate goals," *BBC News*, Last modified January 22, 2014, http://www.bbc.com/news/science-environment-25841134.
[50] Bilgin, "Avrupa Komisyonu," 184.

Şekercioğlu

The Commission's administrative units are composed of lower service units dealing with different fields, and technical units like legal, economic etc. These are cabinets responsible for providing communication between administrative units and the Commissioners. Members of the cabinet directly depend on the Commissioner and does its consultancy and is a bridge between technical units. In this sense it is possible to say that members of the cabinet play a key role within the decision-making mechanism.

An intense coordination can be observed within the Commission's decision-making mechanism. In this context, texts to be prepared on a subject are prepared by the proposal of the Commissariat and Directorate Generals'coordination.[51] First of all, the texts prepared by the Directorate Generals are sent to the Commissioner of the Committee after they are examined by the Commisioner and its cabinet and the final decision is made by the Commissioner of the Committee in weekly meetings.

In this sense the Commission should not be seen as a homogeneous structure. Many of the subjects being related to each other, necessitates different Directorate General sub-units to be included within the process and the process of coming to an agreement can be evaluated as complicated. This first preparation process together with the reading process by the cabinet of the Commisioner, can be evaluated as the most effective processes.

The European Commission, being the institution to prepare law drafts, is in the position of being the first institution that CSOs try to reach. Organizations, before the preparation of the drafts and in the process of public consultations, communicate with the Commission. All four Commission representatives interviewed for this book, are of the same opinion that CSOs are in contact with them at every stage.[52]

According to Adelle and Anderson, groups who lobby the EU on the environment are rather successful in bringing the subject of their interest forward almost at every stage of the process. The Commission generally seems to be the most important communication channel for CSOs. The most important reason for this is the Commission's mission to be the agenda setter. According to Hontelez, the fundamental reason for CSOs to participate in this process is to

---

[51] "Avrupa Komisyonu," 184-185.

[52] In the aforementioned interviews, Commission representatives emphasized the importance given to the participation of civil society. In the period after Rio within the scope of climate change, civil society being constantly in contact with the Commission and new legislations on transparency, show that the interaction between civil society and the Commission will continue.

create a balance mechanism against business organizations.[53] The Commission, in this sense, also benefits from environmental organizations to defend its own proposals against the business world.

The Commission representatives, in order to measure the influence capacity of CSOs on the Commission, were asked how to communicate with CSOs, how their relation with CSOs developed after the White Paper on Governance was published in 2001 and how much influence umbrella and singular organizations have on Commission decisions.

Interviewee 4 emphasized the importance of civil society to participate in the process in terms of public participation and that the Treaty of Lisbon, with its changes on "citizens initiative", made the process become more transparent. The interviewee, remarking that civil society also holding different views from radical to pragmatic within itself, indicated that it would be difficult to analyse the influence by looking at the structures of civil society in terms of their influence.[54]

Interviewee 5 on the other hand, stated that, starting from their establishments, both environment and climate change Commissariats had been conducting interviews with CSOs and in this sense the White Paper published in 2001 did not create a new influence. He/she emphasized that in terms of organizations' influence, the Commission was always open to hear different voices. Moreover, it was emphasized that while Commissariats like the industry Commissariat umbrella organizations are more effective, on the subject of climate change, organizations studying climate change had just as much influence on the process as umbrella organizations.[55]

Similar to other Commission representatives, interviewee 6 also stated that public consultations are not only supported online, but at the same time with activities such as various workshops, conferences and stakeholder meetings. In this meaning he/she emphasized that within the process, sometimes umbrella organizations and sometimes singular organizations are more effective, depending on the situation.[56]

---

[53] Adelle and Anderson, "Lobby Groups," 156.
[54] Interviewee 4 (EU Commission DG Climate consultant), interview by the author, Brussels, September 23, 2015.
[55] Interviewee 5 (EU Commission DG Climate consultant), interview by the author, Brussels, September 23, 2015.
[56] Interviewee 6 (EU Commission DG Energy bureaucrat), interview by the author, Brussels, September 23, 2015.

When the Commission generally puts a draft forward, it has the ability to change the text with the feedback it receives from CSOs. This method indicates that a bottom up process is followed by related institutions. They try to increase participation of the groups and enrich the text in technical terms where integrating the voices of member states' citizens.[57] Through assuming the participation of the citizens into the process, it is predicted that development on democratic participation is ensured.

Interviewee 9, on the other hand, indicated that the consultation process in which CSOs participated was transparent and that even in the 1990s the CSOs had a big infuence. Here influence is emphasized to be a result of expertise. It is pointed out that specialists in their own subjects also make changes among institutions and therefore instead of the influence of only one single organization, the influence of experts is also important.[58]

While the Commission is the first place to be reached, according to Eising and Lehringer, the interest groups reach the Commission not as a whole but through Commissariats.[59] The fundamental actors to lobby the Commission are the employees of the related Commissariat and the Directorate General. The most optimistic part of this process is that lobbying the Commission is less costly as there are not many people to contact. According to Gullberg, the ability of the business world to influence the Commission is greater.[60] There has not been an agreement on which groups are the most influential on the Commission.

Interviewee 5 indicated that the meetings are generally conducted among Directorate Generals and General Secretariats of Energy, Industry, and Transportation. Here which of the Directorate Generals is more influential changes according to its political preference and its representatives. One of the main reasons of the creation of the ETS is that Industry and thus the Directorate General supported the proposal.[61]

Here the main reason for the industry to influence the Commission is having more capacity for lobbying activities. In this context the negotiations divide into two. While institutional participation includes legal negotiations, non-institutional participation includes bureaucrats and politicians together with

---

[57] Eising and Lehringer, "Interest Groups and the European Union," 194.

[58] Interviewee 9 (EU Commission DG Climate consultant), interview by the author, Brussels, September 25, 2015.

[59] Eising and Lehringer, "Interest Groups and the European Union," 192.

[60] Gullberg, "Lobbying friends and foes in climate", 2967.

[61] Interviewee 5 (EU Commission DG Climate consultant), interview by the author, Brussels, September 23, 2015.

unofficial meetings. On the subject of renewable energy, Commission members and parliamentarians can be evaluated in this context.[62]

The information that the EU institutions need changes depending on the subject. The Commission, while preparing the proposal, needs information both on the subject and on common European interests. On the other hand, the Parliamentarians, as they are chosen for European and national interests, are in need of information on national interests. Finally the Council, because of its intergovernmental structure, considers the learning of national interests as a top priority. While expert knowledge is needed more in the stage of preparation of proposals, it is at this stage that lobbying activies are most influential.[63]

Although it is highly difficult to measure the success of CSOs, it can be said that within the framework of multi-level governance theory, with the transition to common decision-making mechanism, many different actors are integrated into the process in different stages of the process and try to influence the final decision/document. Here it would be meaningful to say that fundamental arguments of multi-level governance determined by Gary Marks, Liesbeth Hooghe and Kermit Blank, are directly related to evolution process of climate and energy policies.

The combination of the Commission should also be handled importantly in making influence. The process starting with Romano Prodi, who conducted the Commission Presidency between 1999 and 2004, continued with José Manuel Barroso, Commission President between 2004 and 2014. In this context, Stavros Dimas and Janez Potočnik, who conducted the Environmental Commissariat, Andris Piebalgs and Günther Oettinger who conducted the Energy Commissariat and Connie Hedegaard who conducted the Climate Commissariat can be indicated to have played an important role in the formation of energy and climate change acquis. As a way to prove their success, Barroso indicated that 20% greenhouse gas emission objectives until 2020 were the "most ambitious commitment ever made to tackle climate change." In this context, Barroso, stating that the decision to be taken in EU Summit will be watched by all around the world carefully, also emphasized the EU's global leadership.[64]

In the interviews it is pointed out that from the change made by the Commission, policies were influenced. In accordance with this, interviewee 4 and 5 mentioned that the Juncker Commission, compared to the Barroso Commission

---

[62] Gullberg, "Pressure or Information?", 613.

[63] Gullberg, "Pressure or Information?", 615.

[64] Stephen Mulvey, "Summit to test EU climate resolve," *BBC News*, Last modified March 7, 2007, http://news.bbc.co.uk/2/hi/europe/6427015.stm.

followed a more transparent process and tried to form more integrated policies. Therefore they are of the opinion that in the process starting with Juncker, the Commission can act more effectively.[65]

From this point of view, it can be inferred that the meetings the Commission conducts with CSOs are highly important especially in terms of the Environment and Climate Change Commissariats' activities and that since the foundation of Commissariats, an effective communication has been provided with CSOs. As already mentioned, this cooperative platform that Union institutions conduct with CSOs actually integrates both sides. The link developed between the Commission and CSOs is remarkable in this sense. Hermansson also points out in his studies that some interest groups, because of their positions, have, as a privilege, the ability to reach EU institutions. However, he observed that although he himself examined it in detail, Brussels-based organizations do not have the expected level of success.[66]

European Council

The process of the Council's decision-making starts with study groups formed by member state representatives. Then it is discussed in the Committees and finally in the Council of Ministers. The subjects of Environment and Energy are discussed in COREPER I. The meetings of this committee are arranged once a week.[67]

While the subject is being discussed in the Council of Ministers, there is also a cooperation between the Council and the Parliament. In this context, as long as a general approach is provided, reconciliation during the First Reading becomes easier. The stage of forming political reconciliation is connected to the attitude of the Council in the First Reading. In the stage of providing political reconciliation, "Trilogue" meetings are unofficially arranged.[68] These meetings are very important in terms of providing reconciliation.

In the interview conducted with a European Council representative, the importance of the decision-making mechanism was discussed. The representative was asked questions on how the agreement was reached in the Council after the proposals of the Commission. The representative emphasized

---

[65] Interviewee 4 (EU Commission DG Climate consultant), interview by the author, Brussels, September 23, 2015; Interviewee 5 (EU Commission DG Climate consultant), interview by the author, Brussels, September 23, 2015.
[66] See Hermansson, "The European Commission's environmental".
[67] Tezcan, "Avrupa Birliği'nde Politika Yapımı", 303.
[68] Tezcan, "Avrupa Birliği'nde Politika Yapımı", 304.

that their fundamental principle was reconciliation and said that the functioning of study groups were important. According to this, the study groups within the European Council constantly gather under different agendas. The effect of this platform is very important in terms of reaching an agreement, because in each proposal, the interest of states may be different. Thus state representatives who are not in favour of an agreement, do not take the risk that while discussing another subject, other states may constantly be against, similar to their arguments.[69]

In the Council's decision-making process, different interests clash with each other. Each state struggles more for its own interest. Thereby, it may take sides with another state that is predominant over a subject that does not affect itself much. And in the next stage it may ask for help from the state that it previously supported, on decisions to be made on a subject that the state itself is more interested in. As Moravcsik says, this situation of asymmetrical interdependency emerging from intercommitment, is especially valid for climate policy. Because while the discussions that occured during the acceptance of Energy and Climate Package could even have resulted in deadlock, they were able to come to an agreement only by the guarantee of supporting different interests. Interviewee 11 also stated that the Council was prone to find the lowest common denominator.[70]

When the working order in European Council is examined, coming to an agreement became the fundamental principle and within this frame, the decisions sent to the Council are handled. In the interview conducted with a European Council representative, he/she was asked questions on the influence rates of CSOs on the mechanism. The interviewee indicated that not only CSOs, but also different actors like business world representatives were to reach them and that lobbying studies constantly continued. He/she also pointed out that in this platform they tried to listen to the opinions of the lobbyists' coming to the Council with different arguments, and tried to come to an agreement.

The Council is the hardest EU institution to be influenced by CSOs. The most important reason for this is that the subject becomes more concrete until it arrives at the Council. Moreover, the characteristic of intergovernmental negotiations decrease the power of observation and influence. Therefore, the

---

[69] İnterviewee 3 (European Council consultant), interview by the author, Brussels, September 22, 2015.

[70] Interviewee 11 (FoE representative), internet interview by the author, June 21, 2016.

institutions in favour of influencing the Council generally act through national states.[71]

The Council, COREPER and study groups do not possess a structure that is easily reached by interest groups. The states in the Council are more influenced by national interest groups reaching their own national institutions.[72] At this point the interviewee, confirming the findings in literature, stated that CSOs active on a national level were prone to lobby their own governments. Generally, large interest groups perform studies to reach the Council's bureaucracy.[73]

An interesting point in the interview was the indication that in order to create a blocking minority, CSOs try to influence the countries in the Council with lobbying activities. Interviewee 3 said: "There are two states: a leverage state and a problematic state. Sometimes it is better to try to affect the leverage state to affect the problematic state."[74] Therefore, it can be interpreted that state representatives are not only directly influenced by lobbying studies but are also influenced indirectly by civil society activities.

During the determination of climate objectives, Poland was trying to create a blocking minority and Italy and Germany were concerned that the competitive power of their industry sector would decrease.[75] But they confronted the contradiction that making free allowance to some sectors would affect European economy negatively in the long term. In this situation, the Parliament requested that by confirming the draft as soon as possible, wanted the necessary infrastructure to be provided for COP in 2009.[76] In addition to these states, Bulgaria, Esthonia, Latvia, Hungary, Lithuania, Romania, and Slovakia also had concerns on the enactment of climate change package. These states requested the planning to be based not on the levels of 1990 but of 2005. France, the president of the period, tried to come to an agreement on this subject.[77]

---

[71] Adelle and Anderson, "Lobby Groups," 158.
[72] Eising and Lehringer, "Interest Groups and the European Union," 193.
[73] Gullberg, "Lobbying friends and foes in climate", 2967.
[74] İnterviewee 3 (European Council consultant), interview by the author, Brussels, September 22, 2015.
[75] "EU leaders united on crises, divided over climate", *Euronews*, Last modified October 17, 2008. euronews.com/2008/10/17/eu-leadersunited-on-crisis-divided-over-climate/.
[76] "Euro MPs stick to climate targets," *BBC News,* last modified October 7, 2008, http://news.bbc.co.uk/2/hi/europe/7656478.stm.
[77] "Nations challenge EU climate plan," *BBC News,* last modified October 15, 2008, http://news.bbc.co.uk/2/hi/europe/7672335.stm.

Interviewee 3 emphasized that well known actors' campaigns, apart from CSOs, also play an important role in influencing EU decisions. For example he/she indicated that the campaign organized under the leadership of the singer Bono, influenced the decisions made on the climate.[78]

They expressed that during the discussion of 2020 objectives, a huge burden was created on some countries. The Minister of the Environment of Denmark at the time, Connie Hedegaard, while thinking that the emission objective would create a huge burden on Denmark, criticized that Germany and Britain were to make less emission. While Sweden also shared the concerns of Denmark, states like Britain, Germany, Ireland and France indicated to act in accordance with the objectives determined by the Commission.[79]

The fundamental concern of Germany was the production to be passed to other countries. After all, one of the most important arguments used by the business world during lobbying activities is the claim that it would direct its investments to other countries. However, in terms of the Parliament and the Council, the concern to lose votes may be effective in their decisions.[80] The point that civil society would break the influence of the business world seems to be this.

During the approval of the climate package, as the attitudes of the countries were not very positive, it was concerned that it would not get approved. Energy commissar Dimas, indicating that the crisis effective at that time had the potential to influence states' attitudes, said that because of that, delays in some sectors were put on the agenda. CSOs like WWF insisted that it was important for EU to take a step on this subject before 2009 climate negotiations.[81]

France, wanting to come through in summit meeting with a "cost-effective" solution, contrary to the influence of blocking minority, tried to change the states' approaches. The main concern of these states was to avoid the burden

---

[78] "Open letter to World leaders: 2015 will see major decisions for the millennium," *Euractiv*, last modified January 15, 2015, http://www.euractiv.com/sections/developmentpolicy/open-letter-world-leaders-2015-should-seemajor-decisions-millennium.

The singer Bono established an organization under the name of "ONE Campaign" and organizes various campaigns together with famous people able to make influence on world politics. Within this scope in the letter emphasizing UN Summits to be organized in 2015, it was indicated that the reconciliation of world leaders was important for the planet's future. The importance of the organization is that by working with many famous political and social people, its ability to attract the attention of global public opinion and as a result of political pressure to be created by this interest, more binding international treaties to be signed.

[79] "EU faces tough climate change road," *BBC News*, last modified January 23, 2008, http://news.bbc.co.uk/2/hi/europe/7205221.stm.

[80] Gullberg, "Pressure or Information?", 614.

[81] Roger Harrabin, "Climate plan concern as EU meets," *BBC News*, Last modified October 15, 2008, http://news.bbc.co.uk/2/hi/europe/7670814.stm.

that would come to their economies with the mentioned legislation because of having a coal intense industry.[82] And France, before leaving the presidency term to Czech Republic, wanted to gain the support of East Europe. For this, President of the Republic of France, Sarkozy, made intense efforts.[83]

The member states, acting all together with the support of the industry using more energy, caused differences between the proposal and the directive. These discussions among member states caused these fundamental differences between the proposal and the directive:

1. Ten Eastern European member states that are particularly dependent on fossil fuels in their power generation were given the right to apply for reduced auction rates.

2. The Commission's suggested aim of full auctioning in the industry by 2020 was modified to a less demanding 70% in 2020, 'with a view to reaching no free allocation by 2027'.

3. Industries that can demonstrate that emissions trading will generate costs that exceed 5% of their gross value-added and that have a non-EU trade intensity above 10% "qualify for the free allocation of its allowances".[84]

While the influence of CSOs was visible in Council meetings, in accordance with the interests of the states, the Council made the final decision. As the states' own interests and their industries would be directly affected to a large extent, national lobbies worked very actively. In accordance with both literature and the interviewees' opinions, it was claimed that the Council was mostly affected by national lobbies.

During the determination of 2030 objectives, many discussions were made. According to Oettinger, the Energy Commissar of 2013, the main goal of forming the 2050 Road Map was to form the binding renewable objectives. However during this period, the states were not in favour of it. Apart from Denmark and Holland, no state was willing to enter into obligation.[85] New objectives brought up for discussion with the Green Paper published on March

---

[82] "EU set to backtrack on emissions," *BBC News*, last modified October 16, 2008, http://news.bbc.co.uk/2/hi/europe/7673411.stm.

[83] "No deal amid EU climate deadlock," *BBC News*, last modified December 6, 2008, http://news.bbc.co.uk/2/hi/europe/7768758.stm

[84] Skodvin, Gullberg and Aakre, "Target group influence", 863.

[85] "EU: No action on 2030 renewables target is 'no real option'," *Euractiv*, last modified October 17, 2012, http://www.euractiv.com/section/climateenvironment/news/eu-no-action-on-2030-renewablestarget-is-no-real-option/.

27, 2013, were criticised by various experts and CSOs for being of minimum value.[86]

In a lengthy discussion process, environment and economy ministers of Germany, France, Italy, Austria, Belgium, Denmark, Ireland and Portugal sent a letter to the Commission and requested stronger 2030 objectives. These states believed that the transition to renewable energy will strengthen the competition and will provide more employment and growth.[87] It would be meaningful in this sense to say that the states act in a way to influence public opinion through the media. It can also be mentioned that a kind of public diplomacy study was conducted.

With the notification published on January 22, 2014, the objectives of 40% emission mitigation and 27% renewable energy were determined, but energy efficiency objectives were not. However, in the Commission's analysis, in order to achieve the objective of 40% emission mitigation, 25% energy efficiency should be achieved. While Hadegaard defended the fact that a lot of effort was needed to achieve a 40% emission reduction, the text was not successful.[88] The most fundamental reason for this was that member states did not want to commit to this target.

With all legislation made in the last 10 years, CSOs have pointed out that the subject of energy efficiency should be binding. But as no reconciliation was reached on the subject of binding objectives for energy efficiency, the influence of CSOs was also inadequate on this subject.

European Parliament

There is a certain process for the European Parliament to state its opinion. An opinion of the Parliament to become concrete is possible after the Parliament's detailed analysis of the related commission's proposal or of the subject and after the report prepaped by the Parliament.[89]

---

[86] "Debate rages as Brussels fires starting gun on 2030 energy strategy," *Euractiv*, last modified March 22, 2016, http://www.euractiv.com/section/energy/news/debaterages-as-brussels-fires-starting-gun-on-2030-energystrategy/.

[87] "Big EU guns fire for 'crucial' 2030 renewable targets," *Euractiv*, last modified January 7, 2014, http://www.euractiv.com/section/energy/news/big-euguns-2030-renewable-targets/.

[88] "EU sets out 'walk now, sprint later' 2030 clean energy vision," *Euractiv*, last modified January 23, 2014, http://www.euractiv.com/section/sciencepolicymaking/news/eu-sets-out-walk-now-sprint-later-2030-clean-energy-vision/.

[89] Tezcan, "Avrupa Birliği'nde Politika Yapımı", 307.

Şekercioğlu

The proposal first arrives to the Parliament and the speaker sends the proposal to the related committee. One or two rapporteurs related to the subject are assigned and they are asked to prepare a report on the subject. Other deputies that are not from the rapporteurs' parties may be assigned as shadow rapporteurs to follow the process. The report is first discussed within the committee. After the opinion of the committee is prepared, it is taken to the General Assembly. The General Assembly's acceptance of the report makes it official.

Interviewee 12, one of the former deputies of the European Parliament, indicated that the consensus in Parliament was made through negotiations. In addition to the determined rapporteur for each report, political groups also determine shadow rapporteurs, and these rapporteurs discuss the details. The proposal formulation here depends on the rapporteurs. And these rapporteurs do their best in the reports' style to gain wide support.[90]

The people that interest groups try to reach in the European Parliament are generally head of Committees and rapporteurs. As the parliamentarians are assigned by election and as they are more open to national preferences, they do are not heavily influenced by interest groups.[91] However, institutions with large financial opportunities try this way too. Therefore, reaching the rapporteurs initially seems to be the most important and effective channel in Parliament.

According to the information given by Interviewee 12, CSOs meet with committees' members, primarily with rapporteurs. As lobbying activities are rather costly, while organizations with higher budgets conduct lobbying activities with members of the related committee and also other MEPs, most of the CSOs only meet with the related committees' members. The interviewee pointed out that during the preparation of the REACH Regulation in 2005, the rich chemical industry made contact with almost every parliamentarian. When examined specifically to climate, it was indicated that the lobbyists of energy intense industry was very active.[92]

Truman indicated that decision-makers are basically in need of two kinds of information: technical information and political information. While technical information is information on the content of the subject, political information can be seen as a projection on what results may occur if alternative decisions are taken in the decision-making process. While the first kind of information is mostly provided by associations with field engineering, this situation provides

---

[90] İnterviewee 12 (EP former parliamentarian), internet interview by the author, June 28, 2016.

[91] Eising and Lehringer, "Interest Groups and the European Union," 192.

[92] İnterviewee 12 (EP former parliamentarian), internet interview by the author, June 28, 2016.

them a kind of legitimacy. Technical information, in this sense, can be qualified as more important than political information.[93]

Business organizations benefit from this and conduct intense lobbying activities on the Parliament. While the lobbying activities of business organizations are continued with invitations, lunch and dinners, other organizations also conduct lobbying activities and are usually influential, although not as much as the business world. But it does not seem possible that CSOs are always influential.[94]

Therefore the European Parliament is one of the targets of CSOs. Accordingly, informal groups consisting of parliamentarians and stakeholders, attract the attention of CSOs.[95] They try to influence parliamentarians with meetings, e-mails, campaigns, brochures and media activities.[96]

According to Truman, penetrating the Governments' decision unofficially stems from the need for up-to-date information and the existence of the groups that would support the decisions made related to this information.[97] Therefore providing the need of information of people within the decision-making mechanism, can be seen as the precondition to influence the decision-making mechanism. CSOs also use this way.

For parliamentarians, especially the opinions of field experts, are important. Here, instead of the opinions of the business world indicating at every environmental legislation that European industry will weaken, reports prepared by scientists have more influence on the parliamentarians. These reports are generally delivered through lunch meetings where parliamentarians invite the experts. Another interesting point here is when the lunch invitation comes from the representatives of the business world, the meeting is usually held in restaurants, but when the request comes from a parliamentarian to an expert, the proposal of having lunch or eating a sandwich inside the Parliament comes from the parliamentarian.[98]

In fact it can be said that parliamentarians try to provide a balance. While parliamentarians try to hold meetings within the Parliament in common areas, on the other hand the business world send invitations in a more organized way,

---

[93] Truman, The Governmental Process, 334.
[94] İnterviewee 12 (EP former parliamentarian), internet interview by the author, June 28, 2016.
[95] Adelle and Anderson, "Lobby Groups," 158.
[96] İnterviewee 12 (EP former parliamentarian), internet interview by the author, June 28, 2016.
[97] Truman, The Governmental Process, 333.
[98] İnterviewee 12 (EP former parliamentarian), internet interview by the author, June 28, 2016.

to increase its ability of persuasion and to show its financial possibilities to make influence.

As it is stated in literature, business establishments conduct lobbying activities both with the Parliament and the Commission, but ECSOs point out that they conduct their lobby activities more with the Parliament. According to the WWF, reaching the Parliamentarians representing the non-institutionalized part of the decision-making process is much easier. However, on the other hand, the number of people to be reached at the Parliament also increases the cost of lobbying activities.[99]

Thus it can be said that the CSOs' influence on the factors of decision-making mechanisms cannot only be measured by their closeness to one group and that it is also possible to observe a difference of opinions while coming to an agreement on one subject. In this situation it is possible to get better results by not handling the CSOs' influence as a general influence but as subject based.

When five directives and one decision[100] within the scope of this book and the voting in the Parliament are examined, especially the voting of the first legislation in 2003 on emission trade and the legislation on aviation sector added to this legislation in 2008 can be said to have been difficult. Both of the directives could go in effect after the second reading of the Parliament. When the rate of the voting is examined, amendments proposed on the subjects like the acceleration of the process of inclusion of other sectors besides energy intense sectors to the scope of the directive on Emission trade of 2003 (amendment number 9), the article on how the country allowances will be determined (amendment number 24), the facilities to stay outside the directive temporarily (amendment number 50) and Clean Development Mechanism (amendment number 53) were mostly accepted. While some of the articles of the legislation made by the Commission were not accepted, some of them were invalidated.[101]

During the second reading, amendments proposed by the Committee of the Environment of the Parliament within the scope of the first bloc and 16 amendments proposed by seven political groups were accepted. However 17 amendments proposed by the committee of environment within the scope of

---

[99] Truman, The Governmental Process, 2967.

[100] When the rate of voting within this scope are examined, the legislations are as such: Directive 2003/87/EC, Directive 2008/101/EC, Directive 2009/28/EC, Directive 2009/29/EC, Directive 2009/31/EC, Decision No 406/2009/EC.

[101] Greenhouse gas emission allowance trading, *Official Journal of the European Union*, C279/E, Vol. 46, Assented to 20 November 2003, 30.

bloc 2 were invalidated. Apart from these, some of the amendments made by the committee were invalidated and some were withdrawn.[102]

When amendments on aviation are examined, it can be seen that the articles were not approved one by one, but as a bloc. Some of the proposals of political groups and the committee were accepted, but while most of them were denied with a small difference of the votes, some were invalidated.[103] But in the second reading, it can be seen that the amendments proposed by political groups were accepted as a bloc, but the proposals of the committee were not accepted.[104]

The EP acted highly willingly on the subject of aviation sector emissions coming under ETS. In the voting, with 640 positive votes against 30, the aviation activities coming under ETS were accepted. The EP, by taking a step that the USA opposes, tried to create the appropriate ground to reach an international treaty.[105]

During the negotiations of Renewable Energy Directive that entered in force within the scope of Energy and Climate Package in 2009, the amendments proposed by the committee were invalidated and amendments proposed by the political groups were accepted. Finally the proposal of the legislation was accepted with 635 positive votes.[106] On the legislation made in 2009 on the subject of greenhouse gas emission, only amendment number 180 proposed by the political groups was accepted and other amendments were invalidated. At last with 610 acceptancies, 60 denials and 29 non committal votes, the proposal of legislation was accepted by the Parliament.[107]

On the subject of the Effort Sharing Decision, again while most of the amendments were similarly invalidated, the proposal of legislation was

---

[102] Greenhouse gas emission allowance trading, *Official Journal of the European Union*, C 74 E/130, Assented to 24 March 2004.

[103] Annex I Point 14: Amendment of Directive 2003/87/EC so as to include aviation activities in the scheme for greenhouse gas emission allowance trading within the Community ***I, *Official Journal of the European Union*, C 282E, Vol. 51, Assented to 6 November 2008.

[104] Annex I Point 19: Amendment of Directive 2003/87/EC so as to include aviation activities in the scheme for greenhouse gas emission allowance trading within the Community ***II, Official Journal of the European Union, C 256/E, Vol. 51, Assented to 9 October 2008.

[105] "EU includes aviation in CO2 curbs" *BBC News,* last modified July 8, 2008, http://news.bbc.co.uk/2/hi/europe/7495567.stm

[106] Annex I Point 1: Promotion of the use of energy from renewable sources ***I, *Official Journal of the European Union*, C 58E, Vol. 52, Assented to 12 March 2009.

[107] Annex I Point 2: Greenhouse gas emission allowance trading system ***I, *Official Journal of the European Union*, C 58E, Vol. 52, Assented to 12 March 2009.

accepted with small amendments by putting to the vote.[108] In geological storage directive, the directive proposal was accepted with 623 votes with small amendments.[109] According to the information given by Interviewee 12 on the subject of the reports prepared by the committees arriving to the Parliament, the situation of the proposals that environmental committee examined is generally as such:

> *"During my years in the EP, if the ENVI vote was very tight with a 'proggressive' majority (GUE, S&D, Greens, ALDE) the plenary many times switched the majority (EPP, ECR, right wings of ALDE and S&D), but not always..."*[110]

Starting from this, it can be said that the parliamentarians are influenced by lobbying studies and that they act based on the subject regardless of the amendments' field. Nevertheless, the Parliament is seen as the most environment friendly institutions among all EU institutions. Because within the process of change in 2009 of ETS Directive, the aviation sector coming under ETS and greenhouse gas emission objectives and the renewable energy objectives to be higher, were proposed.[111]

The CSOs' attitude towards the parliamentarians is affected by both their level of knowledge and the general attitude of the parliamentarians. For example, the groups in the European Parliament that Greenpeace mostly contacts within the scope of emission trade are the Greens and European Free Alliance. Within the scope of long-term objectives, Greenpeace provides information flow and assumes a common attitude with these groups. However there has been disagreements on the subject of CCS, because the parliamentarians could not reconcile at a common point.[112] On the other hand, the European Office of the WWF keeps its distance from the Greens and is more interested in forming environmental organizations in other parties.[113] And this situation shows that each civil society organization assumes different attitudes and thus should be evaluated separately.

---

[108] Annex I Point 3: Shared effort to reduce greenhouse gas emissions ***I, *Official Journal of the European Union*, C 58E, Vol. 52, Assented to 12 March 2009.

[109] Annex I Point 4: Geological storage of carbon dioxide ***I, *Official Journal of the European Union*, C 58E, Vol. 52, Assented to 12 March 2009.

[110] İnterviewee 12 (EP former parliamentarian), internet interview by the author, June 28, 2016.

[111] Truman, The Governmental Process, 2967.

[112] Gullberg, "Lobbying friends and foes in climate", 2966.

[113] Gullberg, "Lobbying friends and foes in climate", 2968.

Civil Society Impact on the EU Climate Change Policy

The legislation that was most attractive should be evaluated as ETS legislation. The aforementioned legislation brought a lot of discussions with it and it took a long time to form the ground of reconciliation. Therefore, the Commission's proposal underwent a change and concessions were made. The draft could only be accepted by granting privileges to some sectors because of the states that are against climate draft and that indicate that their economies cannot bear this burden.

The ETS rapporteur of the Parliament, Avril Doyle, commented that with the agreement, the environmental integrity was preserved and elbow room was left for industries in Europe. The Greens parliamentarian Satu Hassi, while defining coming to an agreement as historical, also reflects her concern of the possibility of emission mitigations moving to other countries. The spokesman of the Conservatives John Bowis, on the other hand, indicated that the mitigation of ETS provisions in basic fields was disappointing, whereas ECSOs accused the Union to be under the influence of industrial lobby.[114] The European Parliament, besides the 2020 objectives, also supported the binding sectoral objectives, but in the negotiations, the bindingness of sectoral objectives was not accepted.[115] Actually, it would be useful to state that the binding objectives here were formed similiar to ECSOs' request.

During legislation making in Parliament committees, if the proposal coming from political groups has an effect on the parliamentarians, the language of the amendment also tends towards the proposal. According to interviewee 12, if the proposal of amendment is coming from an institution outside the Parliament, the source of it should be stated. The currently used method is that the institutions influencing the Parliamentarians and political groups stating amendment proposal towards this direction. Interviewee 12 pointed out that during the legislation of REACH, the Greens and the European Free Allaince (EFA) did not present any amendment proposals, whereas the Progressive Alliance of Socialists and Democrats (S&D), influenced by the chemical industry, presented amendment proposals. However, it was indicated that the most of the amendment proposals came from the Alliance of Liberals and Democrats (ALDE) and the European Public Party (EPP).[116]

While this clearly shows the lobbying influence, to the question posed of which legislation of renewable energy, and carbon capture and storage are more open

---

[114] "Euro MPs seal major climate deal," *BBC News*, last modified December 17, 2008, http://news.bbc.co.uk/2/hi/7787504.stm.

[115] Gullberg, "Pressure or Information?", 621.

[116] İnterviewee 12 (EP former parliamentarian), internet interview by the author, June 28, 2016.

to lobbying, interviewee 12 responded: "Concerning ETS, RES, CCS Directives I cannot say in which lobbying was more open/secretive."[117] When looked at in this context, while it can be commented that the Parliament assumes a different attitude for each legislation with the effect of the lobbie, it is also evident that the differentiation on the penetration of this effect cannot be made clear.

European Court of Justice

The position of the ECJ generally provides ground for the development of environmental policy. When seen in this context, it can be said that it directly effects from three aspects: "1) Consistently supporting the view that the EU should have competence in the field of environmental policy, 2) backing up the Commission in the sometimes difficult job of overseeing the implementation of EU law in the member states, and 3) clarifying the meaning of key elements of the treaties."[118] When the development process of the EU's environment and climate policies are examined, it can be inferred that in the formation of agreement between member countries of the EU and EU institutions, the decisions and institutional role of the ECJ are influential. The Court, in one sense, functions to find the balance between EU institutions and member states.

The ECJ firstly supported the development of environmental policy, and with its decisions on the protection of environment, overcame the dilemma of free trade and protection of environment, and provided environmental law to be built on a strong foundation.[119] Climate policy was also built on a strong foundation with the opinions the ECJ has developed since the 1980s. According to Ludwig Krämer's data, more than 700 cases came in front of the ECJ between the years 1976 and 2010. Two thirds of these cases were about the member states being unwilling to transfer EU environment directives into domestic law and were brought by the Commission. Besides according to clause 4 of article 263, unless they are directly affected, CSOs and people do not sue anyone at the ECJ. Therefore, most of the mentioned cases were filed by EU institutions and the states.[120]

The disputes on the subject of environment form an important part of EU law, whereas disputes on the subject of climate, separately from the environment, played a role on the formation of international institutional framework. Although the mentioned cases on climate have rather technical aspects, the

---

[117] İnterviewee 12 (EP former parliamentarian), internet interview by the author, June 28, 2016.

[118] John McCormick, *Environmental Policy in the European Union* (Hong Kong: Palgrave, 2001), 133.

[119] McCormick, Environmental Policy in the European, 133.

[120] Krämer, "The European Court of Justice," 116-119.

public is informed about the subject in the process of the case. Secondly, these disputes, by providing the democratization of environmental law, are open to the participation of different components such as CSOs. When all of the process is analysed, it can be seen that the courts try to make decisions in cases where a lot of different actors including governments, the business world and CSOs are involved.[121] Thus, one of the driving powers of the development of the legislations on the subject of climate, in which a wide range of components are involved, is the judicial system. The role of the courts cannot be underestimated not only in terms of the EU, but also in terms of the development of global climate policy.

When the subject is examined specifically to the EU ETS, independently from the international system, the taken binding decisions within the EU affects the EU law's development process related to the subject. Within the EU structure, the authorization to prepare new legislation proposals belongs to the Commission. The proposals prepared by the EU Commission, can be implemented with the approval of the Parliament and the Council. Therefore, the legal texts that come into effect are approved finally by member states. Here, the fundamental actors in the emergence of legal disagreements are those that will be affected negatively from the current legislation (companies, people, etc.) or the discrepancies arising from domectic legislations of member countries.

The situations where the ECJ is authorized relating to the ETS can be lined up as such. Firstly, according to article 263 of the Treaty on the Functioning of the European Union, the ECJ can use this authorization to supervise the EU institutions' savings and to decide in cases such as rule violation with lack of jurisdiction. In this context, the most seen dispute is seen within the scope of reviewing National Allowance Plans prepared for the allowances within the ETS. States can be involved in the case even if they do not have any special benefit, and the private sector – thinking that its interests are damaged – sue the Commission within the scope of this article of the Treaty. However, as legislations within ETS include extremely open expressions, most of the time their request to sue through the ECJ is denied.[122]

According to article 264 of the Treaty, the ECJ can declare the saving that is the subject of case, as null and void. The power exceeding cases of Poland (Case T-183/07) and Estonia (Case T-263/07) against the Commission can be evaluated in this context. Although the Court is authorized to evaluate the plans of member

---

[121] Sanja Bogojević, "EU Climate Change Litigation, the Role of the European Courts, and the Importance of Legal Culture," *Law&Policy* 35, no. 3 (July 2013): 186-187.

[122] Bogojević, "EU Climate Change", 190.

states on the subject of the Commission's National Allowance Plans, it decided that they are not to make power exceeding these allowances.[123] The Court of Justice, by mentioning the supremacy of law, commands that everyone in the Union should stay within their own jurisdiction.

Secondly, according to article 267 of the Treaty, the ECJ has the authorization to make predecisions in certain cases. Although in many cases within the scope of the ETS, this article of the Treaty was asked to be used, only in two cases was this decision made: the first case was the question of French administrative court on the harmony of the principle of equal treatment of the ETS Directive (C-127/07) and the other was Britain's question of 2008/101 Directive (the directive where the amendment was made in the ETS Directive dating 2003, to include the aviation sector) on the harmony between international law provisions and international practice law (C-366/190).[124]

Furthermore, in accordance with article 258 of the Treaty, the Commission can sue member states in the ECJ, claiming that they do not fulfill their obligations. Again within the scope of the ETS, Italy (C-122/05) and Finland (C-107/05) were being sued by the Commission. In parallel with the Commission's opinions, the ECJ declared the decision that member states were late to transfer Directive provisions into domestic law.[125]

In the period between 2003 and 2009, until the ETS revision in 2009, the mentioned cases enabled the revision of the Directive, and at the same time made the disagreements between member states and the Commission visible. After the preparation of 2003 Directive, there have been many cases on the subject of National Action Plans. The most important cases sued by the member states to the Commission are: Britain (Case T-143/05), Germany (Case T-374/04), and Poland (Case T-183/07).

The common point of all three cases is that the dispute arose during the review of the Commission of their own National Action Plans. Generally, the attitude of ECJ was that the Commission should not exceed its power. While in Britain's case, it defended the right of member states to revise their National Action Plans to be reserved. In the case of Germany, it made the decision that by differentiating between the Directive's fundamental objectives and sub-

---

[123] Bogojević, "EU Climate Change", 195-197.
[124] Bogojević, "EU Climate Change", 191.
[125] Bogojević, "EU Climate Change", 191.

objectives, the Commission was to evaluate these national plans separately from article 10 of the Directive.[126]

The Commission, on the other hand, sued Italy and Finland, claiming that they failed to transfer the Directive into the domestic laws of the related states.[127] Some of the cases related to the subject, except the states and the Commission, were brought by interest groups. One of the most famous cases is the case brought by EnBW Energie against Germany's National Action Plan. The claim here was that the national plan provided more advantages to its competitors. The ECJ presented its opinion that cases where this and similar National Action Plans are mentioned should be dealt with national courts.[128]

The most important case seen recently to affect the developments on ETS is the case brought by Poland against the Commission (Case T-370/11). In the decision of 2011/278/EU relating to the distribution of emission allowances that the Commission made within the scope of article 10 of the Directive numbered 2003 in the year 2011, legislation about the allowances of the period after 2013 took part. Poland, with this decision, pointed out the concerns of chemical industry and rafineries and claimed that the decision was against the principle of proportionality.[129]

The general view of Poland is that the Commission interfered in the formation of member states' own energy profiles. In this context, it was claimed that the limitations put by the Commission on the free distribution of CO_2 permissions created stricter rules than were necessary for the protection of the climate. However, the court indicated in its final decision that the decision made by the Commission does not hinder the formation of the energy profiles as they want.[130]

The aforementioned claim of Poland was already mentioned in the first preparation of energy and climate package. Poland claimed that the ETS would

---

[126] J.A.W. van Zeben, "The European Emissions Trading Scheme Case Law," *Amsterdam Center for Law and Economics Working Paper No. 2009-12*, Accessed June 15, 2016, http://papers.ssrn.com/sol3/papers.cfm?abstract_id=1462651, 3-5.

[127] van Zeben, "The European Emissions", 6.

[128] van Zeben, "The European Emissions", 7-8.

[129] "Judgement of the General Court," *General Court,* Last modified March 7, 2013, http://www.emissionseuets.com/attachments/356_Judgment%20of%20the%20General%20Court%20of%207%20March%202013.pdf.

[130] Stephanie Bodoni and Ewa Krukowska, "Poland Loses EU Court Appeal of Carbon Permit Hand-Our Rules," *Bloomberg,* Accessed June 16, 2016, http://www.bloomberg.com/news/articles/2013-03-07/poland-loses-eu-court-appeal-of-carbon-permithand-out-rules-1-.

annihilate the member states's energy independencies and the Council stated that Poland was making the effort to create blocking minority.[131]

Generally, in the studies, the results that the ECJ does not force EU decisions and that member states do not directly affect the policy-making processes of member states were achieved.[132] The decisions of the ECJ have more of a legislative function. When the cases that were brought to the ECJ relating to climate change are examined, it can be seen that these cases influenced the legislation of the ETS process.

The operations of the organizations at EU level and the analysis of their success levels

CSOs in the EU have the opportunity to provide a transnational interest and represent unity. Most of the time, when EU institutions want to make better legislation, they support the participation of CSOs as it will increase the legitimacy of the legislations.[133] Thereby into the area to be legislated, the opinions of CSOs are articulated.[134]

The Commission also supports CSOs that gained the ability to act EU-wide and gives these groups the chance of privileged communication.[135] For example, when the 2015 budgets are examined, 40% of the EEB's budget, 35% of CAN Europe's budget, 16% of WWF's budget and 55% of FoE's budget are formed by funds from the EU.[136]

Therefore, the agenda setting function that the Commission officially holds for these groups also passes to CSOs, because these CSOs need the funds from the EU to continue their daily operations. These funds are used in the policy's formulation as a pressure group by the employees of Brussels based organizations.[137] According to Wurzel and Connelly, there are five stages of a decision-making mechanism: These are:

---

[131] "Euro MPs stick to climate targets," *BBC News,* last modified October 7, 2008, http://news.bbc.co.uk/2/hi/europe/7656478.stm.

[132] Bogojević, "EU Climate Change", 189.

[133] Kohler Koch, "Civil Society and Democracy, 7.

[134] Beate Kohler-Koch and Vanessa Buth, "The balancing act of European civil society," *De-Mystification of Participatory Democracy,* edited by. Beate Kohler-Koch et al. (Great Britain: Oxford University Press, 2013), 127.

[135] Wurzel and Connelly, "Environmental NGOs," 216.

[136] It was formed by the use of the data of EU's transparency register page aforementioned in the subtitles of the organizations.

[137] Lenschow, "Environmental Policy," 319.

Civil Society Impact on the EU Climate Change Policy

1. Agenda setting
2. Consultation
3. Negotiating
4. Decision-taking
5. Implementation[138]

In these stages, the fields that civil society is most likely to succeed in are agenda setting and implemantation. In agenda setting, civil society organizations can try to pressure the Commission by raising public awareness. As organizations within the G10 have privileged access opportunities compared to other organizations, they influence the stage of agenda setting. In a sense, citizens are also given "responsibilities." And this is explained by the principle of transparency.[139]

The field of implementation is the part where national CSOs are successful. The function of the CSOs is to follow the implementations of the states, after the legislation in the related field is made. In accordance with this, national CSOs inform the Commission if the states are late in transferring the legislation into domestic law or if they present an attitude against the EU legislations.[140]

Wurzel and Connelly indicate that in the stages of consultation, negotiation and decision-making, EU institutions and member states are influencial.[141] However, according to Finke, since 1992 when the authorization of the Treaty of Maastricht was increased, CSOs started to be articulated into the decision-making mechanism.[142]

According to Koch: "If the EU is a "multi-level quasi-government," then CSOs are intermediaries giving citizens a voice and bringing the plurality of interests to the attention of decision-makers."[143] An interesting simile is that CSOs are influenced by the Commission just as the Commission is influenced by CSOs,

---

[138] Wurzel and Connelly, "Environmental NGOs," 226.
[139] Kohler Koch, "Civil Society and EU Democracy", 110.
[140] Lenschow, "Environmental Policy," 319.
[141] Wurzel and Connelly, "Environmental NGOs," 226.
[142] Barbara Finke, "Civil society participation in EU governance," *Living Rev. Euro. Gov.* 2. No. 2, 2007, Accessed June 15, 2016, http://www.europeangovernancelivingreviews.org/Articles/lreg-2007-2/download/lreg-2007-Color.pdf, 6.
[143] Kohler Koch, "Civil Society and Democracy", 8.

especially when the structure of umbrella organizations are similar to Directorate General structures in the Commission.[144]

But most of the time these CSOs take action in the subjects of which their supporters have little or no knowledge and may carry out acts in which their own supporters cannot participate.[145] In this situation, although there is the claim that democratical representation increases as a result of the relation formed by CSOs and Union institutions, the in-house operation in CSOs is determinant.

When analysing the influence of CSOs on the EU, one of the main arguments that was examined was the variation of CSO's participation in legal legislation.

CSOs do not participate in every legislation process at the same rate. Practically there are two main reasons for this: 1) If the relevant legislation is highly technical, the low number of CSOs studying this subject causes the CSOs to be less visible.[146] 2) The fact that the subject on which legislation is to be made or was made, causes change in the infuence of civil society.

At this point, when the current information in literature, textual analysis and interview outcomes are compared, the prediction that CSOs try to influence the decision at every stage of the process is validated. All the interviewees indicated that CSOs use every method to influence EU decisions and are in relation with every EU institution. Especially the collaboration built in daily functioning in the Commission and the Parliament, results in faster articulation into decision making mechanism in the next period.147

As already mentioned, the interviews conducted with the Commission and civil society respresentatives disclosed the existence of CSOs at every stage of the process. The visibility of CSOs differ based on their organizational structures, recognizability, lobbying abilities and technical knowledge. Thus, the organizations' rate of influence in the EU are different and that this originates not only from themselves but also from the character of the legislation to be made. Therefore the stages that are most influential are not the first and fifth stages as Wurzel and Connelly predicted. It should be indicated that even if not at the same rate, CSOs are influential in different levels at the stage of decision making.

---

[144] Kohler-Koch and Buth, "The balancing act of European", 119.

[145] Warleigh, "Europeanizing' Civil Society", 634.

[146] While making impact analysis, it can be said that not only CSOs but all interest groups are involved in the process. But while making technical legislations, it can be said that not only CSOs but other interest groups are less involved in the process. At this point the numerical fewness of CSOs most of the time brings along the lowness of lobby abilities.

[147] Kohler-Koch and Buth, "The balancing act of European", 118.

Klüver's definition of "influence" defends that the influence of CSOs is not the same all the time and a CSO's success on one subject is formed according to the coalition it is in. Therefore, when the subject is examined from the perspective of democratic legitimacy, she suggests to view the subject from the perspectives of "input legitimacy," including the increase in the ability of citizen participation, and "output legitimacy," handling the interest groups' contribution to problem solving.[148] She shows the Commission's strategy, which uses CSOs' participation to solve the legitimacy crisis, including CSOs.[149]

To identify this compex relation network, it is suggested to use the definition of "intertwined asymmetrical relation" based on the observations. Here the word "intertwined" is used in the meanings of working together and being an inseparable entity. The word "asymmetrical" is preferred to be used for the institutions in relation with each other and to reflect the different roles of CSOs. Here a triple differentiation can be seen. With CSOs, the complex structure of the relation developed among EU institutions, especially the Commission and a process in which states are included through these institutions are attempted to be explained. In short, neither EU institutions nor the states or the CSOs cannot act independently from the relations they have with each other.

Therefore, the development of the relationship between civil society and EU institutions is very interesting. They try to develop concepts like legitimacy and democratic representation through each other, and a kind of symbiosis can be seen. Structures that could not exist independently from each other were formed.

CSOs try to be one of the fundamental factors of the decision-making mechanism by gathering legitimacy from the government. Thereby it can be emphasized that not only the EU but also CSOs transform within the process. In parallel with the development of EU law, the states found the Commission' and the Parliament's increased authorization acceptable. Therefore, while the authorization of the Commission to make legislation increased, at the same time the Parliament's activity that would strengthen the decision-making mechanism of the Union in terms of democratic representation expanded. This situation accelerated the influence of CSOs and the transformation in EU institutions made them a part of the process. Therefore, CSOs learned how to direct the process as a condition to exist within this mechanism.

The most important condition of this is the professionalization and the state to present scientific reports that will influence EU reports. CSOs, instead of

---

[148] Klüver, Lobbying in the European Union, 204-214.
[149] Barbara Finke, "Civil society participation in EU", 4.

preparing drafts on just one subject for the benefit of society, started to present by reporting in a way that would be of multiple use for the institutions. This transformation and CSOs rasping its activist sides in accordance with the EU system and developing its relations through EU institutions and the Council in a way not to be away from the process, expresses the word "intertwined."

Each of the EU institutions, states and CSOs included in the process represent a different level, and their relations in this sense show a variation. And this necessitates their relation to be defined as asymmetrical. Therefore, the relation between CSOs, EU institutions and states are evaluated as intertwined and asymmetrical.

However, this new kind of relation actually results in not determining CSOs becoming a part of the process, at what rate it works for its benefits and at what rate it reflects the views of member institutions. Civil society started to be seperated from its seperative structure that forms its own self and the general description emphasizing public participation. A kind of monopoly formation starts to come into question.

In other words, it should be emphasized that also civil society went through a transformation. Here as Wurzel and Connelly indicated, ECSOs being against carbon markets at the beginning, with reconciliation into the system within the process, preparing reports on carbon markets[150], show that by rasping their radical sides, they transform into a company that has a strong tie with the state.

From this perspective, we can say that climate policy developed as a "learning by doing" process not only in terms of the Commission but also in terms of CSOs. It would be meaningful in this sense to emphasize that this common development process results in the state of co-existence.

In order to measure the participation of civil society, the interviewees were asked to line up the three directives within the scope of the study. Interviewee 4, while making the evaluation of civil society participation, lines the civil society participation as such: ETS Directive, Renewable Energy Directive and finally Geological Storage Directive.[151] Interviewee 10 on the other hand lined up the directives as renewable energy, ETS and CSS.[152]

The main reason for these differences is that one of the interviewees is a member of the Commission and the other one is a member of a CSO. Within the

---

[150] Wurzel and Connelly, "Environmental NGOs," 226.

[151] Interviewee 4 (EU Commission DG Climate consultant), interview by the author, Brussels, September 23, 2015.

[152] Interviewee 10 (Greenpeace former employee), internet interview by the author, April 25, 2016.

framework of the lobbying activities for the Commission, while CSOs' influence of civil society on ETS can be seen, within the scope of the Renewable Energy Directive, Greenpeace and the WWF make a great effort. On the subject of ETS, it should be stated that CAN and the WWF make a more intense effort.

As it can be seen, upon the same texts, both sides of the subject can be thought differently. Therefore generally this difference in interpretation originating from the distinctive intertwined asymmetrical relation emerging between EU institutions and CSOs, makes it difficult for acedemical studies to obtain a clear result.

The process of acceptance of the Union's 2020 objectives is a process in which lobbying activities are very intense. Although 20% renewable energy objective in 2020 accepted on March 2007 on the subject of renewable energy became a law on December 2008 under Energy and Climate Package, Gullberg binds the denial of temporary objectives in the second proposal to industrial lobbyists' activities.[153] Besides, on the steps to be taken on the subject of especially climate change, the opposing lobby is always heavy industrial lobby.

In 2008, while the legislations of energy and climate package were being prepared, renewable energy industry, and civil society organizations such as FoE and Greenpeace made lobby together on binding temporary objectives. Therefore the part to make traditional energy production and the parts to make investments on renewable energy follow different lobbying strategies. By CAN Europe, FoE, Greenpeace and WWF, the campaign of "Time to Lead" was organized. Greenpeace, having a more pragmatic influence on European industry, defended energy revolution. CAN Europe on the other hand is in the position to be the main actor on the subject of climate.[154]

The lobby of civil society organizations, continued in different fields without cooperating with industrial representatives. They also succeeded in gaining the support of the Parliament (when considered that rapporteurs and shadow rapporteurs are from different parties). However the Council, except Germany and Denmark, did not accept these objectives.[155] Because, as mentioned before, as heavy industry is directly related with national interests, it tries to make influence through the Council and the risk of deterioration in economy prevents the states to take steps.

---

[153] Gullberg, "Pressure or Information?", 612.

[154] Wurzel and Connelly, "Environmental NGOs," 220.

[155] Gullberg, "Pressure or Information?", 622.

On the subject of 2030, according to Commission bureaucrats, between 1990 and 2013, while the GNP of EU countries increased at the rate of 45%, the emissions mitigated at the rate of 19%. From this point of view it is interpreted that economical growth and emission mitigation can be simultaneous. Besides, it is stated that also business wold expected long term policies rather than short term related to environmental legislations and on this basis the leaders also come to an agreement within 2030 Framework.[156] The reactions of civil society and as far as it was reflected in media, this document will not be very functional. İnterviewee 11 characterized the non-binding texts like Road Map and Objectives as useless.[157]

Here the Commission representatives actually try to show that the growth of the states is possible by taking these precautions. However the separated structure of states' domestic policies, present the ideal. What Moravcsik indicates is that as the difference in states' domestic political structures finally effects their attitudes in the Council, the only condition for the states' being willing to make legislations is possible by different actors within the inner mechanism, developing a close attitude of the Commission's and the Parliament's. The parliamentarians having the worry to be reelected, will be in the position to effect the direction of the decisions to be made both in national parliaments and in EP most.

As its frame was drawn in the first part, as the mentioned decision types in Mintz's theory are to be reconciled at a common point of member states when applied to EU climate policy, we can say that the decisions are interactive decisions. Here, it can be said that not only one part of climate policy, but all decisions related to climate are related to each other. In short, the decisions within the EU system are taken as multidimensional and intertwined. Therefore, CSOs certainly has a role within this process. As the interactive process has many variables, it makes the participation of CSOs as well as the classical actors visible.

CSOs may be included within the process in different stages. As our findings also shows, CSOs, by studying more actively through national centres in more political subjects, try to influence their own inner mechanisms. Other methods include trying to influence the EU's decisions by following from Brussels, as well as influencing national policies through umbrella organizations in which national CSOs generally come together for a common purpose.

---

[156] Delbeke and Vis, "Editors' Introduction", 3.

[157] Interviewee 11 (FoE representative), internet interview by the author, June 21, 2016.

It can be said that the roles of the actors in classical decision-making mechanism vary, especially the parties who interact more with CSOs, make the effort for legislation to be made as they want with the claim that they reflect the view of the public.

National organizations whose studies are directed by the European office include Greenpeace and the WWF. Greenpeace, because of its own management structure, to make more influence, by activating its national CSOs can create a wide action network. And this causes its increase in recognizability and thus its increase of pressure power. When the WWF is examined, the establishment tries to exert more influence by publishing scientific reports and that it acts with the possible effect over the decision makers of science. Also Greenpeace, which is mostly known for its reports as well as its activist ventures, separates from the working methodology of WWF. Thereby, it is obvious that organizations with an hierarchical organizational structure can be mobilized faster but this hierarchical situation, as mentioned before, by ruining the in-house democratic structure, causes results that each of its components would not approve.

Organizations like FoE, benefiting from grassroot activities are also active at EU level. These organizations fundamentally using the outside lobbying methods, try the power of the society to transform the decisions. The important point here is the effort to inform the public and getting mobilized. Through the developed actions, by maintaining the interest of the public, it is the pressure capacity to the institutions are tried to be increased.

When CAN Europe and the EEB are examined, these organizations, as umbrella organizations, are organized to provide these mobilized actions more coordinatively. Each of the institutions, together with reporting, use both inside and outside lobbying methods. Bureaucratic structure of the EEB separates it from other CSOs and results in its having a special position.

When it is looked from this point of view, Greenpeace and FoE can be identified as dark green, the WWF as light green and CAN Europe and the EEB in the scale as in the middle of these organizations. As the ad hoc alliance situation stated by Warleigh is seen for these organizations, especially during the preparation of climate and energy package, it is concluded that the classification of these organizations do not effect the cases of cooperation.

When the relations of CAN Europe, Greenpeace, FoE and WWF with Union institutions are examined, it was concluded that they influenced the development of climate policy. The representatives of all four institutions mentioned professionalism and the importance of having a good network, and indicated that professionalism developed within the process. Therefore, these institutions are not only CSOs, but also work like professional lobbying institutions.

CSOs' representatives regularly meeting with EU Commission employees or the parliamentarians contribute a positive side to those who conduct these meetings. Managing this network is considered to be more important than gaining experience as CSO. Because the most important condition to make effective lobbying is to have gained this professionalization. And the most important contribution to this professionalization is provided again by EU that is funding these organizations. The increase in recognizing CSOs will help to develop policies that will be produced by the Commission in the related field. Finally, professionalization provides CSOs with a voice in the decision-making mechanism and to gain representation abilities.[158]

One of the most important observations to support this situation is the business to business expert transitions and the existence of situations that support observation like CSO employees starting to work in Union institutions.[159] In terms of the interviews made with the Commission, it should be pointed out that Commission employees are more open and gave more explanatory information compared to CSOs.

The information gained from the literature is that CSOs are more open but because of the bureaucratic structure of public institutions, they are more difficult to reach. While CSOs should be acting more willingly to explain their activities, the EU institutions should be more protective.

The idea that the rate of CSOs' specialization increased their lobby abilities[160] proves that the Commission representatives influence the preparation of the Commission's proposals by CSOs. In this case, the argument that CSOs influence EU decisions, put forward by Klüver et al and Koch is corroborated.

In addition to this, there is a very interesting comment related to CSOs. While Greenpeace was evaluated as radical, the WWF was evaluated as pragmatic, and umbrella organizations are seen to be successful in finding a common ground. In the period between 2010 and 2014 when the climate commissariat was conducted by Connie Hadegaard, CAN Europe decided which CSOs would be participating in the meetings organized within the Commission's stakeholder

---

[158] Kohler-Koch and Buth, "The balancing act of European", 138-142.

[159] Joris den Blanken, who was referred as a Greenpeace representative in the current study, now works in the Parliament.

[160] Interviewee 9 (EU Commission DG Climate consultant), interview by the author, Brussels, September 25, 2015.

meetings.[161] The rule of being democratic is managed by the Commission but the representation of civil society was under the dominion of several institutions. In short, CAN Europe became a kind of authority, and on the subject of climate change, there is a hierarchy among the organizations.

When the performance of ECSOs and the lobbying studies conducted by the business world on the same subject are examined, it can be stated that both sides are succesful. When the ETS Directive is analysed, it can be seen that CSOs were actively interested with the process. In the report about ETS prepared by CAN Europe, FoE, Greenpeace and the WWF in 2007, the need of 30% mitigation until 2020 was emphasized. Because of the difficulty of the states' coming to an agreement, the objective could only stay as 20%, but in case of an international treaty, it gained the possibility to rise to 30%.

The distribution of incomes that will be obtained from the auction made within the scope of the ETS is seen as an effective method both in the 2030 and in 2030 frameworks. The ETS is considered to be a transparent process and although it was the ideal solution to distribute the whole allowance by auction, to prevent the industrial production centers to get outside the EU, it could not be made possible in practice. In this context near half of the allowances were given to the manufacturing industry free of charge and they tried to prevent the risk of carbon escape. Finally, with the legislation brought on aviation, although all the flights concerning EU countries was intended to be included within ETS, this situation was postponed to 2017.[162] If the data of the European Council section of the chapter four are examined, especially with the influence of Poland, it can be considered that the Eastern European states contracted the scopes of these legislations.

ETS is fully compatible with Kyoto. During the first emergence of emission trade, while the EU was not in favor, it became the best formation in the present situation. Within this scope, the punishments given by member states to the operators not suitable for ETS actually originate from the fact that rather than being suitable for ETS, it makes it difficult for the member states to fulfill their Kyoto obligations. However, the success of ETS should be evaluated independent from the UNFCCC. The biggest proof of this is the fall of greenhouse gas emissions in the last 10 years from 14% to 9%.[163]

---

[161] Interviewee 4 (EU Commission DG Climate consultant), interview by the author, Brussels, September 23, 2015.

[162] Meadows, Slingenberg and Zapfel, "EU ETS: pricing carbon", 29-43.

[163] Meadows, Slingenberg and Zapfel, "EU ETS: pricing carbon", 54-55.

If a general impact assessment is made, it can be stated to be acted in parallel with the methodology developed by Betsill and Corell in the fourth chapter. However, when the situation is considered in terms of accession, all the members of the EU that could be contacted for interviews state that CSOs are influential. In addition to this, one of the most important situations to be observed within the decision-making mechanism was the attitude of the Parliament. In the reports prepared by the rapporteurs Claude Turmes in the Renewable Energy Directive, Avril Doyle in ETS Directive, Chris Davis in CCS Directive and Satu Hassi in the Effort Sharing Decision and in the Parliament negotiations, a similar view was taken. And the most important indication of this is the Parliament's effort to make allowances in the ETS Directive at EU level.

Although final documents generally depend on the states' reconciliation, at least in the emission mitigations in the 2020 framework and the creation of binding objectives in renewable energy, we can say it to be in relevance with the skill of civil society to raise a question on the subject. After the decisions are made, CSOs continue to work and follow the process.

According to the data obtained from both literature and field work, it was confirmed that the influence of civil society was not an absolute influence and could be changed depending on three different variables: 1) the size and the lobbying skills of the part of society represented by civil society; 2) the need of information of the institutions; 3) its rate of consistency with the vital interests of the states.

During the Energy and Climate Package negotiations in 2008, it can be stated that the states spent a long period of negotiation with the strategies they determined in accordance with their own interests. The blocking minority tried to be formed by Poland on the one hand and international pressure, caused by the obligations of Kyoto on the other, pushed on the intergovernmental negotiation in the Council.

Here, although intergovernmental negotiation was on the agenda, it can also be stated that both Parliament and the Commission tried to influence the negotiations in the Council by taking a stance similar to the opinions of CSOs. In this sense Greenpeace, attracting public attention and FoE controlling the grassroot movements, provided these groups to be taken into consideration by the decision makers. As CAN Europe and the EEB with the organizations they represent and Greenpeace with its national structuring, can easily organize themselves nationally, it is obvious that they conduct studies on changing the attitude of the Council.

Civil Society Impact on the EU Climate Change Policy

At the same time, the effort of all levels to articulate into decision-making mechanism confirms that the theory of multi-level governance is successful theoretically in creating a background for the examination of civil society.

WWF on the other hand, as acting like a specialty institution, draws attention with the reports it publishes. The most visible activity of WWF was the report it demanded from Utrecht University in 1995 and in which the mitigation objectives of EU was discussed. According to the report, only 14% out of 20% mitigation objective of EU until 2005 seemed possible. This report provided WWF a relative fame and although it was not accepted by decision makers, in 1997 the government of Holland demanded a national report from the same researchers.[164]

As it is stated in Klüver's analysis, CSOs provide information supply, as they mostly act commonly in this context or make similar requests, can gain citizen support and economically, although not as much as industrial enterprises, have enough budget to conduct lobbying activities. In this sense, the mission of creating common ground suggested by Eising is being provided.

At last when the strategies in Table 6 are evaluated, both proactive and reactive actions of civil society can be seen. CSOs producing direct policy as driving power most of the time purposely focus on one subject. And it should be indicated that they indirectly developed a defensive policy strategy.

Within EU institutions, the Parliament and the Commission are willing to make stricter legislations in legal steps to be taken in the subject of energy related climate change but the states, under the intense influence of national interest groups in the Council, by suggesting the idea of economic development, try to block up this process. Still the positive influence of the states that are introduced as a green blocking minority should not be excluded. In this case, if we sort the institutions' support, it can be interpreted that legislations on this subject are at least supported by the Council.

---

[164] Long, Salter and Singer, "WWF: European and Global", 95-96.

Conclusion

The EU's energy related climate change policy has been discussed in this book. The transformation in the policy of climate change, the transformation of EU institutions and the increasing influence of civil society in this process were analysed. Within the scope and the aim of this book, the influence of civil society was analysed from different views. And in order to make this analysis, the literature was analysed.

Along with the influential developments that took place, this book includes the years between 1990 and 2014. The main prediction in this period is that the influence of civil society increased within these 24 years. Here, influence is used to define the relation developed among the actors included in the political process and are considered successful in terms of these actors' ability to shape final decisions according to their own interests. The link among actors is taken as pre-condition and it was concluded that the tightness or looseness of this link shows the rate of influence of the decision.

The first prediction formed in the light of the information obtained from literature data, is that the influence of the Commission would get the chance to be analysed the most. In this study, similar to the technique used in Hermansson's study, all the texts were evaluated and instead of single work difference, the change in general view was observed.

Therefore, not only Commission documents, but also CSO reports published and the Parliament's amendments and the outputs of EU Summit meetings were evaluated in terms of the language they used, their bindingness, the expressions they include and the point where they are alike or different.

In addition to these, the crosscheck of literature data and information obtained via interviews were made and it was evaluated whether the present situation of the conciliation pointing that there is influence in general in literature was being reflected or not. In this context, the integration of climate policy with other fields was also examined. The changes of the states' level of commitment from low to high within climate policy, can also be evaluated within this integration.

After reviewing the literature to determine the CSOs to be evaluated in the book, five criteria were determined by the author. In accordance with these criteria, CAN Europe, WWF, Greenpeace, FoEE and EEB were chosen among CSOs organized in the EU that conducted activities on climate change and energy that would influence EU policies during the period analysed, are included in G10, and have connection with national organizations.

In the beginning of the research it was thought that EEB was the speaker of CSOs in the EU. However, as the conclusion of comprehensive study and interview results show, the EEB had the least effect out of the five chosen CSOs.

Again, in the beginning of the book it was determined that decisions that are the foreign policy output of the states, were formed only by people and institutions within the state mechanism. However, based on the findings of the study, it was concluded that in making these decisions, stakeholders were also influential. Accordingly, although they are not influential at the same rate at every subject, the different sides of the subject are included within the process.

While the current theories developed explaining the EU are mostly related to integration, the literature on decision making are mostly used on determining framework. Therefore, it becomes difficult to make a theoretical explanation. Thereby, in order to explain this interaction, the author tried to use the theories of multi-level governance and liberal intergovernmentalism. The basic objective was to see how much the research corresponds to the theory. According to the theory of liberal intergovernmentalism, in a platform where interdependency is taken as a basis, the Council, being a continuous structure, provides the continuity of the bargain. Here, in the interview carried out with the Council representative, while he/she mentioned that the negotiations in the Council are formed on grounds of reconciliation, also states that actually as a result of states' bargains, the decision is made by mutual sacrifice on different subjects.

In this respect although there is the emphasis that the Theory of Liberal Intergovernmentalism is inadequate in explaining the argument, it is important in terms of seeing the logic behind the Council's decision making mechanism. The decision making on the other hand, as Synder expresses, is defined as making a choice among the preferences, the diversification of these preferences necessitates the inputs coming from different sides to the institutions to be taken into consideration. Here although the emphasis of rationality is tried to be made, it is impossible to avoid the psychological factors influencing the process.

When looked at in terms of multi-level governance, it can be mentioned that in the process policy making of EU, the authority lost its traditional characteristics and that a governing mechanism is formed in which governing from one single point is not possible. At this point the relation among states and the institutions of the EU cannot be explained by traditional forms. In this case developing a new theoretical framework would be extremely meaningful. Although the theory of multi-level governance points out to actors articulated into the process in different points of the process, it is not adequate to explain the ongoing bargaining process. In this sense the concept "a horizontally as well as vertically asymmetrical negotiating system" found place in literature, reaches a deeper point as it actually expresses multi-level governance.

Lenschow, while claiming that policy making process in EU shapes this governance structure, emphasized that interdependency of the relations of the EU and its member states. As it can be seen from here, in terms of the theories of both liberal intergovernmentalism and multi-level governance, interdependency is very important. *Intertwined asymmetrical relation*, the name that the book gives to the relations of CSOs, the EU institutions and the states, is again the result of the same approach.

With the Treaty of Lisbon, both the increase of Union authorization and the influence of subsidiarity, institutionalizing the participation of the local, made the lobby studies to be multi-layered and varied the number of the actors that are to be reached. At the same time, the decision making with qualified majority in the Council voting, increased the importance of lobbying studies to be presented to the Commission. In this sense the Commission CSO relation periodization suggested by Qittkat and Finke is important. Accordingly the consultation relation in 1960–70s transformed into partnership in 1980–90s in the next period.

If civil society organizations, as Skodvin suggests, make lobbying activities in this participation process primarily with the two effective actors that are agenda setters and veto players, their chance to be successful in these activities increase.

When EU environmental policy and EU institutions are examined, it can be seen that in this process, the Commission, the Council and the Parliament are directly included in the decision making and CJEU, with its feature of aversiveness, is indirectly included in the process. In the Commission, the foundation of Environmental Directorate General in 1981 and Climate Directorate General in 2010, gave speed to the coordination within the Commission. Within the structure of the Commission founded as sui generis in 1958, climate service was firstly in a vertical structuring. Under the Environment Policy Committee formed by the cooperation of the Environmental Directorate General in one hand and the state and the Commission on the other, they tried to conduct activities.

The Council, on the other hand, is seen as a reconciliation platform. It reaches this reconciliation by the system of qualified majority of votes. The decisions to be taken on climate change are taken within Environment Council. Although they do not always share the same opinion, Germany, Denmark, Holland, Sweden, Finland and Austria, being the green blocking minority, is one of the points to be taken into consideration. In this sense it can be said that Denmark, Sweden and Finland, known as the Northern Block, are more influential in Council meetings on the subject of environment.

When European Parliament is considered, it can be stated that Environment, Public Health and Food Security from 20 sub-committees, conduct activities on the decisions to be taken on the environment. Here, solution-focused studies are conducted and the parliamentarians, as they are chosen directly by the public, feel themselves responsible. As a kind of ad hoc decision-making process, it should be stated that a lot of actors on the environment are articulated to the process.

In terms of the CJEU, it can be mentioned that generally indirect influence is provided through the cases. Most of the cases that are brought to the CJEU by the Commission are the cases that they are sure that they would win. CSOs, at this point, by following the national process, try to pull the Commission inside this process.

In terms of climate change policy, we can gather the policies under two titles: mitigation and adaptation. Accordingly, adaptation policies are left out of the scope of the book and only mitigation policies were focused on. In this process, the Commission presents the political development through the model of "learning by doing". In this context, the policy is handled not only from one perspective but as a whole.

Climate change, being first mentioned in the fifth Environmental Action Plan could only become an article in the sixth Environmental Action Plan and in 2000 became more extensive with European Climate Change Programme. Therefore, it can be said that after 2000, climate change was included in the plannings completely.

Among many official documents on the subject of 2020 objectives analysed in this study, the ETS Directive comes to the forefront. The most cost-effective solution that the Commission struggles with climate change, is the Emission Trade System. This system functions with upper limit trade logic. The most important problem encountered during the preparation of this Directive was at the point of the emission allowance. On this subject, civil society and especially Eastern European states differ from each other.

While the Commission and the Parliament defends the idea of determining the emission upper limit at EU level, the states do not agree with this. Another problem is about the allowances that will be distributed free of charge. While the Parliament and the Commission try to limit the rates of these, in the Council negotiations, states with weaker economies like Poland, gained the right of more free allowances.

Another point discussed by CSOs, is that a functional emission trade system could not be created, as emission quotas were very high. To create this system, CSOs indicate that every year the rates should be reduced. As the system lost its functionality, two measures were taken as short and long term. The short-term measure is withdrawal and the long-term is market stability reserves. The Commission, this way, believes that the system will find its balance.

Within the scope of 2020 objectives, another important legislation is the Effort Sharing Decision, brought as an addition to the ETS. Accordingly, in the sectors of transportation, building, agriculture and waste, that are outside the scope of the ETS, emission legislations are suggested. Again the same way, it is aimed to achieve a mitigation of 20%.

On the subject of renewable energy, the objective of achieving 20% renewable energy share in 2020, determined in the directive of 2009, is close to realization. Within the scope of this directive, the sectors of electricity, heating and cooling and transportation are regulated. The most criticized point of this directive by the civil society is that 10% biofuel objective determined within the framework of transportation is not sustainable and the possibility that it would result in the destruction of agricultural fields. During the preparation of this directive, although heavy industry lobby indicated that it was hard to achieve the objective because of the expensiveness of this system, in practice, the system did not function in this way.

The subject of carbon capture and storage is another important legislation area; coal is the most used fossil fuel in the present and developing countries continue using coal. Moreover, within the EU, Poland has big coal reserves and wants to use these reserves. In the summit of March 2007, the idea to have a technology with environmental security came to the forefront. In this context, the directive of 2009 is a rather technical text. Its fundamental aim is to capture the carbon dioxide appearing during energy production and to store it to secure areas.

CSOs, within the scope of this book, is handled as a community which is composed of citizens and inwhich social and political participation is aimed. In this context, not only the definition of CSOs, but also the definitions of pressure and interest groups mentioned in various researches are made. While pressure groups effect state and social sectors with more experienced and organized structures, interest groups are used more generally to indicate that different groups gained the power to influence the government. And this power is the key of the influence.

The EEB is the first institution to start EU-wide activities among the examined institutions. In this sense, it should be said that it has a great skill to represent. CAN Europe, by representing 44 million citizens, has the ability to reach and represent an almost triple mass compared to EEB. It is already an institution to conduct coordination on the subject of climate. It becomes evident in this sense that it generally conducts subject-based activities.

Greenpeace is one of the biggest institutions not receiving any funds from EU. Their most intense activities are on the fields of energy and emission. It conducts studies on the necessity of the realization of energy revolution and at the same time presents opinion on the subjects like climate change and CCS. WWF differs itself from the others strategically and rather acts as an institution of speciality. Its European part mostly focuses on the climate and promotes the preparation of important reports. FoE is a grassroots organization. It focuses mostly on actions. Besides this, there are employees within the organization, conducting lobbying studies with EU.

Generally, within this framework of background, when EU reports and civil society are evaluated, it can be said that CSOs makes longer term of planning and tries for more strict and binding measures to be taken as a result of Kyoto obligations. In return, the states avoid binding measures.

The reason for bringing binding provisions within the scope of 2020 objectives is the suitability of the conjuncture of the period. Besides this, no steps could be taken on the subject of the bindingness of energy efficiency. 2030 and 2050 objectives formed within the framework of middle and long-term plannings after 2020 objectives, could not be functional. As they were left only as advice, states do not feel any pressure on themselves. After all, the objectives they determined at present, are at a very low level compared to CSOs.

In this process, CSOs, by conducting lobbying activities, tried to increase the objectives. In the fourth chapter this relation is handled with its different dimensions. The basic output of this book is that the Commission and the Parliament are the most active institutions of the process and the Council, most of the time, is the side softening the proposals.

In terms of CSOs, without doing research with concrete data in literature, the studies indicating the influence of civil society were crosschecked. Here, both through text analysis and interviews, the existence of the influence was determined. Still, civil society organizations are known to exist at every stage of the process, even if not with the same influence.

Civil society organizations influence EU decisions but the rate of this influence is changeable. The main reasons of this change are, as far as it could be determined, the conjuncture, formed alliances, the technical level of the subject, states' attitudes and the existence of opposite lobbying. The point where this book differs from other studies is that only certain organizations studying EU wide were analysed. As most of the studies handled civil society organizations as interest groups along with industrial unions, they were insufficient in analysing the singular influence of CSOs.

Besides, they are also insufficient in showing the transformation of CSOs within the process. Accordingly, CSOs developed a new kind of relation as their ties with EU and the funds they use increased. With the development of this relation evaluated to be intertwined asymmetrical relation, the Union institutions turned to be an inseparable whole with CSO. In this process, while softening the radical parts of these organizations, the EU also increased its contact with the public. This situation can also be evaluated as a matter of image, because EU Commission is making the effort to look equalitarian.

The advice of this book to those that will conduct studies with CSOs is to make a classification among CSOs. Although organizations with different internal structures and strategies can cooperate, the classification of these organizations with new criteria to be produced will pave the way for further studies. Because of Turkey's candidateship to EU, it could be possible to closely follow the conformation studies of its own legislations to environmental acquis and in this process to direct a scholarly study by analysing the visibility and demands of civil society.

Among the CSOs to be observed up until today, only the ones that have close relations with the state, that are not involved in activisim and that are less radical are called to the meetings. To understand at what rate this situation reflects the reality, will be possible by the discursive analysis of the relation between CSOs and the state.

The overall suggestion of this book is to use the concept of intertwined asymmetrical relation to explain the relations between EU institutions and CSOs. It is expected that this concept can explain this relation for all policy areas. To verify this prediction, it is necessary to conduct a variety of studies that cover different policy areas.

References

"About Us." *Green10*. Accessed May 12, 2014. http://www.green10.org/aboutus/.

"About Us." *CAN Europe*. Accessed June 2, 2015. http://www.caneurope.org/about-us.

Adelle, Camilla and Jason Anderson. "Lobby Groups," in *Environmental Policy in the EU*, edited by Andrew Jordan and Camilla Adelle, 152-269. 3rd ed. London: Routledge, 2013.

Akdemir, Erhan. "Avrupa Bütünleşmesinin Tarihçesi," in *Avrupa Birliği – Tarihçe, Kurumlar ve Politikalar*, edited by Belgin Akçay and İlke Göçmen, 35-66. Ankara: Seçkin Publishing, 2012.

Alden, Chris and Amnon Aran. *Foreign Policy Analysis*. New York: Routledge, 2012.

Alemdar, Zeynep. "Baskı Grupları ve Sivil Toplum," in *Karşılaştırmalı Siyaset*, edited by Sabri Sayarı and Hasret Dikici Bilgin. 169-188. 3rd ed. İstanbul: İletişim Publishing, 2015.

Andersen, Mikael Skou and Lise Nordvig Rasmussen. "The Making Environmental Policy in the European Council." *Journal of Common Market Studies* 36, no. 4 (December 1998): 585-597.

Annex I Point 1: Promotion of the use of energy from renewable sources ***I. *Official Journal of the European Union*. C 58E, Vol. 52, Assented to 12 March 2009.

Annex I Point 2: Greenhouse gas emission allowance trading system ***I. *Official Journal of the European Union*. C 58E, Vol. 52, Assented to 12 March 2009.

Annex I Point 3: Shared effort to reduce greenhouse gas emissions ***I. *Official Journal of the European Union*. C 58E, Vol. 52, Assented to 12 March 2009.

Annex I Point 4: Geological storage of carbon dioxide ***I. *Official Journal of the European Union*. C 58E, Vol. 52, Assented to 12 March 2009.

Annex I Point 14: Amendment of Directive 2003/87/EC so as to include aviation activities in the scheme for greenhouse gas emission allowance trading within the Community ***I. *Official Journal of the European Union*. C 282E, Vol. 51, Assented to 6 November 2008.

Annex I Point 19: Amendment of Directive 2003/87/EC so as to include aviation activities in the scheme for greenhouse gas emission allowance trading within the Community ***II. Official Journal of the European Union. C 256/E, Vol. 51, Assented to 9 October 2008.

Bache, Ian and Stephen George. *Politics in the European Union*. Great Britain: Oxford University Press, 2006.

Belge, Murat. "Sivil Toplum Nedir?." in *Sivil Toplum ve Demokrasi Konferans Yazıları*. edited by Nurhan Yentürk and Arzu Karamani. no:1. 2003. http://stk.bilgi.edu.tr/media/uploads/ 2015/02/01/belge_s td_1.pdf.

Benson, David and Camilla Adelle. "EU Environmental Policy After the Lisbon Treaty," in *Environmental Policy in the EU*. edited by. Andrew Jordan and Camilla Adelle. 32-48. 3rd ed. London: Routledge, 2013.

Bernauer, Thomas. "Climate Change Politics," *The Annual Review of Political Science* 16, no. 13 (2013): 1-28.

Betsill, Michele M. and Elizabeth Corell. "NGO Influence in International Environmental Negotiations: A Framework for Analysis," *Global Environmental Politics* 1, no. 4 (November 2001): 65-85.

Betsill, Michele and Matthew J. Hoffmann. "The Contours of "Cap and Trade": The Evolution of Emissions Trading Systems for Greenhouse Gases," *Review of Policy Research* 28, no. 1 (2011): 83-106.

"Better Regulation." *European Commission.* Accessed November 3, 2015. http://ec.europa.eu/ smart-regulation/index_en.htm.

"Big EU guns fire for 'crucial' 2030 renewable targets." *Euractiv.* last modified January 7, 2014. http://www.euractiv.com/section/energy/news/big-euguns-2030-renewable-targets/.

Bilgin, A. Aslı. "Avrupa Komisyonu," in *Avrupa Birliği – Tarihçe, Kurumlar ve Politikalar*. edited by. Belgin Akçay and İlke Göçmen, 179-200. Ankara: Seçkin Publishing, 2012.

Black, Richard. "EU's energy plans – how revolutionary?." *BBC News*. Last modified January 10, 2007. http://news.bbc.co.uk/2/hi/science/nature/6247723.stm.

Bodoni, Stephanie and Ewa Krukowska. "Poland Loses EU Court Appeal of Carbon Permit Hand-Our Rules." *Bloomberg.* accessed June 16, 2016. http://www.bloomberg.com/news/ articles/2013-03-07/poland-loses-eu-court-appeal-of-carbon-permithand-out-rules-1-.

Bogojević, Sanja. "EU Climate Change Litigation, the Role of the European Courts, and the Importance of Legal Culture". *Law&Policy* 35, no. 3 (July 2013): 184-207.

Bomberg, Elizabeth. Green Parties and Politics in the European Union. London: Routledge, 1998.

Bouwen, Pieter. "Corporate Lobbying in the European Union: the Logic of Access," *Journal of European Public Policy* 9, no. 3 (2002): 365-390.

Börzel, Tanja A. "Pace-setting, Foot-dragging and Fence-sitting: Member State Responses to Europeanization," *Journal of Common Market Studies* 40. no. 2 (2002): 193-214.

Budak, Sevim. *Avrupa Birliği ve Türk Çevre Politikası*. İstanbul: Büke Yayınları, 2000.

Bulmer, Simon and Martin Burch. "The 'Europeanisation' of central government: the UK and Germany in historical institutionalist perspective" in *The Rules of Integration Institutionalist Approaches to the Study of Europe.* edited by. Gerald Schneider and Mark Aspinwall, 73-96. Great Britain: Manchester University Press, 2001.

CAN Europe. CAN Europe's Response to the European Commission's Greenpaper Consultation on a 2030 Climate and Energy Framework. Transparency Register Number: 55888811123-49, Accessed 26 June 2013.

"CAN Europe Transparency Register." *European Commission Transparency Register page*. Accessed June 3, 2015. http://ec.europa.eu/transparencyregister/public/consultation/displaylobbyist.do?id=55888811123-49.

"Carbon Capture and Storage." *European Commission.* Accessed May 20, 2015. http://ec.europa. eu/energy/en/topics/oil-gas-andcoal/carbon-capture-and-storage.

Chryssochoou, Dimitris N. et al. *Theory and Reform in the European Union*. 2nd ed. Great Britain: Manchester University Press, 2003.

Cini, Michelle. "Intergovernmentalism," in *European Union Politics*. edited by. Michelle Cini and Nieves Pérez Solórzano Borragán, 86- 103. 3rd ed. United States: Oxford University Press, 2010.

"Climate Action." *European Commission*. Accessed December 1, 2014. http://ec.europa.eu/ clima/aboutus/mission/index_en.htm.

Coen, David. "Lobbying in the European Union," *DG Internal Policies Briefing Paper*. 2007. http://www.eurosfaire.prd.fr/7pc/doc/1211469722_lobbying_eu.pdf.

Connelly, James and Graham Smith. *Politics and the Environment*. London: Routledge, 1999.

"Consultations." *European Commission*. Accessed December 1, 2013. http://ec.europa.eu/ yourvoice/consultations/index_en.htm.

Corell, Elizabeth and Michele M. Betsill, "A Comparative Look at NGO Influence in International Environmental Negotiations: Desertification and Climate Change," *Global Environmental Politics* 1, no. 4 (November 2001): 86-107.

Council of the European Union. [Council Directive 96/61/EC] concerning integrated pollution prevention and control, Assented to 24 September 1996.

Council of the European Union. *Brussels European Council Presidency Conclusions 23/24 March 2006 (7775/1/06)*, Assented to 8 July 2006.

Council of the European Union. Brussels European Council Presidency Conclusions 8/9 March 2007 (7224/07), 9 March 2007.

Council of the European Union. Brussels European Council Presidency Conclusions 8-9 March 2007 (7224/1/07) REV 1, 2 May 2007.

Council of the European Union. Brussels European Council Presidency Conclusions 13/14 March 2008 (7652/1/08) REV 1, 20 May 2008.

Council of the European Union. Brussels European Council Presidency Conclusions 19/20 June 2008 (11018/1/08) REV 1, 17 June 2008.

"Council of the European Union." *European Union*. Accessed December 2, 2013. http://europa.eu/about-eu/institutions-bodies/councileu/index_en.htm.

Çokgezen, Jale. "Avrupa Birliği Çevre Politikası ve Türkiye", Marmara University İİBF Journal 23. no. 2. (2007): 91-115.

"Debate rages as Brussels fires starting gun on 2030 energy strategy". *Euractiv.* last modified March 22, 2016. http://www.euractiv.com/section/energy/news/debaterages-as-brussels-fires-starting-gun-on-2030-energystrategy/.

"Decision Making Mechanisms." *European Union Turkey Delegation*. Accessed December 1, 2013. http://www.avrupa.info.tr/tr/avrupa-birligi/ab-nasilcalisir/karar-alma-mekanizmalari.html.

de Conninck, Heleen and Karin Bäckstrand. "An International Relations Perspective on the Global Politics of Carbon Dioxide Capture and Storage," *Global Environmental Change*. No. 21 (2011): 368-378.

Delbeke, Jos and Peter Vis. "Editors' Introduction," in *EU Climate Policy Explained*, edited by. Jos Debeke and Peter Vis. 1-4. Oxon: Routledge, 2015.

Delbeke, Jos and Peter Vis. "EU Climate Leadership in a Rapidly Changing World," in *EU Climate Policy Explained*. edited by. Jos Debeke and Peter Vis. 5-28. Oxon: Routledge, 2015.

Dupont, Claire, "Combating Climate Complexity in Integration of EU Climate and Energy Policies," in *Energy and Environment in Europe: Asssessing a Complex Relationship, European Integration Online Papers (EIoP)*. edited by. Jale Tosun and Israel Solorio. Special Mini-Issue 1 15. no. 8 (2011): 1-20.

Dür, Andreas. "How Much Influence Do Interest Groups Have in the EU? Some Methodological Considerations". *Opening EU Governance to Civil Society Gains and Challenges*. edited. by. Beate Kohler Koch, Dirk De Bièvre and William Maloney. Mannheim. CONNEX Report Series no. 5, (February 2008): 45-68.

Dür, Andreas and Gemma Mateo. "Who lobbies the European Union," *Journal of European Public Policy* 19. no. 7. (September 2012): 969-087.

Duru, Bülent. "Avrupa Birliği Çevre Politikası," in *Avrupa Birliği Politikaları*. edited by. Çağrı Erhan and Deniz Senemoğlu. Ankara: İmaj Publishing House, 2007. http://kentcevre.politics. ankara.edu.tr/duruabcevre.pdf.

Dutch, Steven I.. *Encyclopedia of Global Warming*. USA: Salem Press, 2010.

"ECCP EU ETS Review Process: Written Comments CAN-Europe, Friends of the Earth Europe Greenpeace and WWF." *CAN Europe, Friends of the Earth Europe, Greenpeace, WWF*. June 2007.
http://ec.europa.eu/clima/events/docs/0065/caneurope_ngo_en.pdf.

Eden, Sally. "Greenpeace," *New Political Economy* 9. no.4. (2004): 595-610.

Eising, Rainer and Sonja Lehringer, "Interest Groups and the European Union," in *European Union Politics*. edited by. Michele Cini and Nieves Pérez Solórzano Borrogán. 189-206. 3rd ed. Oxford: Oxford University Press, 2010.

"Environment Action Plan to 2020," *Avrupa Komisyonu*. Accessed January 4, 2014. http://ec.europa.eu/environment/pubs/pdf/factsheets/7eap/en.pdf .

"Environmentalists criticise new EU climate goals," *Euronews*. last modified January 23, 2014. http://www.euronews.com/2014/01/23/environmentalist s-criticise-new-eu-climate-goals/.

"EU faces tough climate change road." *BBC News*. last modified January 23, 2008. http://news.bbc.co.uk/2/hi/europe/7205221.stm.

"EU includes aviation in CO2 curbs." *BBC News*. last modified July 8, 2008. http://news.bbc.co.uk/2/hi/europe/7495567.stm.

"EU reveals energy plan of action." *BBC News*. last modified January 23, 2008. http://news.bbc.co.uk/2/hi/science/nature/7203514.st m.

"EU set to backtrack on emissions." *BBC News*. last modified October 16, 2008. http://news.bbc.co.uk/2/hi/europe/7673411.stm.

"Euro MPs seal major climate deal." *BBC News*. last modified December 17, 2008. http://news.bbc.co.uk/2/hi/7787504.stm.

"Euro MPs stick to climate targets." *BBC News*. last modified October 7, 2008. http://news.bbc.co.uk/2/hi/europe/7656478.stm.

"EU sets out 'walk now, sprint later' 2030 clean energy vision." *Euractiv*. last modified January 23, 2014.
http://www.euractiv.com/section/sciencepolicymaking/news/eu-sets-out-walk-now-sprint-later-2030-clean-energy-vision/.

"EU: No action on 2030 renewables target is 'no real option'". *Euractiv.* last modified October 17, 2012. http://www.euractiv.com/section/climateenvironment/news/eu-no-action-on-2030-renewablestarget-is-no-real-option/.

"EU leaders united on crises, divided over climate". *Euronews.* Last modified October 17, 2008. euronews.com/2008/10/17/eu-leadersunited-on-crisis-divided-over-climate/.

"European Climate Change Program." *European Commission.* Accessed December 15, 2015. http://ec.europa.eu/clima/policies/eccp/index_en.htm.

European Commission. [COM(2000) 200 final] Reforming the Commission: A White Paper Part I. Brussels: European Commission, 2000.

European Commission. [COM(2001) 581 final] Proposal for a Directive of the European Parliament and of the Council establishing a scheme for greenhouse gas emission allowance trading within the Community and amending Council Directive 96/61/EC, Assented to 23 October 2001.

European Commission. [COM(2002) 680 final] Amended proposal for a Directive of the European Parliament and of the Council establishing a scheme for greenhouse gas emission allowance trading within the Community and amending Council Directive 96/61/EC, Assented to 27 November 2002.

European Commission. [COM(2003) 463 final] Opinion Of The Commission pursuant to Article 251 (2), third subparagraph, point (c) of the EC Treaty, on the European Parliament's amendments to the Council's common position regarding the proposal for a Directive of the European Parliament and of the Council, Assented to 18 July 2003.

European Commission. [COM(2006) 105 final] Green Paper A European Strategy for Sustainable, Competitive and Secure Energy, Assented to 8 March 2006.

European Commission. [COM(2006) 843 final] Communication from the Commission to the Council and the European Parliament Sustainable power generation from fossil fuels: aiming for near-zero emissions from coal after 2020, Assented to 10 January 2007.

European Commission. [COM(2006) 848 final] Communication from the Commission to the Council and the European Parliament Renewable Energy Road Map Renewable energies in the 21st century: building a more sustainable future, Assented to 10 January 2007.

European Commission. [COM(2007) 2 final] Communication from the Commission to the Council, The European Parliament, The European Economic and Social Committee and the Committee of the Regions Limiting Global Climate Change to 2 degrees Celsius The way ahead for 2020 and beyond, Assented to 10 January 2007.

European Commission. [COM(2008) 18 final] Proposal for a Directive of the European Parliament and of the Council on Geological Storage of Carbon Dioxide and Amending Council Directives 85/337/EEC, 96/61/EC, Directives 2000/60/EC, 2001/80/EC, 2004/35/EC, 2006/12/EC and Regulation (EC) No 1013/2006, Assented to 23 January 2008.

European Commission. [COM(2008) 19 final] Proposal for a Directive of the European Parliament and of the Council on the promotion of the use of energy from renewable sources, Assented to 23 January 2008.

European Commission. [COM(2008) 30 final] Communication From The Commission To The European Parliament, The Council, The European Economic And Social Committee And The Committee Of The Regions 20 20 by 2020 Europe's climate change opportunity, Assented to 23 January 2008.

European Commission. [SEC(2008) 85/3] Impact Assessment Document accompanying the Package of Implementation measures for the EU's objectives on climate change and renewable energy for 2020, Assented to 23 January 2008.

European Commission. [COM(2009) 147 final] White Paper Adapting to climate change: Towards a European framework for action, Assented to 01 April 2009.

European Commission. COM (2011) 112 Final] Communication From The Commission To The European Parliament, The Council, The European Economic And Social Committee And The Committee Of The Regions A Roadmap for moving to a competitive low carbon economy in 2050, Assented to 08 March 2011.

European Commission. [COM(2011) 885] Communication From The Commission To The European Parliament, The Council, The European Economic And Social Committee And The Committee Of The Regions Energy Roadmap 2050, Assented to 15 December 2011.

European Commission. [2013/162/EU)] Commission Decision on determining Member States' annual emission allocations for the period from 2013 to 2020 pursuant to Decision No 406/2009/EC of the European Parliament and of the Council, Assented to 26 March 2013.

European Commission. [COM(2013) 169 Final] Green Paper A 2030 framework for climate and energy policies, Assented to 27 March 2013.

European Commission. [COM (2014) 15 Final] Communication From The Commission To The European Parliament, The Council, The European Economic And Social Committee And The Committee Of The Regions A Policy Framework for Climate and Energy in the Period from 2020 to 2030, Assented to 22 January 2014.

European Commission. [SEC(2008) 85/3] Impact Assessment Document accompanying the Package of Implementation measures for the EU's objectives on climate change and renewable energy for 2020, Assented to 23 January 2008.

European Community. "Single European Act," *Official Journal of European Communities*. No L 169/1, Assented to 29 June 1987.

European Council. *[(2003/C 125 E/05)] Common Position (EC) No 28/2003*, Assented to 18 March 2003.

European Council. *European Council Conclusions 23 and 24 October 2014 EUCO 169/14*, Assented to 24 October 2014.

European Environmental Bureau. The EEB's Response to the European Commission's Consultation on a 2030 Framework for Climate and Energy Policies. Transparency Register Number: 06798511314-27, 01/07/2013.

"European Environmental Bureau." *EEB official web page*. Accessed May 25, 2015. http://www.eeb.org/index.cfm/about-eeb/.

European Environmental Bureau Transparency Register. *European Commission Transparency Register page*, Accessed June 1, 2015.

http://ec.europa.eu/transparencyregister/public/consultation/displaylobbyist.do?id=06798511314-27.

European Parliament and the Council. [Directive 2003/87/EC] establishing a scheme for greenhouse gas emission allowance trading within the Community and amending Council Directive 96/61/EC, Assented to 13 October 2003.

European Parliament and the Council. [Directive 2004/101/EC] DIRECTIVE 2004/101/EC amending Directive 2003/87/EC establishing a scheme for greenhouse gas emission allowance trading within the Community, in respect of the Kyoto Protocol's project mechanisms, Assented to 27 October 2004.

European Parliament and the Council. [Directive 2008/101/EC] amending Directive 2003/87/EC so as to include aviation activities in the scheme for greenhouse gas emission allowance trading within the Community, Assented to 19 November 2008.

European Parliament and the Council. [Regulation (EC) No 219/2009] adapting a number of instruments subject to the procedure referred to in Article 251 of the Treaty to Council Decision 1999/468/EC with regard to the regulatory procedure with scrutiny, Assented to 11 March 2009.

European Parliament and the Council. [Directive 2009/28/EC] on the promotion of the use of energy from renewable sources and amending and subsequently repealing Directives 2001/77/EC and 2003/30/EC, Assented to 23 April 2009.

European Parliament and the Council. [Directive 2009/29/EC] amending Directive 2003/87/EC so as to improve and extend the greenhouse gas emission allowance trading scheme of the Community, Assented to 23 April 2009.

European Parliament and the Council. [Directive 2009/31/EC] on the geological storage of carbon dioxide and amending Council Directive 85/337/EEC, European Parliament and Council Directives 2000/60/EC, 2001/80/EC, 2004/35/EC, 2008/1/EC and Regulation (EC) No 1013/2006, Assented to 23 April 2009.

European Parliament and the Council. [Decision No 406/2009/EC] on the effort of Member States to reduce their greenhouse gas emissions to meet the Community's greenhouse gas emission reduction commitments up to 2020, Assented to 23 April 2009.

European Parliament Committee on the Environment, Public Health and Food Safety. Report on the proposal for a directive of the European Parliament and of the Council on the geological storage of carbon dioxide and amending Council Directives 85/337/EEC, 96/61/EC, Directives 2000/60/EC, 2001/80/EC, 2004/35/EC, 2006/12/EC and Regulation (EC) No 1013/2006 (COM(2008) 0018 – C6-0040/2008 – 2008/0015 (COD)), Assented to 16 October 2008.

European Parliament. [P5_TA(2002)0461] Legislative resolution on the proposal for a European Parliament and Council directive establishing a scheme for greenhouse gas emission allowance trading within the Community and amending Council Directive 96/61/EC (COM(2001) 581 – C5-0578/2001 –2001/0245(COD)), Assented to 10 October 2002.

European Parliament. [P6_TA(2007)0038] European Parliament resolution on climate change, Assented to 14 February 2007.

European Parliament. [P6_TA(2007)0406] European Parliament resolution of 25 September 2007 on the Road Map for Renewable Energy in Europe, Assented to 25 September 2007.

European Parliament. [EP-PE_TC1-COD(2008)0016] Position of the European Parliament adopted at first reading on 17 December 2008 with a view to the adoption of Directive 2009/.../EC of the European Parliament and of the Council on the promotion of the use of energy from renewable sources and amending and subsequently repealing Directives 2001/77/EC and 2003/30/EC (EP-PE_TC1-COD(2008)0016), Assented to 17 December 2008.

Finke, Barbara. "Civil society participation in EU governance," *Living Rev. Euro. Gov.* 2. No. 2. 2007, Accessed June 15, 2016. http://www.europeangovernancelivingreviews.org/Articles/ lreg-2007-2/download/lreg- 2007-2Color.pdf.

"Focus: Adaptation," *UNFCC.* Accessed December 17, 2015. http://unfccc.int/ focus/ adaptation/items/6999.php.

"Focus: Mitigation – Action on mitigation: Reducing Emissions and Enhancing Sinks," *UNFCC.* Accessed December 17, 2015. http://unfccc.int/focus/mitigation/items/7171.php.

"Focus: Mitigation – NAMAs, Nationally Appropriate Mitigation Actions," *UNFCC.* Accessed December 17, 2015. http://unfccc.int/focus/mitigation/items/7172.php.

"Freezing Climate Change WWF Position Statement EU Climate and Energy Package," *WWF.* Accessed May 24, 2016. http://awsassets.panda.org/downloads/effort_sharing.pdf.

Friends of the Earth. Submission on the European Commission's Green Paper on a 2030 framework for climate and energy policies. Transparency register number: 9825553393-31, 07/2013. 2-4.

"Friends of the Earth Europe Transparency Register." *European Commission Transparency Register Page.* Accessed April 15, 2016. http://ec.europa.eu/transparencyregister/public/ consultation/displaylobbyist.do?id=9825553393-31.

Gibbins, John and Hannah Chalmers. "Carbon Capture and Storage," *Energy Policy.* 36 (2008): 4317-4322.

"Green groups upbeat over EU energy/climate package". *Euronews.* last modified July 9, 2007. http://www.euronews.com/2007/03/09/green-groupsupbeat-over-eu-energyclimate-package/.

Greenhouse gas emission allowance trading. *Official Journal of the European Union.* C279/E, Vol. 46, Assented to 20 November 2003.

Greenhouse gas emission allowance trading. *Official Journal of the European Union.* C 74 E/130, Assented to 24 March 2004.

Greenpeace. Submission to the European Commission Public Consultation on a 2030 Framework for Climate and Energy Policies. Transparency Register number: 9832909575-41.

"Greenpeace European Unit Transparency Register." *European Commission Transparency Register page.* Accessed June 3, 2015. http://ec.europa.eu/transparencyregister/public/ consultation/displaylobbyist.do?id=9832909575-41.

Greenwood, Justin. "Regulating Lobbying in the European Union," *Parliamentary Affairs* 51. no.:4, (1998): 587-599.

Gullberg, Anne Therese. "Rational Lobbying and EU Climate Policy," *International Environmental Agreements: Politics, Law and Economics*. 8. (2008a): 161-178.

Gullberg, Anne Therese. "Lobbying friends and foes in climate policy: The case of business and environmental interest group in the European Union," *Energy Policy*. 36. (2008b) 2964- 2972.

Gullberg, Anne Therese. "Pressure or Information? Lobbying for Binding Renewable Energy Targets in the European Union," *Review of Policy Research* 30 no. 6. (2013): 611-628.

Harrabin, Roger. "UK opposes green aviation target," *BBC News*. Last modified September 26, 2008. http://news.bbc.co.uk/2/hi/science/nature/7636780.stm.

Harrabin, Roger. "Climate plan concern as EU meets," *BBC News*. Last modified October 15, 2008. http://news.bbc.co.uk/2/hi/europe/7670814.stm.

Hasson, Anders and Mårten Bryngelsson. "Expert Opinions on Carbon Capture and Storage – A Framing of Uncertainties and Possibilities," *Energy Policy*. 37 (2009): 2273-2282.

Hermansson, Henrik. "The European Commission's environmental stakeholder consultations: Is lobbying success based on what you know, what you own or who you know?," *Interest Groups and Advocacy*. (2016): 1-23.

Hill, Christopher. *The Changing Politics of Foreign Policy*. China: Palgrave Macmillan. 2003.

"History." *Friends of the Earth International*. Accessed April 12, 2016. http://www.foei. org/about-foei/history.

"How EU Decisions are made." *European Union*. Accessed December 1, 2013. http://europa.eu/eu-law/decisionmaking/procedures/index_en.htm.

"Impact Assessments." *European Commission*. Accessed December 1, 2013. http://ec.europa. eu/governance/impact/index_en.htm.

"In graphics: The EU and emissions." *BBC News*. last modified January 10, 2007. http://news.bbc.co.uk/2/hi/europe/6244465.stm.

IPCC. "Adaptation and Mitigation Options," *Fourth Assessment Report: Climate Change 2007*. Accessed March 28, 2015. https://www.ipcc.ch/publications_and_ data/ar4/ syr/en/ spms4.html.

IPCC. "Observed Changes and in Climate and their Effects," *Fourth Assessment Report: Climate Change 2007*. Accessed March 27, 2015. https://www.ipcc.ch/publications_and_ data/ar4/syr/en/mains1.html.

IPCC. *Fourth Assessment Report Glossary A-D*. Accessed November 16, 2015. https://www.ipcc.ch/publications_and_data/ar4/wg2/en/annexessglossary-a-d.html.

IPCC. *Fourth Assessment Report Glossary E-O*. Accessed November 16, 2015. https://www.ipcc.ch/publications_and_data/ar4/wg2/en/annexessglossary-e-o.html.

Jaggard, Lyn. *Climate Change Politics in Europe*. London: Tauris Academic Studies, 2007.

Jordan, Andrew. "The European Union: an evolving system of multi level governance or government?," *Policy and Politics* 29. no. 2 (2001): 193-208.

Jordan, Andrew and Camilla Adelle. "EU Environmental Policy: Context, Actors andPolicy Dynamics," *Environmental Policy in the EU*. Edited by. Andrew Jordan and Camilla Adelle. 1-9. London: Routledge, 2013.

"Judgement of the General Court." *General Court*. Last modified March 7, 2013 http://www.emissionseuets.com/attachments/356_Judgment%20of%20the%20General%20Court%20of%207%20March%202013.pdf.

Karakaş, Işıl. "Avrupa Birliği'nde Egemenlik Yetkilerinin Devredilmesi Sorunsalı," *Avrupa Birliği Hukuku*. edited by. İdil Işıl Gül and Lami Bertan Tokuzlu. 43-50. İstanbul: Şefik Matbaası, 2003.

Kıvılcım, İlge. *İKV Değerlendirme Notu AB'nin En Büyük Sınavlarından Biri "AB ETS" Olacak*. Last modified October 2014,. http://www.ikv.org.tr/images/files/AB_nin_En_Buyuk_Sinavlar%C4%B0ndan_Biri_AB_ETS_Olacak.pdf.

Klüver, Heike. *Lobbying in the European Union*. Great Britain: Oxford University Press, 2013a.

Klüver, Heike. "Lobbying as a Collective Enterprise: Winners and losers of Policy Formulation in the European Union," *Journal of European Public Policy* 20, no. 1. (2013b): 59-76.

Knill, Christoph and Duncan Liefferink, "The Establishment of EU Environmental Policy," *Environmental Policy in the EU*. edited by. Andrew Jordan and Camilla Adelle, 13-31. 3rd ed. London: Routledge, 2013.

Kohler-Koch, Beate and Barbara Finke. "The Institutional Shaping of EU Society Relations: A Contribution to Democracy via Participation?," *Journal of Civil Society* 3. no. 3. (2007): 205-221.

Kohler-Koch, Beate. "Civil Society and EU Democracy: 'astroturf' representation?," *Journal of European Public Policy* 17. no. 1. (2010): 100-116.

Kohler-Koch, Beate. "Civil Society and EU Democracy: 'astroturf' representation?," *Journal of European Public Policy* 17. no. 1. (2010): 100-116.

Kohler-Koch, Beate. "Civil Society and Democracy in the EU: High Expectations under Empirical Scrutiny," *De-Mystification of Participatory Democracy*. edited by. Beate Kohler-Koch et al. 1-17 Great Britain: Oxford University Press, 2013.

Kohler-Koch, Beate and Vanessa Buth. "The balancing act of European civil society," *De-Mystification of Participatory Democracy*. edited by. Beate Kohler-Koch et al. 114-148. Great Britain: Oxford University Press, 2013.

Kolstad, Charles et al. "Social, Economic and Ethical Concepts and Methods," Climate Change 2014: Mitigation of Climate Change (Contribution of Working Group III to the Fifth Assessment Report of the IPCC). edited by. O. Edenhofer et al.. 207-282. UK: Cambridge University Press, 2014.

Karhonen, Kaisa. "Guardians of Subsidiarity: National Parliaments Strive to Control EU Decision Making," *FIIA Briefing Paper*. no. 84. (May 2011).

Krämer, Ludwig. "The European Court of Justice," *Environmental Policy in the EU*. edited by. Andrew Jordan and Camilla Adelle. 113-131. London: Routledge, 2013.

"Legislative Powers." *European Parliament*. Accessed December 2, 2013. http://www.europarl.europa.eu/aboutparliament/en/0081f4b3c7/Law-making-procedures-in-detail.html.

Lenschow, Andrea. "Transformation in european environmental policy," *Transformation in European Environmental Governance*. edited by. Beate Kohler Koch and Rainer Eising. 37-58. London: Routledge, 1999.

Lenschow, Andrea. "Environmental Policy in the European Union: Bridging Policy, Politics and Polity Dimensions," *Handbook of European Union Politics*. edited by. Knud Erik Jørgensen, Mark A. Pollack and Ben Rosamond. 413-432. Great Britain: Sage Publications, 2006.

Lenschow, Andrea. "Environmental Policy," *Policy Making in the European Union*. edited by. Helen Wallace and William Wallace. 305-327. Great Britain: Oxford University Press, 2010.

Liefferink, Duncan and Mikael Skou Andersen. "Strategies of the 'green' member states in EU environmental policy making," *Journal of European Public Policy* 5. no. 2. (1998): 254-270.

Long, Tony, Liam Salter and Stephan Singer. "WWF: European and Global Climate Policy," *European Union Lobbying: Changes in the Arena*. edited by. Robin Pedler. 87-103. New York: Palgrave, 2002.

McCormick, John. *Environmental Policy in the European Union*. Hong Kong: Palgrave, 2001.

McGrath, Matt. "Burnt ou' EU likely to curb climate goals," *BBC News*. Last modified January 21, 2014. http://www.bbc.com/news/science-environment-25828181.

McGrath, Matt. "EU outlines 2030 cimate goals," *BBC News*. Last modified January 22, 2014. http://www.bbc.com/news/science-environment-25841134.

Meadows, Damien, Yvon Slingenberg and Peter Zapfel. "EU ETS: pricing carbon to drive cost effective reductions across Europe," *EU Climate Policy Explained*. edited by. Jos Delbeke and Peter Vis. 29-60. Oxon: Routledge, 2015.

"Members." *CAN Europe*. Accessed July 22, 2016. http://www.caneurope.org/membership/index.php?option=com_civicrm&task=civicrm/profile&gid=50&reset=1&force=1&search=0.

Michalowitz, Irina. "What determines influence? Assessing conditions for decision-making influence of interest groups in the EU," *Journal of European Public Policy* 14, no. 1. (2007): 132-151.

Mintz, Alex and Karl DeRouen. *Understanding Foreign Policy Decision Making*. New York: Cambridge University Press, 2010.

Monaghan, Elizabeth. "Making the Environment Present: Political Representation, Democracy and Civil Society Organisations in EU Climate Change Politics," *Journal of European Integration* 35. no. 5. (2013): 601-618.

Moravcsik, Andrew. Theorizing EU Policy-Making," in the European Community: A Liberal Intergovernmentalist Approach," *Journal of Common Market Studies* 31. no. 4. (December 1993): 473-524.

Moravcsik, Andrew. "Taking Preferences Seriously: A Liberal Theory of International Politics," *International Organization* 51. no. 4. (Autumn 1997): 513-553.

Moravcsik, Andrew. "In Defence of the 'Democratic Deficit': Reassessing Legitimacy in the European Union," *Journal of Common Market Studies* 40. no. 4. (2002): 603-624.

Moravcsik, Andrew and Frank Schimmenfelling. "Liberal Intergovernmentalism," *European Integration Theory*. Edited by. A. Wiener and T. Diez. 67-87. 2nd ed. Oxford: Oxford University Press, 2009.

Mulvey, Stephen. "Summit to test EU climate resolve," *BBC News*. Last modified March 7, 2007. http://news.bbc.co.uk/2/hi/europe/6427015.stm.

"Nations challenge EU climate plan." *BBC News*. last modified October 15, 2008. http://news.bbc.co.uk/2/hi/europe/7672335.stm.

"No deal amid EU climate deadlock." *BBC News*. last modified December 6, 2008. http://news.bbc.co.uk/2/hi/europe/7768758.stm.

"Open letter to World leaders: 2015 will see major decisions for the millennium." *Euractiv*. last modified January 15, 2015. http://www.euractiv.com/sections/developmentpolicy/open-letter-world-leaders-2015-should-seemajor-decisions-millennium.

"Our History." *Friends of the Earth Europe*. Accessed April 12, 2016. https://www.foeeurope.org/about/history.

Paker, Hande. "Çevre Rejimleri ve Türkiye'de Sivil Toplum Örgütlerinin Rolü: Akdeniz'de Sürdürülebilirlik," *Marmara Avrupa Araştırmaları Dergisi* 20, no. 1. (2012): 151-175.

Pollack, Mark A. "Theorizing EU Policy-Making," *Policy Making in the European Union*. edited by. Helen Wallace, William Wallace and Mark A. Pollack. 13-48. Great Britain: Oxford University Press, 2005.

Qittkat, Christine and Barbara Finke. "The EU Commission Consultation Regime," *Opening EU Governance to Civil Society Gains and Challenges*. ed. By. Beate Kohler Koch, Dirk De Bièvre and William Maloney. Mannheim: CONNEX Report Series no: 5. (February 2008): 183-222.

Risse-Kappen, Thomas. "Exploring the Nature of the Beast: International Relations Theory and Comparative Policy Analysis Meet the European Union," *Journal of Common Market Studies* 34. no. 1. (March 1996): 53-80.

Romanova, Tatiana. "The Partnership for Modernisation Through the Three Level of Analysis Perspectives," *European Politics and Society*. 16. no. 1 (2015): 45-61.

Rosamond, Ben. *Theories of European Integration*. Great Britain: Palgrave, 2000.

Rosamond, Ben. "New Theories of European Integration," *European Union Politics*. edited by. Michelle Cini and Nieves Pérez Solórzano Borragán. 104-122. United States: Oxford University Press, 2010.

Schön Quinlivan, Emmanuelle. "The European Commission," *Environmental Policy in the EU*. edited by. Andrew Jordan and Camilla Adelle. 95-112. London: Routledge, 2013.

"Second European Climate Programme." *European Commission*. Accessed December 5, 2015. http://ec.europa.eu/clima/policies/eccp/second/index_en.htm.

Skjærseth, John Birger. "The Climate Policy of the EC: Too Hot to Handle?," *Journal of Common Market Studies*. 32. no. 1. (March 1994): 25-46.

Skodvin, Tora, Anne Therese Gullberg and Stine Aakre. "Target group influence and political feasibility: the case of climate policy design in Europe". *Journal of European Public Policy*. 17 no. 6. (2010): 854-873.

Snyder, Richard C., H. W. Bruck and Burton Sapin. "The Decision-Making Approach to the Study of International Politics," *Foreign Policy Decision-Making: An*

Approach to the Study of International Politics. edited by. Richard Snyder, H.W. Bruck and Burton Sapin. 199-206. New York: The Free Press of Glencoe, 1962.

Snyder, Richard C., H. W. Bruck and Burton Sapin. "Decision making as an Approach to the Study of International Politics," *Foreign Policy Decision Making (Revisited)*. edited by. Richard C. Snyder, H. W. Bruck, Burton Sapin et al. 21-152. New York: Palgrave Macmillan, 2002.

Sönmezoğlu, Faruk. *Uluslararası Politika ve Dış Politika Analizi*. İstanbul: Der Publishing, 2014.

Spear, Joanna. "The Environment Agenda," *International Politics in Europe*. edited by. G. Wyn Rees. 111-132. London: Routledge, 1993.

"Structural Reform of the European Carbon Market." *European Commission*. Accessed March 25, 2015. http://ec.europa.eu/clima/policies/ets/reform/index_en.htm.

Tezcan, Ercüment. "Avrupa Birliği'nde Politika Yapımı / Karar Alma," *Avrupa Birliği – Tarihçe, Kurumlar ve Politikalar*. edited by. Belgin Akçay and İlke Göçmen. 281-318. Ankara: Seçkin Publishing, 2012.

"The EU Emission Trading System." *European Commission*. Accessed December 12, 2014. http://ec.europa.eu/clima/policies/ets/index_en.htm.

"The Subsidiarity Control Mechanism (Protocol No. 2)." *European Commission*. Accessed June 20, 2016. http://ec.europa.eu/dgs/secretariat_general/relations/relations_other/npo/subsidiarity_en.htm

Truman, David. *The Governmental Process*. USA: Greenwood Press, 1981.

Umbach, Frank. "The EU and Germany's Policies on Climate Change," *Global Warming and Climate Change*. edited by. Antonio Marquina. 227-252. Great Britain: Palgrave Macmillan, 2010.

Usui, Yoichiro. "Evolving Environmental Norms in the European Union," *European Law Journal*. 9. no. 1. (February 2003): 69-87.

van Zeben, J.A.W., "The European Emissions Trading Scheme Case Law," *Amsterdam Center for Law and Economics Working Paper No. 2009-12*. Accessed June 15, 2016. http://papers.ssrn.com/sol3/papers.cfm?abstract_id=1462651.

Vogler, John. "The European Union as a Global Environmental Policy Actor," *The European Union As a Union in International Climate Change Politics*. edited by. Rüdiger K. W. Wurzel and James Connelly. 21-37. London: Routledge, 2011.

Vogler, John. "The External Environmental Policy of the European Union," *Yearbook of International Cooperation on Environment and Development 2003/04*. edited by. Olav Schram Stokke and Øystein B. Thommessen. 65-72. London: Earthscan, 2003.

Warleigh, Alex. "Europeanizing' Civil Society: NGOs as Agents of Political Socialization," *Journal of Common Market Studies*. 39 no. 4. (November 2001): 619-639.

Warleigh –Lack, Alex and Ralf Drachenberg. "Policy Making in the European Union," *European Union Politics*. edited by. Michelle Cini and Nieves Pérez Solórzano Borragán. 209-224. United States: Oxford University Press, 2010.

"What is the CDM," *UNFCC*. Accessed December 17, 2015. http://cdm.unfccc.int/about/index.html.

"Why did greenhouse gas emissions decrease in the EU between 1990 and 2012?." *European Environment Agency*. Accessed May 23, 2016. http://www.eea.europa.eu/publications/why-did-ghgemissions-decrease.

Wurzel, Rudiger K. W. and James Connelly. "Environmental NGOs," in *The European Union As a Leader in International Climate Change Politics*. edited by. Rudiger K. W. Wurzel and James Connelly. 214-231. New York: Routledge, 2011.

Wurzel, Rudiger K. W. "Member States and the Council," *Environmental Policy in the EU*. edited by. Andrew Jordan and Camilla Adelle. 75-94. 3rd ed. London: Routledge, 2013.

WWF. Response to the European Commission Public Consultation on a 2030 Climate and Energy Package, Transparency Register Number: 1414929419-24.

"WWF European Policy Programme Transparency Register," *European Commission Transparency Register page*. Accessed June 3, 2015. http://ec.europa.eu/transparencyregister/public/consultation/displaylobbyist.do?id=1414929419-24.

"WWF Reaction to the European Commission's 'Consultative Communications on the Future of Carbon Capture and Storage in Europe'," *WWF*. Accessed May 20, 2015. http://ec.europa.eu/ energy/en/topics/oil-gas-andcoal/carbon-capture-and-storage.

"WWF summary position paper on EU Climate and Energy Package poposals," *WWF*. Accessed November 25, 2015. http://www.wwf.se/source.php?id=1185063.

Yurdusev, Nuri. "Analiz Seviyesi" ve "Analiz Birimi": Bir Ayrım Argümanı," *Uluslararası İlişkiler Journal*. 4. no. 16. (Winter 2007-2008): 3-19.

"2030 Climate and Energy Governance: Assessing an Open Method of Coordination Approach." *ClientEarth*. February 2015. http://www.clientearth.org/reports/2030-climate-andenergy-governance-assessing-an-omc-approach.pdf.

Index

Andrew Jordan *21, 22, 38, 40, 44, 47, 50, 55, 109, 191, 199, 200, 202, 204*
Andrew Moravcsik *10, 14, 15, 16, 17, 18, 21, 47, 52, 91, 102, 155, 176, 201, 202*
Austria *50, 51, 79, 159, 186*
Avril Doyle *165, 180*
bargaining process *15, 17, 22, 23, 185*
CAN Europe *iii, 6, 59, 107, 108, 109, 110, 112, 113, 114, 115, 117, 136, 139, 140, 141, 142, 143, 147, 170, 175, 177, 178, 179, 180, 184, 188, 191, 192, 194, 201*
Carbon capture and storage *98*
Carlo Ripa di Meana *48*
Certified Emission Reductions *iii, 86*
Chernobyl *35*
Claude Turmes *148, 180*
Committee of Permenant Representatives *50*
Common Market *10, 14, 16, 20, 30, 39, 50, 57, 65, 77, 134, 136, 191, 192, 201, 202, 203*
Control of Transboundary Movements of Hazardous Wastes and Their Disposal *51*
COREPER *iii, 50, 154, 156*
Council of Ministers *21, 24, 50, 154*
Democratic representation *10*
Denmark *50, 51, 52, 53, 56, 60, 79, 93, 157, 158, 159, 175, 186*
Directorate General for Environment, Nuclear Security and Civil Defence *48*
Directorate General of Climate Action *36*
Directorate General of Environment and Energy *36*
Emission Reduction Units *86*
Emission Trading Directive *67, 139*
Environment, Public Health and Food Security *54, 186*
Environmental Commissariat *111, 153*
Eurocrats *48*
European Climate Change Programmes *5*
European Council *21, 26, 27, 45, 50, 67, 70, 71, 75, 82, 83, 92, 94, 100, 154, 155, 156, 179, 191, 193, 196*

European Court of Justice *iii, 55, 56, 166, 200*
European Single Act *24, 29, 127*
Finland *50, 51, 93, 168, 169, 186*
First Action Plan *38*
Germany *29, 36, 51, 52, 53, 57, 60, 66, 93, 149, 156, 157, 159, 168, 169, 175, 186, 192, 203*
Greenpeace *6, 59, 105, 106, 107, 108, 109, 115, 116, 117, 118, 119, 120, 136, 137, 139, 140, 141, 142, 143, 144, 148, 164, 174, 175, 177, 178, 179, 180, 184, 188, 194, 198*
Greens *iii, 37, 41, 49, 53, 54, 164, 165*
Isil Karakaş *24, 200*
Kyoto *5, 62, 63, 67, 69, 78, 81, 82, 83, 87, 95, 121, 139, 141, 143, 179, 180, 188, 197*
liberal intergovernmentalism *6, 10, 14, 15, 20, 21, 22, 23, 184, 185*
lobbying *4, 5, 7, 29, 30, 31, 32, 33, 34, 47, 49, 52, 53, 57, 58, 59, 60, 66, 105, 108, 113, 114, 115, 116, 117, 120, 127, 131, 132, 133, 134, 135, 138, 145, 146, 148, 152, 153, 155, 156, 157, 160, 161, 162, 164, 165, 172, 175, 177, 178, 179, 180, 181, 185, 188, 189, 193, 199*
Malta *29*
Marc Galle *30, 31*
Mark Pollack *9, 18, 23, 201, 202*
Mitigation policies *64*
multi-level governance *6, 9, 19, 22, 23, 45, 88, 153, 181, 184, 185*
National Allowance Plans *167, 168*
Nordic Council *51, 52*
Nordmann Report *31*
Paris Summit *38, 39*
Poland *36, 89, 102, 148, 149, 156, 167, 168, 169, 179, 180, 187, 192*
Polluter Pays Principle *36*
Richard Snyder *11, 12, 13, 202, 203*
Rio Summit *42, 48, 65, 120*
Satu Hassi *165, 180*
Seveso *35*
Stockholm Summit *35*

subnational actors 22
the Environmental Policy Observation Committee 49
Treaty of Lisbon *3, 5, 24, 25, 26, 27, 44, 45, 54, 151, 185*
Treaty of Maastricht *24, 25, 26, 31, 37, 41, 42, 43, 54, 171*

Treaty of Nice 24
Treaty of Rome *24, 27, 38*
WWF *iv, 6, 58, 66, 107, 108, 109, 113, 115, 117, 120, 121, 122, 123, 124, 125, 126, 138, 139, 140, 141, 142, 143, 146, 147, 148, 157, 162, 164, 170, 175, 177, 178, 179, 181, 184, 188, 194, 198, 201, 204*

www.ingramcontent.com/pod-product-compliance
Lightning Source LLC
Chambersburg PA
CBHW051643230426
43669CB00013B/2423